The Cleaning Bible

To Ada So glad to hear you're so Houseproud! Best Wishes, Kim xxxx

The Cleaning Bible

Kim and Aggie's
Complete Guide to Modern
Household Management

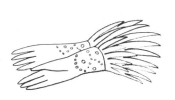

KIM WOODBURN
AGGIE MACKENZIE

WITH JERRY FOULKES

Dec 2008

PENGUIN BOOKS

I dedicate this book to Victoria Coker who saw in me something which I never saw in myself. And not forgetting lovely Ben Frow – thank you for commissioning such a wonderful show. **Kim**
For Dad, whose humour, warmth, humility and enormous appetite for life is an inspiration to all who know and love him. **Aggie**

PENGUIN BOOKS

Published by the Penguin Group

Penguin Books Ltd, 80 Strand, London WC2R ORL, England

Penguin Group (USA) Inc., 375 Hudson Street, New York, New York 10014, USA

Penguin Group (Canada), 90 Eglinton Avenue East, Suite 700, Toronto, Ontario, Canada M4P 2Y3
(a division of Pearson Penguin Canada Inc.)

Penguin Ireland, 25 St Stephen's Green, Dublin 2, Ireland (a division of Penguin Books Ltd)

Penguin Group (Australia), 250 Camberwell Road,
Camberwell, Victoria 3124, Australia (a division of Pearson Australia Group Pty Ltd)

Penguin Books India Pvt Ltd, 11 Community Centre, Panchsheel Park, New Delhi – 110 017, India

Penguin Group (NZ), 67 Apollo Drive, Rosedale, North Shore 0632, New Zealand
(a division of Pearson New Zealand Ltd)

Penguin Books (South Africa) (Pty) Ltd, 24 Sturdee Avenue, Rosebank, Johannesburg 2196, South Africa

Penguin Books Ltd, Registered Offices: 80 Strand, London WC2R ORL, England

www.penguin.com

First published by Michael Joseph 2006
Published in Penguin Books 2007

2

Copyright © Kim Woodburn, Aggie MacKenzie and Jerry Foulkes, 2006

Designed by Smith & Gilmour, London
Illustrations by Dermot Flynn@dutchuncle
Printed and bound in Italy by Printer Trento srl

ISBN: 978–0–141–02700–5

Please note: care and caution should be exercised when using chemicals, products and formulas presented in this book. It is highly recommended that all cleaning treatments should be tested in small inconspicuous areas before application. Always read and follow the information and directions contained on product labels with care. Total success cannot be guaranteed in every case and the authors and publishers hereby disclaim any liability and damages from the use and/or misuse of any product, formula or application presented in this book.

Contents

Introduction

This book is about much more than just cleaning: it's about running your home. This doesn't have to be difficult; in fact it can give a huge amount of satisfaction and pleasure. Really, there's nothing nicer than sitting down and admiring what you've achieved once all the jobs are done.

We're going to share with you two lifetimes of experience and know-how. We've tried so many tips that you can be sure they work. When you tackle a stain, scratch or sticky mark, it'll be just as though we're there advising you.

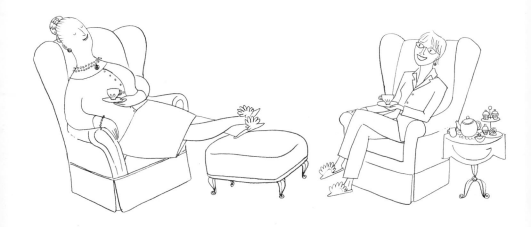

Kim I worked very hard to get my craft going. If you work as a housekeeper that's how you keep a job and word gets around. I don't get it all from books, although they certainly help. If there's a tip I'll try it, but so many of them don't work and they're a big disappointment. For example, pouring white wine on to red to get out a stain. I don't know who said that works, but I've tried it and it doesn't. Your expertise builds up and grows and over the years you're learning a lot without knowing it.

I think I was born with my grandmother's cleaning genes. She absolutely sparkled, she liked everything so clean. She cleaned the schools bless her. It was the 1950s and the war was only just over. Every day she was down on her hands and knees with not so much as a mop – there weren't any modern conveniences.

Aggie My mother taught me how to clean. We were taken round the rooms and shown how to dust, even on the high ledges and the top of the doorframe. No corners were ever cut in our house. In my early teens my sister and I used to babysit for a very ... shall we say 'bohemian' couple's children. While we were there we used to clean the kitchen because we couldn't bear it, everything was so sticky with dirt. I don't know how we had the nerve, really. I had lots of friends who grew up in mucky homes, and when I used to visit them I remember thinking, 'I never want to live in a house like this.'

Kim I've worked in the big houses. I've visited the British stately homes and seen how they're unpacked and packed away at the beginning and end of every season. I've watched them wrapping the drapes in cotton cloth and packing books in acid-free tissue paper; so much of what you learn is invaluable. I'm interested in cleaning so I've spent a lifetime learning my craft. Some of it's common sense – you know what you can and can't clean – but I like my things, and I want to know what I can and can't get away with.

Before you dip inside these pages looking for an answer to your current cleaning conundrum, we have several secrets to share with you. First a few words about clutter.

Kim My approach to clutter is 'don't have it'. I've got two boxes in my attic, but that's it – two boxes! You can't clean with clutter, it just can't be done. Every week more and more papers and things arrive in your home, so unless you can conquer your clutter you're a lost cause in my opinion.

Aggie I'm a minimalist at heart so throwing things out is a pleasure. I'm not a great shopper, so I don't spend a lot of time dragging things back into my house, but in a family home keeping on top of clutter is a daily battle. You just have to be on it the whole time, rather than letting it get so you can't face it.

No one can clean a messy home. You should adopt a zero tolerance approach to clutter – all those things you don't need, don't use, but hang on to anyway 'just in case' they come in handy. When you've finished with something sell it, pass it on to someone else, or recycle it. If you have loads of stuff covering all your surfaces, you won't be able to clean them.

Secondly, please don't save up all your jobs. 'A little and often' is the easiest way to clean. You can give yourself an easy life, or a hard one, but we know which we prefer.

Kim I always carry two dusters in my pockets when I'm at home; one old white face cloth and a fluff-free one. That way, whenever I see something that needs to be done, I can just do it there and then. I don't go saving things up, or giving myself a big headache, in fact I don't even notice I'm doing it.

Aggie Most of the time I don't even notice when I'm doing jobs. On the way down in the morning I straighten the boys' beds. I'll have a heap of stuff in my hands, a glass of water from last night, and I'll be gathering up laundry. When the post arrives I'll open and sort it straight away, pay a bill or check a statement and file them away. Every time you go upstairs take something with you. While I'm having breakfast I'll be planning or preparing dinner and the washing machine will be going. I don't particularly enjoy housework – I find the routine chores such as vacuuming tedious, but I don't mind the bigger occasional jobs. Scrubbing the tile grout, doing the windows or cleaning the oven are things I get more satisfaction from.

Finally, we urge you to adopt our third rule if you haven't already. There are some countries where it's considered disrespectful to bring the dirt from outside in, and we definitely agree. Take your outdoor shoes off at the door and your floor coverings will last years longer and it will save you from a great deal of cleaning.

Kim Even when I was a girl I took my shoes off at the front door and then I would go and wash out my grey school socks ready for the morning. I tell people over and over again, 'If you don't wear your shoes indoors you'll save all that cleaning.' Ooh, it's a magnificent way to save on housework, you know. Do you know, some people even put their shoes up on the sofa – I ask you, on the sofa!

Aggie I think it all started with me a few years ago when we got a new stair carpet and I thought, 'I want this to stay nice.' Living in London the streets are filthy with dogs' mess; people even spit on the pavement. I don't want that inside my house, so we have a 'shoes off before you go upstairs' rule. When people come to visit I just say, 'I'm sorry but everyone has to take their shoes off in this house.'

Of course, we all have to cut our coat according to our cloth. Only you know what you can manage to do around your home.

Kim You can't all do what I do, I'm very careful and respectful of my things. The more disrespectful you are, the harder the work will be. I don't know why people don't look after things more – they must have money to burn.

Aggie I'm number three of four sisters; we grew up in the north of Scotland. None of us is as pristine as our mother, but we all know what the standards should be, even though we fall short of perfection. Perhaps it's a generational thing – looking after the house was my mother's job, that's what she did. I remember her polishing the bathroom floor lino every single day with a tin of Mansion polish until it shone. When we came home from school and made snacks, we got told off for leaving crumbs everywhere. Today, the funny thing is, I don't blame her at all. It's very hard to run a home with four kids and have everything pristine all the time.

When it comes to cleaning there's no time like the present, so we really ought to be getting on.

Kim's housekeeping tales: Prenton, Merseyside

In 1959, when I turned seventeen years old, I had to find a job that provided accommodation. I replied to an advert for a live-in maid's position in the *Liverpool Echo* and went for an interview at a posh house in Prenton, an upmarket area near Birkenhead. Looking back, I think the lady would have taken any girl who was prepared to skivvy for her from morning until night, six days a week. She knew I wasn't experienced, and it must have been obvious that I needed the accommodation. She offered two pounds and ten shillings (£2.50) a week living in and it was very hard work because by that time I hadn't learnt all the skills I needed, not by any stretch.

I would be up at 7.00 am and lay the breakfast table, and didn't finish until 9.30 in the evening when the dinner washing-up was finally done, and then I took a bath and went to bed. The lady did all the cooking, which was a good thing because it's something I came to late, although no wonder she loved to cook because muggins here did all the washing-up afterwards. She taught me how to lay the table and carry the platters through, but I didn't eat with the family, goodness no, I was far too common. No, I ate my dinner in the scullery. The lady would ring a bell between the courses and I would scurry in and collect up all the dishes.

Women in those days didn't have the vast choice of cleaning products there are today. We used soap, scouring powder and bleach. Scouring powder was used for everything, even to get marks off the linoleum. There weren't all the labour-saving devices we have now either, although the lady did have an upright vacuum cleaner, a Hoover it was, with a horrible brown and burgundy cloth bag that filled up with air; they got awfully dusty. At that time it was the thing to have a wall-to-wall fitted carpet.

I used to get all the cobwebs down from the ceilings with a long-handled broom. I would tie the four corners of a duster over the broom head and the cobwebs would come tumbling down all over me.

Then I realized if I dampened the duster first, the cobwebs would stick to it, and that's how you learnt – you wanted to stop the dirt from falling all over you.

I did all the cleaning, but not the laundry. I had to lick backsides to keep a roof over my head. The man of the house, he was one of the first people to open an automatic laundrette, not a wash house, a proper laundrette. All week the clothes would pile up and then once a week he took them away, and the following day was my 'day of ironing'. At 9.00 am I walked the youngest lad to prep school and then went back to the house and got out the iron, an electric one – I'm not that old you know – although there was no such thing as a steam iron, instead you had to fill a rubber spray bottle with water or use a wet pressing cloth. I would just about finish in time for the school bell at 3.00 pm, when it was time to collect the lad again.

There were still a few maids working in the big houses at that time. We were called maids, although 'general dogsbody' was what you were. We were all fed up. We were young girls, most of us had been forced to leave home, and we had nowhere to go. We all felt we should be doing something better than cleaning. You would see the other girls walking their charges to school, but there wasn't much time off. There was no 'five-day week'. I did six days, and got just one day off. I would go and sit in the park because I only had my tiny room, although I kept it spotless, mind. On Fridays the couple would go out and I would be allowed to watch their television in the big posh lounge; I loved that.

After six months the lady announced the family were going on holiday for two weeks. She told me I would have to find somewhere else to stay because she didn't want me to stay in the big house. Well I didn't have anywhere to go did I? When you're broke, people put upon you, and when you've had no education it is hard to get another job. Fortunately the maid opposite had a friend who worked in a hotel, so she found me my next job.

Conquer the clutter

Dealing with clutter

When it comes to clutter we all seem to have a weakness for some kind of collection or another that has grown out of control. No one's perfect – not even us!

Aggie I have the opposite problem from most people when it comes to clutter – I get rid of too much stuff, even things that aren't mine, and that I later regret. When it comes to ornaments, I'm afraid I follow the maxim, 'If it isn't useful or beautiful, preferably both, then it's out the door.'

Kim I don't have a great deal of clutter; I'm really a very tidy person and I like everything in its proper place. My old clothes go to Oxfam because it's a very worthwhile cause and I don't want an overload of clothes in my wardrobe so I can't see what I've got. I'm rather ruthless when it comes to clothes. Even if I like something, but I just know I'll never wear it, out it goes. Please, always wash your clothes before you send them to charity; it's disrespectful to take them in dirty.

Aggie My golden rule when it comes to clutter is never to go upstairs or downstairs empty-handed. If I need to go up I'll always find something to take with me; if I'm not going up I'll leave things by the stairs. I get so irritated when my boys walk past the pile without taking something!

Kim My husband Pete is quite a tidy soul, actually I'm very proud of him and the way he gathers up his things. He does have one weakness: video tapes – he has hundreds of them!

Aggie I love to throw things away. Our local council collects items for recycling once a week. The charity Scope also sends plastic bags about once a month, which are another good excuse for a clear-out.

Kim When I lived in America I would always have three large garbage bins for glass, cans and paper in the garage and put them out for the recycling each week. I do like the bins that are divided into separate compartments.

Aggie Unwanted gifts go to charity, or get recycled and passed on again, and I have regular culls of my wardrobe. Luckily one of my sisters is the same size so she is the main beneficiary. Since I've been appearing on TV my shoe collection has swelled to about thirty pairs, which is a lot for me, but they are all stored neatly in canvas hangers in the wardrobe. I console the clutter-free side of me that shoes last longer if you wear them less often.

Kim I don't put things in the loft. What's the point – you'll only have to carry it all out when you move. Old furniture goes to Oxfam or social services. I might put up a freestanding fan I use in the summer, or some wrapped winter bedding just inside the flap, but nothing more than that. I suppose some people might have family heirlooms they don't want to part with, or put on display, but otherwise ask yourself, 'Do I really need this?' Go on, get rid of it. There's always someone who needs something you no longer have any use for, so let them have the benefit.

Aggie We sort through all the boys' toys and clothes twice a year, once in July before their birthdays, and once in December before all the new Christmas stuff arrives in the house. I usually manage to find homes for unwanted furniture: kids' beds or a small chest of drawers. There is nearly always someone who can use something like that for their own family. It's always worth asking around before you get rid of stuff. There are also charities that will pass furniture on. Because I like a minimalist home, I do get rid of too much. My one exception is a large collection of cookery books. I did go through and weed some out a few years ago, but to be honest I've regretted it ever since.

Kim Let me tell you, every home must have a 'muck' drawer. Mine is in the kitchen, that's where everything goes: keys, safety pins, the odd rubber band, bits of string, batteries, notepads, pens, little things I know I'll need. I'm constantly in and out of it. But despite detesting clutter, I must own up to one collection. I've got eighty-two tiny designer teapots and seventeen large ones, which are designed like market stalls and are made by a Devon firm called Cardew. I bought my first from a stall a few years ago and I haven't stopped collecting since. They're displayed on shelves all around the top of the kitchen and they take some careful cleaning I can tell you.

Where to start?

Today we have more possessions than our parents, or any generation before us ever did. We don't have to save up for things like people used to, but they don't last as long either. This truly is the 'consumer' age – no wonder our homes fill up with clutter faster than ever before.

Clothes are cheaper and fashions change faster. There is an electrical gadget available for every conceivable task, which as soon as we buy is replaced by a newer model that performs even more functions. Newspapers are thicker, and some come delivered free whether we like it or not, along with tons of junk mail. Video tapes, DVDs and CDs all pile up more quickly than we have time to play them.

The question is, how do you know when your stuff has grown to be unbearable rather than pleasurable? People who remember wartime rationing were taught never to throw anything away because it might come in handy. The government of the day even ran advertisements in women's magazines urging readers to 'make do and mend' and save up their clothing coupons. Those days are gone unfortunately so there's no excuse to hoard unused or broken possessions.

Most of us keep far too much stuff that we'll never use again, but which might bring some benefit or pleasure to other people. Friends, family, schools and charities can all benefit from our unwanted clutter. We can even turn it into cash at a car boot sale or by putting it up for online auction. It's much more difficult to clean when the contents of wardrobes, cupboards and drawers are overflowing on to every surface. When there's nowhere left to tidy anything away to, cleaning becomes impossible.

Of course no one can tell us how much stuff we should have in our homes; the real test is how the things around you make you feel. If you don't know where to start when it comes to cleaning, the chances are you need to launch a big clear-out. Once you've recognized the problem, it will become much easier to decide what to keep and what to get rid of.

Recognizing the tell-tale signs of clutter

Does your home suffer from any of the following?

- O Cupboards, drawers and shelves are all full to overflowing and there's nowhere left to store anything.
- O You have so much stuff you're thinking of paying for storage. Once it's stored do you think you will ever miss it? If not, save the expense and get rid of it.
- O Too much furniture, either from parents or previous houses, which is no longer useful. It is broken, the wrong style or size.
- O Too many clothes that are unlikely ever to be worn. They don't fit, are out of fashion, need alteration or repair, or were a mistake.
- O Linens and towels, which are never used, taking up valuable storage space.
- O Envelopes of photographs awaiting albums, video tapes without labels, stacks of DVDs by the television, piles of books without shelves.
- O A collection that has grown out of control. There is nowhere to store or display it all, there are too many duplicates, and it is an annoyance to others in the home.
- O Unused kitchen gadgets that take up surface or cupboard space. Broken televisions, video players, or music players. Obsolete computers, printers and fax machines, old telephones and mobile phones.
- O Hobby equipment that is no longer used. Musical instruments, sports or exercise equipment, craft materials, or redundant DIY tools and projects.
- O Children's toys that have been outgrown, broken, or are no longer played with.
- O Grown-up children's possessions still stored in the family home.

Nearly all of us will admit to one of these problems, but if you can identify with more than three, you probably already have a clutter problem.

Kim & Aggie The Cleaning Bible

Friends, family and bereavement

Unwanted gifts from friends and family can pose a dilemma. Should you display gifts whether you like them or not? Is it acceptable to recycle unwanted but expensive gifts? Only you can decide what is acceptable to you, but remember it's *your* living space, and you should put your enjoyment of it first and foremost. If you do recycle gifts frequently, keep a note of where they came from to avoid embarrassment when you pass them on!

Sometimes we inherit things from friends or family that we don't like, but we keep them anyway out of a sense of loyalty or obligation. These may also include things grown-up children have asked us to 'temporarily' store for them, or 'borrowed' furniture. Just because you decide to let go of these things doesn't mean you forget the people who gave them to you, but do check before you dispose of anything you may be expected to return.

Dealing with possessions children leave behind when they finally move out can be difficult. Once they've set up a permanent home, give them a deadline to collect the things that you're storing for them. Have it all ready for them next time they visit and offer to get rid of the things they don't take away. This is usually a good way of getting them to focus on what they really do and don't want to keep.

Sorting through possessions can be especially difficult after bereavement. You may feel unable to part with anything associated with someone you've already lost. Clothes are among the most difficult personal effects to admit will not be worn again, but sending them to a favourite charity can provide a little comfort, knowing that they may bring some benefit to someone else.

An incentive to declutter

If you need an incentive, begin by imagining how you will use all the extra space: perhaps for a home office, a playroom or some new entertainment equipment. If you're planning to sell something, calculate how much money you might raise, and think how much time you'll save by not cleaning and searching for things.

Dealing with clutter has become big business; there are even experts who will happily charge to help decide which things to get rid of! If nothing else, calculate how much money you will save by doing it yourself.

You may have both too much stuff and too little storage – even for the things you absolutely must keep. Don't use this as an excuse to delay having a sort-out. It's easier to think of extra storage ideas when you've discovered exactly what it is you need to store.

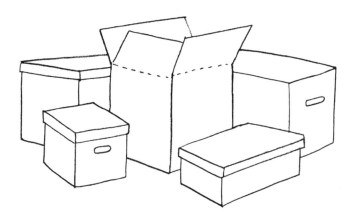

Getting started

Don't try to reorganize your whole home in one go. If you tackle it one room at a time, you're more likely to see the job through. It's sometimes easier to start with one of the least cluttered rooms because you'll have an incentive to keep going. Before you start:

- Prepare to declutter by stocking up with bin bags and boxes.
- If you need some encouragement, invite a friend to come and urge you on.
- Set a time limit for the session and put on some of your favourite music to help it go quickly. When the time is up, stop.
- It's very easy to get sidetracked into reading old letters, looking at photographs or reminiscing. Avoid this by putting together things that need further sorting, and tackling them later one at a time.

When you've finished think about any additional storage that would be useful. Freestanding units can be taken with you when you move; built-in designs are more flexible for awkward spaces.

Conquer the clutter   Dealing with clutter

Sorting clutter: The traffic light method

Take three boxes and mark them red, yellow and green. These traffic light colours will help you decide how to proceed with every item – stay, wait or go.

RED – stay or keep These are the things you use regularly. They are important to you and must be given a permanent home where you can find them easily.

YELLOW – wait These are the things you instinctively want to keep, but actually haven't used for over a year. These things need to be repaired, returned, finished or new homes found for them.

GREEN – go or recycle This is stuff you haven't used in over two years. Anything broken that will never be repaired, anything you don't like, and anything you'll probably never use again.

Empty every surface or cupboard you declutter into the three categories. Put anything that is obviously rubbish into bin bags. Once the space is clear, vacuum it and wipe it clean. Line drawers and cupboard shelves with attractive paper, which will make them easier to clean in future.

Examine the red/keep items. These are the things you use regularly and must hang on to. Group everything associated with the same activity together: jewellery, stationery, photography, travel, sports, etc. Create a permanent home for each of these groups. Once you have each group assembled, edit it again, removing any duplication for sale or recycling.

Now the yellow/wait items. This is probably a large and daunting collection of things that grew rapidly. Start with the broken items. If you're unlikely ever to get round to fixing them, put them into the rubbish or recycling. Next make plans to return anything borrowed. Set a deadline for all half-finished projects, for example by the end of next week, and put a tag on them with the date. If you miss the deadline, promise you'll definitely get rid of it next time you declutter.

Finally the green/recycle items. It's time for these things to go. You might have decided to raise some cash from your clutter. Work out where to sell each item, for how much, and set a deadline for its disposal. If you haven't managed to sell everything by, say, the end of the month, consider giving away what's left to a charity shop to sell. Donate anything you know you won't be able to sell (old paperback books are a good example) and recycle anything that isn't saleable. All local authorities operate recycling centres that are free to use and are a good way to avoid simply putting everything into household rubbish, which mainly ends up as environmentally damaging landfill.

Staying on top of clutter forever

Once you've spent time sorting out your clutter you'll want to try and keep everything in its place. Most of us are constantly acquiring new objects so an ongoing routine keeps things under control. Put articles away as you use them or at the end of the day to stay on top of clutter.

The daily ten-minute tidy
Make this a part of your daily routine before going to work, or to bed.
- Pick up everything left on the floor.
- Empty all shopping bags.
- Recycle all discarded newspapers and junk mail.
- Put things ready to go upstairs/downstairs.
- Return things to their correct homes.
- If you live with someone less tidy, gather their stray things together in a nominated space in a box or shelf.

The weekly tidy
- Find just half an hour a week to keep on top of clutter forever.
- Collect together the week's correspondence. Pay bills, respond to letters and file away.
- Pack away anything there wasn't time to deal with during the week.
- Clear out one drawer, shelf or cupboard when you return something to a crowded space. Keep in mind the traffic light colours to help sort things.

The ongoing tidy

These are the routines you won't need to carry out every week,
but they are good habits to help keep on top of your possessions.

○ Don't pile up unwanted clutter in lofts, cellars, sheds and garages. Tackle each of these in turn and promise never to have to do them again.

○ Adopt the mantra 'one in, one out'. For every new major item you bring into your home, look for one existing item to dispose of.

○ When you have some spare time on your hands, pick one room and return things to their correct homes. If you do this regularly, your home will stay entirely clutter-free.

○ Edit your collections. Whenever you add an item to a collection, look for something to discard.

○ Stick photographs into albums or frames. Throw away the prints that don't make it on to the page and keep the negatives or disks instead.

○ Dispose of equipment you update: TV, audio and computers, cooking and DIY gadgets.

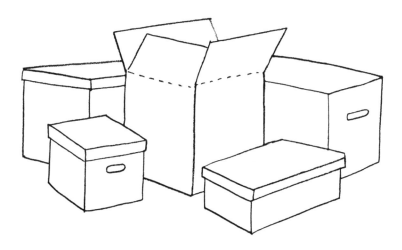

Getting into a routine

'A little and often' is the secret to getting everything done. How you decide to schedule your jobs is entirely up to you, but if the time has come to rethink your routine, here is how we manage.

Kim I'm always being asked, 'When should you clean?' Well my advice for a life of leisure is, 'Do it as you go along dear.' Once you get your house in order life is easy. If something is dropped, then mop; if something spills, then wipe; clear out the fridge while you're putting away the milk. When you do a little bit here and there, your life is your own.

Aggie When it comes to routines I'm a stickler. A little every day is best and I believe in spacing out the jobs during the week rather than saving them up. A little bit of cleaning and ironing every day is the secret to making your home run smoothly. Keeping mini sets of cleaning materials where I need them helps me because I'm more likely to get things done as I notice them. I keep extra rubber gloves in the bathroom and even a microfibre dusting cloth in the bedside cabinet – what a passion booster that is!

Kim I don't let a daily cleaning routine ruin my life. If the house is always nice when you receive an unexpected invitation, you're free to get up and go without worrying about leaving any mess behind. Now don't get me wrong, that doesn't mean there aren't things I do every day. I sort the incoming mail, gather up newspapers and keep the kitchen straight. I'll have a quick flick round with the duster, and run the vacuum over the areas where the walking gets done; but it's not plugged in for more than five minutes – it doesn't need to be. Do as you go, that's what I say.

I don't have set days for the bigger jobs. Just slot them in: polish a mirror here; mop a floor there. If I see something that needs to be done, then I do it. If in the evening there's nothing I fancy watching on television, I'll go and straighten a room I don't often use – that way you're never wasting your time.

Aggie There isn't quite the need for spring cleaning that there once was with sooty fires burning all winter, but it's still nice to freshen up any rooms that need it by repainting in the spring.

Kim I don't do spring cleaning because I don't need to. Homes don't get dirty like they used to with open fires. We don't have that filth any more – we're pretty lucky. If I notice a rug or a pair of curtains that aren't looking as fresh as they should, then I'll arrange to get them washed or cleaned there and then; I don't go saving it up until the spring.

Why follow a routine?

Every day we continue a ceaseless domestic cycle. Our bed linen, soiled by our bodies and perspiration, needs airing; the bathroom has to be cleaned; crockery and cutlery must be washed and dried ready for the next meal. A daily cleaning routine provides a cleaner, safer and more hygienic living environment and helps us stay healthy. Our furnishings and possessions will last longer and when the time comes to put the house on the market, it's much more likely to sell quickly.

Whatever your attitude to household chores, today they've never been so easy. We have a whole battery of weapons at our disposal in our war on grime, from washing machines to dishwashers, the option of microwaves, and even duvets to do away with struggling with sheets and blankets. Our only difficulty is finding time to get around to it all. Domestic duties are no longer down to women. More of us live alone than ever before, and in family homes many mothers also have full- or part-time jobs. People with clean and tidy homes don't have any extra hours in the week, they just make sure they devote some of them to keeping their home clean.

A history of housekeeping

If today's chores seem like hard work, take comfort from the harsh routines followed by our ancestors. Almost 150 years ago Mrs Beeton wrote one of the earliest manuals on household management. In it she records that housemaids should be at work by 6.00 in the summer and 6.30 in the winter. In winter, the grates had to be cleaned and the fires lit before the breakfast parlour, stairs and drawing room were swept and dusted. The drudgery went on like this all day until dinner, and in the evening the housemaid was expected to do needlework; there was no time off.

Of course not all homes had servants, but despite the passing decades, domestic routines remained written in stone until the middle of the twentieth century. Even until the early 1960s, the days of the week dictated the order in which household tasks were carried out. Monday was laundry day, and woe betide you if your sheets weren't out on the line by midday. Tuesday was for ironing; Wednesday for mending; Thursday for cleaning; Friday was payday and with the onset of the weekend came baking and shopping. Sunday was for your roast dinner, and rest, and the whole cycle began again in earnest the following day. For many it was a routine of joyless drudgery, almost unaided by labour-saving devices. Laundry was washed in the sink, squeezed through a mangle and flattened with an iron heated on the coals. The front step was scrubbed daily, for the sake of appearances and what the neighbours might say. Extra seasonal cleaning was necessary because when spring came, the sun showed up the sooty residue from winter coal fires and gas lamps. For many people this was a routine that carried on until the '60s and '70s, when clean central heating was finally installed.

The secret to keeping your home clean and organized

If you're looking for a single pearl of wisdom – the secret to domestic bliss – then 'little and often' is it. Do a few minutes each day and they'll quickly become part of your routine. Your home will stay cleaner; you'll spend less leisure time doing housework; and have more opportunity to enjoy your free time.

One frequent complaint is that unlike decorating, housework is never finished. We all like the satisfaction of seeing a job done, so it's best to set yourself a target or standard, so you'll know when it's been met and you've finished. You have to review what's possible from time to time: when you're busy at work, unwell, or caring for someone else. At these times you may decide you can happily live without cleaning the windows, but you must have clean bed linen every week. Whatever you decide is right for you, don't put off doing so many jobs that the task becomes too frightening to ever begin.

So how do you find the time to clean? The only routine that works is the one you'll stick to. It's no good designing a lovely rota and sticking it up on the fridge if you then delay the new regime until tomorrow. The bossy approach to routines isn't very inspiring; none of us really wants to be told which day to do things during the week, or even throughout the year. We would all rather divide our jobs up into the odd few minutes we have available. Who wants to clean for three solid hours a week – unless they're getting paid for it?

Finding time to clean

You can make more time for cleaning by following a few simple rules:

- Do a few minutes each day to be more productive. Don't set out to vacuum the whole house. Do one bedroom before work and another one tomorrow.
- Mess definitely breeds mess. Keep your home as uncluttered as possible so that cleaning is easier and quicker.
- If you find your housework is never finished, make a list and decide in advance when to start and when to stop. Starting jobs, rather than worrying about them, definitely makes life easier. Allocate your most productive time to the most difficult tasks. If you're a morning person, someone who has time for an extra cup of coffee at breakfast, then you can probably fit some tasks into your morning routine. If, on the other hand, you flap out of the door in a frenzy to catch the bus, but stay up watching TV until midnight, then look to the evening to do your chores.
- Set priorities and, when time is tight, review what you can realistically manage and don't fret about untouched jobs you can't possibly achieve. But don't put off doing so many jobs you're too frightened to start.
- Whenever possible do double duty. File some bills while you are chatting on the telephone; wipe the splashbacks while you're waiting for the kettle to boil; clean the basin while the bath taps run; and so on.

Doing 'a little and often'

Here are some suggestions for the kinds of jobs you can fit into the spare moments throughout the day. Make a list in the morning, slot the jobs in along the way, and do the things you enjoy least while you're at your best.

Regular jobs you can do in five minutes
In the kitchen:

- Replace the dishcloth and drying cloths.
- Wash a few breakfast dishes.
- Empty the dishwasher.
- Empty the bin.
- Make a shopping list.
- Wipe fingerprints from handles and switches.

Elsewhere:

- Open the windows and allow bedding to air.
- Throw out old newspapers and put five things away.
- Hang out the washing.
- Make an appointment.
- Pay a bill and file it.
- Water the houseplants.
- Dust the living room.
- Clean a pair of shoes.

Regular jobs you can do in ten minutes

In the kitchen:

- Sort out and clean the fridge.
- Vacuum and mop the floor.
- Clear and wipe all the surfaces.
- Handwash some clothes.

Elsewhere:

- Put in a load of washing.
- Clean the bathroom basin and toilet.
- Vacuum the living room and hall.
- Shine all the mirrors.
- Sort through a pile of magazines.
- Strip and make up a bed.
- Tidy out a drawer.

Regular jobs you can do in thirty minutes

In the kitchen:

- Scrub the oven shelves.
- Sort through a set of cupboards.
- Iron a basket of clothes.

Elsewhere:

- Vacuum cushions, curtains and underneath furniture.
- Change bed linen.
- Clean the windows.
- Clean the bathroom from top to bottom.
- Polish the furniture.
- File paperwork.
- Hem a pair of trousers.

Is spring cleaning still necessary?

More women work full time these days, so there isn't the time available today. But however fastidious you normally are, when spring arrives you may notice some dirt you've missed during the dark winter months. That doesn't mean you should save up jobs for the spring because if you do a 'little and often' you should do them as you notice them.

Most of us make a few extra preparations for summer, even if it's just getting a lightweight duvet. Why not also tackle the garage when you drag out the garden chairs and barbecue? Some people also mark the arrival of autumn with a burst of activity. When the days grow shorter and the kids go back to school, you might want to pack away the garden furniture and swap summer clothes for your winter wardrobe.

Once or twice a year jobs
- Change over seasonal clothing in wardrobes.
- Dispose of clothing not worn in over two years.
- Launder and pack away winter duvets.
- Clean underneath and behind kitchen appliances.
- Dispose of electrical gadgets no longer used.
- Unpack/repack garden chairs and barbecue.
- Hose down the patio.

Cleaning a new or neglected home

If you're unlucky, at least once in your life you'll be faced with a mammoth cleaning task, such as moving into a neglected new home. These jobs can be daunting and calling in professional help is an attractive alternative, but it can be hard to find reliable contractors and they tend to come with an equally daunting price tag.

Taking on a large cleaning job requires some advance planning. There may be considerable quantities of furniture and rubbish to get rid of and professional repairs may be required. These things are best organized before the cleaning begins because it's impossible to work around the clutter and pointless to clean before the workmen are finished.

Estimate how long the job will take you so you don't bite off more than you can manage or feel like giving up halfway through. For the television programmes, it takes a team of four to eight helpers two days to clean a four-bedroom house. Of course these were extreme cases where there was a year's worth of clutter and dirt, but it may help you calculate the size of your job.

You may want to tackle the kitchen and bathroom first because these rooms must be clean to be hygienic. As a rule it's best to do all the wet work first – washing walls and shampooing carpets – and then work through to vacuuming and polishing.

CHECKLIST: CLEANING OR MOVING INTO A NEGLECTED HOME
- Prepare by organizing any necessary repairs.
- Dispose of unwanted furniture and clutter before cleaning commences.
- Begin with kitchen, bathroom and bedroom if you are living in the property.
- Work from the top of the house down to avoid spoiling work already done.
- Wash down walls and floors and shampoo carpets.
- Wipe down surfaces, polish and vacuum.

The home office

Many of us don't have the space for a home office, but every home needs to keep track of bills, insurance policies, warranties and instruction manuals. No one wants to receive a letter threatening to cut off the telephone or to discover the insurance cover expired the week before we were burgled.

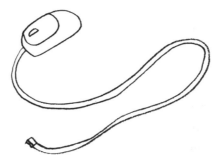

Kim Managing paperwork is an important part of running the home. Paying bills on time is essential. Who wants to have to pay extra, or receive one of those red letters saying you haven't paid? That's just embarrassing. I open the post every day in the kitchen and immediately throw away anything I don't want. All the bills go into the bureau in my living room to be dealt with during the next day or so. I love my roll-top bureau with its drawers; it's absolutely invaluable. I've had it about five years now and it makes dealing with paperwork a pleasure.

I mark reminders in my diary a month ahead of when things like house insurance will fall due; that way, if they forget to write to you (and there can be glitches) you'll always be insured.

When the bills are paid they go into a file. We keep all the files in Pete's computer room, which is our office. He used to have a terrible habit of throwing all the paperwork into heaps so he couldn't find anything without going through it all. 'Oh come on Pete!' I said, so now we've got a set of drawers with files and he keeps the office lovely and tidy. I keep twelve months' worth of bills before I shred them. In fact, I shred all my personal paperwork. They're fantastic things shredders; they keep your details secure. I let a local boy have the shredded bits for his rabbits – they love my old paperwork!

Aggie I'm absolutely fastidious when it comes to paperwork. Whenever possible, I open mail in the office and file it away immediately either into the bin or into the appropriate place in my four-drawer filing cabinet. If I'm in a hurry, I plonk it into my in-tray, but if I do I make sure I clear it later in the day. If I don't do it quickly, I know something important will go missing.

Once a year I go through all the files – usually when they start bulging – and give them a good clear out. We once did some research at the Good Housekeeping Institute about how long you need to keep paperwork, so I loosely follow what I learnt then: a year for old utility bills, two years for bank statements, that kind of thing. I keep warranties, guarantees and instruction books in the filing cabinet too, but warranty cards are less important than manufacturers would like us to think. Proof of purchase gives just as much protection under the Sale of Goods Act.

I keep my laptop computer locked in a cupboard. I'm afraid this is one lesson I learnt the hard way after we were burgled last year and the thieves took everything that was portable and electronic, which was a total pain and very disruptive. Keeping your records locked away so that intruders can't steal your identity is a sad fact of modern life.

Every home needs a home office

The home office doesn't have to take up a whole room. It could just be a cupboard with a desk top that folds out, or a shelf under the stairs for the computer and some drawers for the household accounts. If you work from home full or part time, you probably do need an actual room dedicated to the task, which will also help you keep 'office hours' and stop you from being interrupted when you're busy. Studies have shown that homeworkers put in more uninterrupted hours than office workers.

Household filing system

Wherever your office space is, it will only work efficiently if you keep it organized. It mustn't become a dumping ground for piles of correspondence, things that will 'come in useful' and unfinished projects. Unfiled paperwork soon accumulates, making important documents devilishly difficult to find when you need them.

Dealing with paperwork

One of the biggest headaches is the amount of paperwork that turns up – mainly through the letterbox. The amount of unsolicited direct mail we receive has doubled in the last fifteen years. The best place for it is straight into the recycling box.

If you find junk mail a nuisance, the Mailing Preference Service can take your name off 95 percent of direct mailing lists and their service is free (www.mpsonline.org.uk; 0845 703 4599). A similar service exists to remove your telephone number from sales callers' databases. The Telephone Preference Service is at www.tpsonline.org.uk; 0845 070 0707.

Household bills need to be dealt with quickly to avoid hefty late payment and interest charges. Find a system that suits you. If putting things aside means you forget them, then dealing with them as they arrive is the only way. If, on the other hand, you're disciplined and can set an hour aside at a fixed time each week, then start an 'in-tray' and deal with everything once a week.

Set up a file for each of the companies you regularly receive correspondence from, or group them into subjects such as utilities, money and insurance, etc. Find a file type that you enjoy using: expandable, hanging or a ring binder.

Dealing with correspondence

Deal with your incoming mail every day or once a week. If you sort the paperwork weekly, you must set aside time every week to clear your in-tray. If you never get round to it, switch to a daily routine.

- Open all incoming mail daily.
- Recycle unwanted paper.
- Pay bills immediately or add to weekly in-tray.
- Check that bank and credit card statements are correct.
- Add paperwork to filing system, noting date paid.
- Leave outgoing post by the front door and take with you next time you go out.

Dealing with utility bills

If you find keeping up to date with bills a challenge, then set aside some time and arrange to switch to monthly direct debit payments. This is a service that most companies offer and ensures you will never miss a payment as long as your bank account remains in credit. Some utility companies will give you a small discount for this method of payment, but check they don't overestimate your consumption and accumulate too much of your money.

However you pay your accounts, you'll have some paperwork to deal with. How you file your utility bills will depend on how many suppliers you have. Most of us have to pay for gas, electricity, water, telephone, council tax and TV licence. You should keep copies of these bills for twelve months, which will also help you keep track of how much you are spending if you decide to change supplier.

Most utility companies bill quarterly, so you should receive four invoices every year. Don't throw all four away at the same time, just the oldest one as you add the most recent. The bills also contain useful contact information for when things go wrong or you move home.

Every home with a television receiver (television, video or computer with a tuner) must have a valid TV licence. Seniors over seventy-five are entitled to a free licence and blind people get a 50 percent discount.

CHECKLIST: UTILITY BILLS

- Set up monthly direct debits.
- Keep bills on file for 12 months.
- Don't throw out all previous bills at the same time: 'one in, one out'.
- Once a year check how much you could save by consuming less energy or switching energy supplier. You could try contacting www.uswitch.com; 0800 093 0607, www.ukpower.co.uk; 0800 093 2447 or www.simplyswitch.com; 0800 781 1212.

Dealing with bank accounts, credit cards and savings

It is essential to keep track of financial records: bank statements, the mortgage, credit card bills, savings and any investments such as Premium Bonds or a pension. Some of these generate paperwork more frequently: monthly for current accounts and credit cards, once a year for the mortgage and personal pensions.

You should check through bank statements and credit card bills to ensure all the listed debits and credits are correct. Keep receipts that you pay by card and check them off each month – these are your proof if there is a mistake. If you return goods and receive a credit, check it shows up on your statement. Paying by credit card can also provide some additional protection if a supplier fails to supply goods or ceases trading. If you use your credit and debit cards for online shopping, you should be especially vigilant.

If you frequently incur late payment or overdraft charges on your accounts, see if you can reschedule payments to coincide with your monthly salary credit. Credit cards are safest paid off in full by direct debit, but if you can't manage to do this, then change to a zero or low interest rate card and check the rate regularly to make sure your deal is still current.

Financial records should be kept for longer than utility bills – especially if you are self-employed and are required to keep tax records for up to six years. Store two years' worth of your financial records in readily accessible files and put the previous years in a sturdy, clearly marked box somewhere safe. When you add another year of completed accounts at tax return time, you can shred the oldest year of accounts on file.

It's safest to shred your financial records before you dispose of them because they provide enough detail for other people to access your money should they fall into the wrong hands. It's not unknown for criminals to rifle through bins and household rubbish looking for bank statements and credit card receipts. For the same reason, financial records should be locked away in case you're burgled. A fireproof metal storage box is also worth considering.

CHECKLIST: BANK ACCOUNTS, CREDIT CARDS AND SAVINGS

- ☺ Keep receipts and check against bank and credit card statements.
- ☺ Query any errors immediately, especially if you shop online.
- ☺ If you frequently incur overdraft charges on your bank account, reschedule regular bills to coincide with your salary credit.
- ☺ If you incur late payment credit card charges, pay by direct debit. Try and clear the balance in full or move to a low or zero interest card and monitor the rates regularly.
- ☺ Keep financial records for two years (six years if self-employed).
- ☺ Lock bank statements away so that your identity cannot be stolen if you're burgled.
- ☺ Shred financial documents before disposal.

Dealing with insurance policies

Insurance policies – buildings, contents, car and travel – all generate plenty of paperwork. Keep these together and, when they arrive, read them through to check that all the details are correct and that they provide the cover you need. Insurance companies adhere strictly to the wording of the policy when it comes to dealing with claims.

Home buildings insurance is a condition of a mortgage, but you don't have to take home insurance with your mortgage lender. It's often cheaper not to because they tend to rely on the assumption that you won't check around for a more competitive quote.

Home contents insurance is optional and can be extended to provide accidental cover to electrical goods and furnishings. The annual premium might be several hundred pounds, but if your home is burgled or even burns down, could you afford to replace the lost contents from your own pocket? That is the risk that insurance covers. Three out of four homes are covered by contents insurance – just one claim could be worth many years of premiums.

Owning and driving a car without third party insurance cover is a criminal offence. Most insurers also include fire and theft cover with the most basic type of policy.

Fully comprehensive insurance covers damage to your own vehicle in the event of an accident, even if it is your fault.

Travel insurance tends to offer better value when bought as a multi-trip annual policy – especially if you go on holiday more than once a year. An annual policy may cost the same as just two weeks and will cover holidays from the time you book them, which may provide cover if you have to cancel the trip. Make sure you pay the premium at the renewal date or you run the risk of travelling without cover. If you need cover for winter sports or travel to the US, you will have to pay a higher premium.

Save money on insurance

Consider synchronizing your insurance renewal dates for home, car and travel. You'll need to budget to do this, but you're more likely to remember insurance is due for renewal and you won't risk being without cover. For many types of insurance, provided there have been no claims, you don't have to wait until the end of the policy to change provider and unused premiums will be refunded. Many companies also offer a discount if you hold several policies with them and it will cut down on your paperwork. Doing this may mean paying for all your annual insurance in one go – because monthly payment options usually cost more money. If you decide to synchronize your renewal dates, pick a time of the year when you know you'll have time to obtain quotes (the first year is often the most competitively priced, so you should shop around every year).

Use an online comparison service such as www.confused.com, which will compare dozens of quotes for you once you've entered your details. Study the providers that are top rated, looking at their own websites or telephoning direct (there is often a discount for online purchase, and cutting out a middle man can also save money). The reputation of an insurance company is as important as the price of the premium; you need to know they will pay out if you make a claim. You can however appeal to the Financial Ombudsman if there is a dispute with an insurance provider: www.financial-ombudsman.org.uk; 020 7964 1000.

- Buildings insurance is a condition of any loan secured on the property, such as a mortgage.
- Home contents insurance is optional and can be extended to cover accidental damage.
- Third party motor insurance is a legal requirement.
- Annual multi-trip travel insurance is often better value than a separate policy for each trip.
- You can often switch insurance provider mid-policy if you haven't made any claims.
- Ask for a discount if you take out more than one policy with a company.

Dealing with instruction manuals and warranties

Keep the instruction manuals and warranties for all the appliances and gadgets you own in one place. It's much easier to find them when there's a problem. In general, you don't have to return warranty cards to the manufacturer because your sales receipt provides adequate legal proof of purchase. When you dispose of electrical items, throw away the manual as well to save cluttering up your files with unnecessary paperwork.

Think carefully before you pay extra for an extended warranty on household electrical equipment because it can add a considerable amount to the purchase price. These are effectively insurance policies and studies have shown them to be among the most expensive insurance you can buy. Most appliances have a manufacturer's guarantee for the first year, which is when most problems are likely to occur. Sometimes you can buy extended cover at the end of the first year of ownership, by which time you'll know how reliable the equipment has proven to be.

Cleaning a computer

Always follow the manufacturer's specific instructions when you clean your computer and don't use any cleaners or solvents that will scratch or etch the casing or screen. Switch off the computer and unplug it before you start. The main problems are dust, which is attracted to the casing and screen and held by static electricity, and greasy fingerprints and debris, which collect on the keyboard.

Wipe the casing with a barely damp cloth and buff dry. If the dust has become ingrained and the case is blackened, moisten a soft cloth with a tiny drop of dilute washing-up liquid, but never get the casing wet. Dust also tends to cling to the screen because of the static charge. Wipe this away with an antistatic wipe or microfibre cloth.

To clean the keyboard, either tip it upside down and gently shake out the dust and crumbs or vacuum with a dusting brush attachment. Computer suppliers also sell air sprays to blow dust out with. If the keys are greasy from contact with dirty fingertips, moisten a cotton bud with a drop of diluted washing-up liquid and then squeeze out all the excess moisture into a towel by pressing with your thumb and forefinger. Gently wipe over the surface of each of the keys with the tip of the barely damp cotton bud.

Personal correspondence

If, for sentimental reasons, you like to hold on to old letters and cards, make up a special memory box to keep them all together. Sort through the contents from time to time.

Give yourself a financial checkup

All the big companies are audited once a year and you should do the same with your own money. It never seems to be quite the right time to do this, but it can turn up some pleasant and nasty surprises, and save you a considerable amount of money, not to mention worry. You'll feel a fantastic sense of achievement quite out of proportion to the time spent.

Add up how much you are spending on utilities. Check whether you could make savings, for example by turning down your central heating (a 1°C cut can save 10 percent off the bill); line drying your laundry rather than using the tumble dryer; or having a water meter fitted (as a guide, if your home has more bedrooms than occupants, this may produce a saving).

Use an online utility comparison search site to see if you could save money by switching or combining energy providers. The National Audit Office reports that householders switching energy suppliers have saved on average £80 on gas and £45 on electricity bills a year. Do remember to check a new supplier's customer service reputation (most search sites rate this) before switching because there is no saving or benefit if they are inefficient or impossible to deal with.

Check that your council tax bill shows your home in the correct valuation band (there are eight lettered bands from A–H). An explanation of how this is calculated is provided with the bill. Most councils allow you to pay in ten equal instalments over the year without any increased charge, but you cannot do this is if you are in arrears. Make sure you are claiming any discounts that you are eligible for. There is a 25 percent discount if only one adult lives at an address and some people are not counted when the number of residents is calculated, for example full-time students, the severely mentally impaired and some low-pay care workers.

Your mortgage payments are probably your biggest single expense, but the one you spend least time shopping around for. Check what kind of loan you have and how competitive the interest rate is. Changing to a new lender can be time consuming, but could save thousands of pounds over a long loan period. Do get professional advice from an independent financial adviser before making any decisions.

Check your savings accounts are paying you a competitive rate of interest. If your type of account is no longer marketed, it probably pays a very low rate so switch to a new one. If you pay tax, use up your tax-free savings allowance by opening an ISA (Individual Savings Account). If you have investments that are performing badly, don't ignore them and hope things will improve – they rarely do. Make an appointment to discuss them with an independent financial adviser; the introductory session is usually free.

If you contribute to a personal pension, read the statements every year. You are relying on your pension to look after you one day, so in the meantime look after it because when you retire it will be too late. Every year policyholders receive statements tracking contributions and investment performance. If you don't understand or are concerned about any of these figures, then seek independent financial advice.

Remember to tell your bank and savings managers when you change address. Millions of pounds are lying unclaimed in accounts that people simply forgot about once they stopped getting statements.

What is an independent financial adviser?

You can get financial advice from all sorts of places – family, friends, people at work – but they may not be the best source of information for your situation. Professionals who give financial advice are regulated by the Financial Services Authority. There are laws to ensure that the financial advice you are given is suitable for your circumstances and attitude to risk. You can get professional financial advice about loans and investments from your bank or building society, but this may not be independent. They may only sell you their own mortgages or loans, but they must tell you this.

Independent financial advisers will also sell you loans or investments, but they sell products from a wide range of companies. Ask if they search the whole market for products. They will either charge a fee for their advice or take commission on the sale. They must tell you how much commission they will receive. A register of all independent advisers is available at www.unbiased.co.uk or you can get a list of your local advisers by telephoning 0800 085 3250.

CHECKLIST: GIVE YOURSELF A FINANCIAL CHECKUP

- Can you reduce energy consumption or save by switching providers?
- Check your council tax band is correct and you're claiming any discounts. Pay in monthly instalments to spread the cost.
- Check your mortgage lender is charging a competitive interest rate. You could save thousands of pounds by switching lenders. Seek independent financial advice before taking out a new loan.
- Check savings accounts are paying a competitive rate of interest. Accounts no longer marketed often pay very low rates of interest.
- If you pay tax, use up your tax-free savings allowance by opening an Individual Savings Account (ISA).
- Read your annual personal pension statement. If you don't understand any of the information, seek independent financial advice. Don't wait until you retire – it will be too late.

Tax returns

Some taxpayers have to make a Self Assessment return to the Inland
Revenue once a year. There are financial penalties for filing a late return
(after 31 January for the tax year that ended the previous April). This is
a task that most people put off until the last minute, but can take a
relatively short time to do. If you post your return before the end of
September, the tax office will calculate any tax due or, if you file online,
the tax is automatically calculated as you enter the figures.

Organizing your budget

There are some serious financial responsibilities that come with being a householder. If you don't keep up payments to a landlord or mortgage lender, you may even lose your home. If you're having difficulties, ask your local Citizens Advice Bureau for help.

It's well worth drawing up a budget so that you can find out exactly where your money is going and identify where you might cut back or make things stretch further. Regular bills must be your priority, along with planning for unexpected and routine maintenance to your home.

List all your incoming money, after any deductions, and then make a list of all the bills you have to pay every month. Don't forget to include any payments you make only once a year, like water rates and car tax.

If you have debts that are out of control, or are having difficulty repaying them, you need to try and reduce how much you pay. In some circumstances there are organizations that will help you do this, such as the Citizens Advice Bureau. Treat with caution companies that advertise loans to help pay off existing debts (also called consolidating loans).

There are unexpected expenses in maintaining a home (unless you rent your home and your landlord pays for repairs). The central heating may break down or the drains become blocked. You can buy insurance policies that cover you for plumbing, electrical and boiler problems. You may decide the premiums are worth the convenience and peace of mind. Alternatively, you may prefer to put some money aside each month to cover any repairs. If you don't use the money for emergencies, it can go towards regular maintenance such as painting the outside or laying a new drive.

Drawing up a budget

Monthly income

Salary/Wages (after tax)

Other income

Pension

Investments/Interest

Monthly outgoings

Mortgage/Rent

Council tax

Food

Gas

Electricity

Telephone

Water

Insurance premiums

Car/Travel pass

Credit repayments/Loans

TV licence/Pay TV

Pension contributions

Childcare/Nursery/Education

Child maintenance

Medical care/Personal care

Clothes

Entertainment/Holidays

Memberships

House maintenance and repairs

Total:

Total:

If your outgoings exceed your income, you need to identify savings
or seek help with debts.

What to do if bailiffs call at your door

If you fail to pay money to a creditor, they can seek a court order and appoint bailiffs to collect the debt. Utility companies, banks and councils in England, Wales and Northern Ireland all use bailiffs. These are licensed enforcement agents authorized by the courts to collect outstanding debts. In Scotland, sheriff officers or messengers-at-arms carry out enforcement procedures for the court.

It is unlikely that a bailiff will ever arrive on your doorstep before sending you a warning letter asking for payment. If you do receive a letter, respond immediately. Once a bailiff visits your home you will often incur extra costs, which can be much greater than the debt. Contact both the bailiffs issuing the letter and the company they are acting for. If the company that you owe money to believes you will pay, they may call off the bailiffs, which may keep your costs down.

Bailiffs need a distress warrant from a magistrate's court before they can take your goods into possession. They can enter your home only by peaceful means, but they can enter through open doors and windows. Once inside, they make an inventory of anything you have that can be sold at auction to cover the debt, but the goods must belong to you, and can't include clothing, bedding, or tools connected with your work. If you agree to make a payment, the goods may not be removed, but they will be at a later stage if you don't pay up. If your possessions are sold at auction, they may fetch far less money than you paid for them.

Equipping your home

Over the years we all assemble a collection of equipment and materials that we believe does the job best. Through experience we resist the claims made for newer products, and stick with the things we've tried and tested. We all have different preferences, but these are the things we treasure in our cleaning kits.

Kim When I first got a place of my own I couldn't afford a vacuum; I had a Ewbank carpet sweeper. But today my favourite piece of equipment would have to be a really versatile upright vacuum cleaner. It should be able to adapt to wooden floors and have plenty of tools. Don't get talked into buying the most expensive, they aren't always the best. A good tip is to ask a friend you trust what machine they use, and whether it actually does what it claims. I've got one with a see-through container where you can see all the dirt it has picked up – it's better entertainment than the television.

I was seventeen when I moved into my first bedsit, a scruffy place it was in Liverpool. I didn't have much money for cleaning supplies, but I scrubbed it clean with Ajax, toilet soap and elbow grease. I still like old-fashioned scouring powder for the toilet bowl. I keep all my supplies in the laundry room cupboard. I don't like things dotted around the house. I like to see what I've got and I don't want three opened cleaners all doing the same thing. I carry what I need around the house in a plastic caddy with a handle.

Aggie I wouldn't be without a vacuum cleaner. The first one I bought was an Electrolux, probably because that's what my mother always swore by. I prefer cylinder cleaners because that's what I was brought up with. I used to have two vacuum cleaners; one upstairs, one down, but I got rid of the small hand-held one recently because it was so annoying. I spent more time scrubbing about with it than picking anything up – so I suppose that was my least useful gadget.

I keep most of the cleaning materials under the sink, and some strategically placed around the house where they'll come in handy. I go through these quite often and get rid of the ones I'm not actually using. I think we're all guilty of having too many products. I don't like powders and sprays because I worry about how much you end up inhaling. I prefer cream cleaners and I wouldn't be without my microfibre cloths. They'll do almost anything, and they're great on glass and mirrors. Bleach is one essential supply. I like the really thick stuff you can squirt, nothing too thin and sloppy that you might spill on your clothes. I don't really go for antibacterial products.

Kim You certainly don't need more than half a dozen products to clean. I buy them at the supermarket and people always stop me in the cleaning aisle and ask me what I'm buying. I never recommend things but I'll tell them what works for me. People who are always trying out the newest fads are a manufacturer's dream – but I'm not one of them. If you're happy with what you use, why change, you'll just be throwing your money away.

Aggie Like most people I pick up cleaning supplies with the weekly shop, but I love browsing in hardware stores and looking through catalogues. My absolute favourite cleaning thing is the pure bristle long-handled broom I use to sweep my wooden kitchen floor – bliss!

Kim I collect all my dirty cleaning cloths in a bag and then, once a week, they all go into the washing machine. I put them on the hottest wash – 95°C – I don't care if they go into holes, I just want them clean.

What do you really need?

When we go shopping there's a bewildering choice of supplies. There are cleaning materials, tools, appliances and gadgets for every imaginable task. The only really big question is how many do you actually need and which ones work?

Few of us have the time, or the money, to buy an elaborate cleaning kit from scratch. So when you're setting up home for the first time, it's best to stick to the essentials. Over the years you'll add many other tools to your armoury, but these are the ones you'll appreciate to start with.

The ten essential cleaning tools

- Vacuum cleaner
- Long-handled broom
- Dustpan
- Hand-held brush
- Floor mop
- Rectangular plastic bucket (with mop wringer)
- Scrubbing brush
- Chamois leather
- Long-handled dusting brush
- Supply of cleaning cloths

The vacuum cleaner

Used regularly, your vacuum cleaner will do more work than any other appliance to help keep your home clean. It's undoubtedly one of the greatest domestic labour-saving devices ever invented. Look at several models before you make your choice and buy the best you can afford, but don't pay extra for features you're unlikely ever to use.

There are three main kinds of vacuum cleaner: upright, cylinder and stick-type. The higher power ratings tend to indicate the amount of suction the machine is likely to deliver, but they aren't the only measure of effectiveness. Make sure there's a separate control to vary the suction when you're vacuuming curtains or delicate soft furnishings.

Cylinder cleaners used to rely purely on suction for cleaning power, while uprights had a beater bar as well. Now some cylinders come with turbo heads that reproduce the action of beater bars. In other words, today's vacuum cleaners are very versatile so the choice really is down to your personal preference; don't let the sales assistant persuade you otherwise.

There is also a choice between vacuum cleaners with or without bags. If you choose bags, buy spares at the same time. When you fit the last bag take the packaging to the store with you to make sure you come back with the right replacements. Whichever design you choose, empty out the dust regularly. Remove caught threads from the rollers and heads, and wipe the casing over with a soft damp cloth to improve performance and prolong the life of the appliance. If you take the machine outside, perhaps to vacuum inside the car, stand it on a mat to keep the wheels clean and free from scratches, otherwise once back inside they may damage your floors.

Some vacuum cleaners offer increased air filtration. Look for the HEPA mark, which stands for High Efficiency Particulate Air (filter). The HEPA filter is a system that retains more of the microscopic dust particles that would otherwise be pushed back into the room through the exhaust vents. The most efficient machines have a retention value of over 95 percent. This is an added benefit for allergy and asthma sufferers.

Finally, there are some vacuum cleaners that shampoo carpets and suck up liquids as well. These tend to have large drums and are more practical for specialist rather than regular daily use. Decide how often you'll use the shampoo function or need to suck up liquid spills before you buy one because you can easily hire a specialist machine if you want to shampoo carpets.

Stick-type vacuum cleaner

Pros

- Good for smaller homes with less flooring and less storage space.
- Best for a mix of polished floors and rugs.
- Less heavy to use and carry than conventional vacuum cleaners.

Cons

- They require frequent emptying.
- Not versatile – only for floors, not upholstery or curtains.
- They tend to have small motors so are less powerful.

Upright vacuum cleaner

Pros

- Best for large areas of carpet.
- Can also be used with a flexible tube attachment and tools.
- Check beater bar can be switched on and off for hard floors and long-looped carpets.

Cons

- Not easily manoeuvred on stairs.
- Can be heavy to lift.
- Bulky to store.

Cylinder vacuum cleaner

Pros

- Easy to use on stairs.
- Versatile in small rooms and rooms with lots of furniture.
- Light and small to carry and store.

Cons

- Hard work on large areas of carpet.
- More bending required.
- Cylinder can bash into paintwork and furniture when the hose is pulled carelessly.

Tools

Most vacuum cleaners come with a variety of attachments. These are not often interchangeable, so check before you buy additional accessories for your machine. Manufacturers often offer replacement parts direct via their websites. The most common attachments are:

Upholstery nozzle Vacuum your soft furnishings (and curtains) regularly to prolong the life of the fabric by removing particles of dust, dirt and grit, which left on the surface cause permanent damage. The upholstery nozzle has fibre strips on the underside to catch hair and fluff. Remove the debris by gently rubbing with a damp cloth.

Crevice nozzle Useful to get into the fabric folds on sofas and chairs or where carpeting meets the skirting board. From time to time use the crevice nozzle on carpet pile to deep-clean and raise the pile. A long version of the crevice tool can be useful in difficult places such as in between car seats.

Dusting brush This is one of the most useful tools. Dusting furniture with a vacuum cleaner removes dust from the room completely. Ideal for removing cobwebs from ceilings and hard-to-reach corners or dust from lampshades.

Turbo brush Some cylinder cleaners offer the option of a turbo brush that is independently powered to clean carpet pile more deeply. Turbo brushes are ideal for removing hair, which is why they are often featured on models aimed at pet owners. Turbo heads are not suitable for all carpet types because they may pull the threads on looped carpet.

Floor brush An attachment for a cylinder cleaner with rows of bristles like a broom for use on polished wooden floors. The bristles loosen dust and dirt in the grain of the wood and between the boards.

Micro dusting brush These are often included in car vacuum accessory kits and are invaluable for cleaning computer keyboards and electrical equipment.

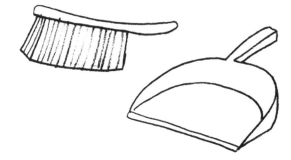

Long-handled broom

Before vacuum cleaners were invented carpets were swept with a brush. This sent up huge clouds of dust so furniture had to be covered with dust sheets. Today, once you own an all-singing and dancing vacuum cleaner, you may wonder what possible use you'll have for a good old-fashioned broom. However, the kitchen floor will always benefit from a quick sweep over and getting out the vacuum can be just too much effort when a broom will have it done in a jiffy.

To sweep a floor expertly, brush towards the centre so the dirt travels the shortest distance. Don't flick the brush head up at the end of the stroke – keep it in contact with the ground. Remove the dirt with a dustpan and soft brush.

Never use the same broom inside and outside. A soft broom is best inside for hard vinyl, wood and tile floors. A stiff broom is best outside for concrete, brick paths and patios. Always store the broom with the head upright, or hang it upside down so the bristles don't get bent.

Dustpan and hand-held brush

Keep a dustpan and brush handy for sweeping up kitchen spills and to save getting out the vacuum cleaner. Choose a dustpan with a soft, flexible lip that will stay in contact with the floor. A soft-bristled brush is best for hard vinyl, wood and tile floors and stiff bristles for carpets, rugs and mats.

Floor mop

There are several types to choose from, but it's really down to personal preference. Mops should always be left upright to dry, never head down in the bucket where harmful bacteria will flourish.

Traditional string type
Pros
- Inexpensive.
- Can be tightly wrung out.

Cons
- Requires a bucket with wringer device.
- Can swish the dirt around if not rinsed out fully.

Cloth strip mop
Pros
- Good for difficult corners.
- Toss into the washing machine when dirty.

Cons
- Requires a bucket with wringer device.
- Can swish the dirt around if not rinsed out fully.
- More expensive than the traditional string.

Square sponge squeeze mop

Pros

o Built-in squeezing mechanism folds sponge in half to remove excess water.

o Flat head sits snugly against the floor surface.

Cons

o Can leave foamy residue behind.

o Refills expensive and not interchangeable.

Triangle-shaped sponge mop with roller squeeze action

Pros

o Roller action squeezes excess water from the sponge.

o Sponge heads have built-in abrasive pads for stubborn marks.

Cons

o Most expensive type to buy and refill.

o Sponges can be unhygienic and wear out quickly.

Rectangular plastic bucket (with mop wringer)

Always use floor washing water from a bucket, never directly from the kitchen sink because this is unhygienic. Use separate buckets for the kitchen and bathroom to avoid cross-contamination of surfaces. Always rinse the bucket after use and allow to dry thoroughly.

Rectangular buckets fit more neatly in cupboards and accept all shapes of mop head. Some buckets are available with two compartments, one for detergent and one for clear rinsing water.

Scrubbing brush

In days gone by, a hard floor was always scrubbed by hand while kneeling down. Modern vinyl and sealed wood surfaces are easier to clean than the old quarry tiles, but there is no substitute for a good scrub every now and again, especially for textured vinyl and grout lines on tiled floors.

Chamois leathers

These last a long time and are worth the investment, so choose genuine leather over synthetic. A rolled chamois will gather pet hair from clothes and upholstery. Avoid using leather with detergent, and don't wring, but squeeze dry. Reshape and allow to dry naturally after use. Rinse in a mild solution of soap flakes to protect the leather and add a drop of olive oil to the final rinse to maintain suppleness.

Long-handled dusting brush

There are three types: feather, microfibre or lambswool. These will dislodge cobwebs from ceilings and remove and trap dust from cupboard tops, shelves and behind radiators. Shake the dust off outside regularly. The microfibre and lambswool types trap and hold more dust than feather.

Supply of cleaning cloths

Soft cotton, fluff-free, loose weave and towelling cloths will cover all eventualities. You can buy cloths, but always recycle old T-shirts, vests, towels and linens. It's much better for the environment to recycle rags and cloths than to buy disposable wipes. White is the best colour because dyes can transfer to other surfaces when used with water or solvents. Always remove any zips or buttons, which could scratch polished surfaces. Save up your dirty cloths for a single machine wash, but don't bother ironing them, they work better creased.

Liquids, powders, polishes and waxes

Supermarket shelves are piled high with cleaning powders, liquids, sprays, polishes and disinfectants for every task imaginable. It's very tempting to buy a product for every job, but completely unnecessary. They're bad for your pocket, bad for the planet and they'll clutter up your cleaning cupboard. Remember not all the best cleaners are in the cleaning aisle – don't forget vinegar, lemon juice and bicarbonate of soda. There are recipes to make your own cleaners elsewhere in the book (*see* The chemistry of cleaning, p. 116).

You only need five daily cleaning products:

- An all-purpose, non-abrasive liquid cleaner.
- An abrasive powder or cream cleaner.
- A mild soap such as washing-up liquid, toilet soap or soap flakes.
- A disinfectant cleaner for the bathroom and toilet.
- Household bleach.

Beeswax polish

This is the kindest wax for wood. You can buy it in tablet form that you have to soften (*see* Furniture, p. 322). Add linseed oil to keep it soft and a couple of drops of essential oil to fragrance. Alternatively, it's available ready formulated. Don't be tempted to wax wood too frequently, it's not necessary.

Bicarbonate of soda

This has been used for scores of jobs over hundreds of years. It provides an excellent alternative to harsh chemical abrasive cleaners for people with allergies or sensitive skin. It makes a powerful paste when mixed with bleach and is a very effective natural deodorizer.

Biological washing powder

Once it looked as if liquids, creams and gels would replace traditional powder, but powder is more economical. Powder allows you to measure exactly how much you need instead of using the manufacturer's measured tablet or capsule dose. Biological powder contains enzymes, which help shift grease and stains. Machine washing can leave trace amounts of detergent in clothes, which some people find causes a skin itchiness or allergy. If you are affected, run an extra rinse cycle or switch to non-biological detergent.

Bleach

Chlorine bleach is the most common household bleach. Ammonia bleach is also available, but the two must never be mixed. Newer oxy bleaches work equally well without the pungent chlorine smell. Don't be tempted to overuse bleach – just a few drops in a bucket of warm soapy water will adequately disinfect. Choose bottles with nozzles for more control over the amount and where it goes, especially when using thin bleach.

Cream cleaner

This has a mildly abrasive action so it's not suitable for surfaces such as acrylic baths or plastic garden furniture, which will scratch. It is however safe for use on enamel baths and tile grout.

Distilled clear vinegar

Vinegar is available in several varieties. The posher, more expensive versions are great for cooking, but wasted on cleaning. Instead, use the cheaper clear 'distilled' type, which is also sometimes described as 'white'. The brown 'malt' vinegar is malted from barley and will also clean, but the smell tends to linger. Vinegar has literally hundreds of uses around the home, so keep some in the cleaning cupboard. Use it for removing limescale (calcium) deposits and cleaning glass and mirrors.

Lemon juice

Either bottled or fresh lemon juice works equally well. The citric acid breaks up limescale deposits left by hard water and, mixed with coarse salt crystals, will rub away the tarnish from brass and copper.

Metal polish

There are different varieties for brass, silver, chrome and stainless steel. Some varieties will clean several metals, so read the label carefully.

Methylated spirits

A solvent that will remove grease, grime and wax from unwashable or hard surfaces such as glass and metal.

Soda crystals

This traditional cleaner has countless uses, mainly for breaking down grease and as a water softener in laundry.

Toilet soap

Very handy for removing stains from clothes and upholstery.

Washing-up liquid

The concentrated variety really does go furthest, but don't save it for the dishes – warm soapy water is suitable for hundreds of cleaning jobs. Antibacterial versions are available, but don't overuse them, they're not necessary and may strengthen the resistance of germs.

Window cleaner

Fill a spray bottle with a half-and-half mix of clear vinegar and water and polish glass with a microfibre cloth for a chemical-free alternative.

Other useful cleaning equipment

Dust mask Always protect your lungs when working with chemicals, especially oven cleaners, or when exposed to dust.

Gloves For tasks involving water and chemicals wear rubber gloves to protect the skin. Latex gloves (as used by medical workers) are good for delicate work, but buy them by the box for best value. Cotton gloves are ideal for protecting hands when polishing wood and metal.

Goggles These are inexpensive and offer additional protection when cleaning inside the oven with spray cleaners.

Cocktail sticks Use them to pick the grime out of switches and screw heads.

Cotton buds These are useful for getting dirt out of fridge door seals and from computer keys.

Microfibre cloths These soft dust-retentive cloths were originally designed for optical use with cameras and spectacles, but are now sold in larger duster sizes.

Paint scraper Good for removing dirt and grease from the hidden sides of cupboards and floors under and around kitchen appliances.

Plastic spatula Good on delicate surfaces or for scraping ice from inside the fridge. Special hob scrapers are best for removing spills from the cooker top.

Razor blade Used with care, a razor blade will remove paint and sticky labels from glass.

Scouring pads These are available in two types: soft white for non-stick cookware, coarse green for tougher jobs.

Toothbrush Never throw away an old toothbrush until it has done at least one other job. They're invaluable for getting into tricky crevices and scrubbing grout lines in tiled surfaces.

Kim's housekeeping tales:
West Chester, New York

It was 1984 before I took another paid cleaning job, when my husband and I decided to look for our first live-in housekeeping job together. Pete was just coming out of the police; I'd been doing shop work and social work. One of the sergeants had been to America and he persuaded us it was a great life out there.

Growing up in Liverpool and watching all the Hollywood movies, I was dreaming of palm trees, sunshine and a mansion in Beverly Hills, so we decided California was the ideal place for us. We went over on holiday and while we were there we placed an advert in the *Los Angeles Times* and received a call straightaway. The gentleman was a Wall Street financier, on vacation in Santa Barbara, but the thing was he wanted a couple for his home near New York. The gentleman was impressed that Pete was coming out of the force. They always like ex-policemen because security is so important for them. So we thought, well at least it's America and we'll get our Green Cards. We got the call in August and we were working for the family just two months later.

It was a huge country house, not old, but then nothing's old in America. It was a beautiful place with about twenty-five rooms, the sort of home you see pictured in magazines. We lived in an apartment in their pool house. Downstairs was a billiards room, table tennis and TV lounge and outside a huge pool and jacuzzi. We hadn't been to the house to meet the couple before we started work, but the Americans are a bit more relaxed so I didn't call them 'sir and madam', they wouldn't have wanted that. But once you're a house-keeper, life changes. It's all 'yes, of course', and people take advantage of you. We'd sold everything to go to America, so we had to make it work, and it was hard. It was very poor money, although we didn't discover until afterwards we were earning the same money that one of us should have been paid.

The lady took us round and showed us what she wanted us to do, and you ask questions, but basically you know what to do – it's cleaning. As soon as you start, they notice the difference, but the jobs soon grow and you spend a lot of time doing washing and ironing. They had two young children who were forever changing their clothes and when someone else is doing the laundry, mum doesn't care. We did full housekeeper duties five days a week. You can give it the most elaborate job title you like, but you are the servants and you do whatever they want: make the beds, clean the house – you're at it from breakfast until dinner. I did all the cooking and babysitting for the two children as well because financiers do an awful lot of deals over dinner so they're often out until late.

They say the Americans are just like us, but everything is on a much bigger scale. You could live inside one of their fridges and they call things different names, a tap is a faucet for example. Of course I'd never been to America, so there were new products to try, and I'd give them all a go. The people don't care what you use, they just want their house cleaned. A lot of Americans have top-loading washing machines, which I have to say I'm very fond of, and I'll tell you why. When you're washing whites you can stop the tub halfway through and leave the whole lot to soak overnight and then finish off in the morning; they come up beautifully. People in this country don't like the top loaders because they don't look good in fitted kitchens, but Americans don't tend to have their washing machines in the kitchen.

The most awful things I saw in New York were the cockroaches; honestly the biggest I've ever seen. Huge things they were, a horrible reddish brown colour, and about two and a half inches across. These don't only scuttle about, they can get off the floor too. Ugh, I hate them.

I remember the winter was cold, very cold, but we'd come to America for the sun, so after two years on the East Coast we once more set our sights on moving to California. We gave our notice, packed up and took a plane to the West Coast. When we arrived we checked into a hotel on Sunset Boulevard and started looking for our next housekeeping job. Finally we were in Hollywood.

Safety and hygiene

Home safety and maintenance

Keeping your home safely maintained is just as important as keeping it clean. Safety first is common sense, but requires some thought and forward planning.

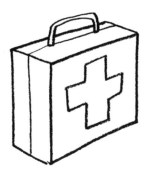

Aggie I have to admit my sisters are much more proficient in home DIY than I am. I can probably do more than I let on, but I prefer it when other people fix things.

Kim Women can do a lot of things around the house today that used to be the man's preserve. I know where the stopcock is; I could free up a sticky lock with some oil; and I'm not afraid to pick up a hammer and bang in a hook for a picture, but I don't like going up ladders. It's very important to keep safe at home, and making sure everything works properly is an important part of that.

Aggie We have plenty of smoke alarms, but we haven't ever discussed how to escape if there was a fire, which we should do. I was staying in a hotel not so long ago when the fire alarm went off at 3.00 am. I certainly didn't waste any time picking up my bag, coat and keys and getting out, and fortunately it turned out to be a false alarm.

Kim I have smoke detectors fitted, which I test regularly, and I never forget to replace the batteries. There's a laminated list of all the telephone numbers I will ever need in an emergency kept in the kitchen drawer. I don't want to have to go ferreting around for numbers when there's a crisis. We all know which numbers we're likely to need, so make your list now.

When it comes to bleeding radiators, don't go round with a tiny tissue to catch the drips, which I have seen some people do. You need a big rag to catch all the drips once the air has escaped. I have a stock of replacement light bulbs standing by. If there's an unusual type that is tricky to buy, then I'll keep in half a dozen. I do know my limitations. If the lights fused and my Pete was out, I'd light a candle and go up to bed.

Aggie I do like things fixed quickly; defunct light bulbs always get replaced within a day or so. I like to keep spare bulbs handy in the kitchen and every now and again, I'll top up the collection with a new batch of the energy-saving type. I can fit a plug; connect up the washing machine; bleed a radiator; hang a picture; and I love unblocking the sink with a plunger, but I wouldn't want to assemble flat-packed furniture or put up a curtain pole because I know I don't have the patience.

There's no meaningful sex-divide when it comes to cleaning and there shouldn't be where home maintenance is involved either.

Most accidents happen at home

Lots of us worry about being involved in a car accident, but statistically we're far more likely to be injured or even killed by an accident in our own home. Taking a few basic precautions and learning a few maintenance skills will minimize the risks.

Preparing for an emergency is something you may feel inclined to put off, but a little preparation now means that when it happens you'll be less inclined to panic, and much more likely to know what to do. Fear and panic set in only when we don't know what's happening and have no idea how to control it.

Home maintenance can be an intimidating business, but when you're trying to do-it-yourself take some comfort from knowing you're not alone. The aisles of vast DIY superstores are crowded with people, just like us, wondering exactly what it is they need, and why none of the staff seems to be anywhere in sight. The good news is you don't need any tools to put most of the following safety advice into action.

What to do in a home emergency

Flooding

The thought of attempting to repair your own plumbing may scare you to death, but there are a few things about the water supply to your home that you should find out about. If you discover water gushing through your ceiling, you'll want to know how to turn off the water. This is not the moment to venture under the sink or into the front garden for the first time in search of the stopcock – especially if it's dark outside.

The stopcock controls the mains water supply to your property. Find out where the stopcock is when you move into a new home. Ask the seller or the developer to show you where it is, and ask whether it needs a key. Shut or off is always the clockwise direction and a few turns should be sufficient to stop the flow. If water is still leaking, that's because it is coming from a water tank or another supply.

WHERE'S THE STOPCOCK?

The stopcock is usually in the front garden under a small metal or plastic cap. You may need a long 'key' to reach down and turn the tap. In newer properties, the stopcock may be located under the kitchen sink. Store the stopcock key somewhere easily accessed, such as just inside the garage door, and keep a torch handy too.

Turning off the water at the stopcock may not immediately stem your leak. Water is also stored in the hot and cold water tanks. If you have hot water leaking, turn on the hot taps to drain the tank. If the water is cold, flush the toilet and run the cold taps to drain the tank. The kitchen tap comes direct from the mains so it won't drain the tank, but because of this, you can check you have successfully turned the stopcock off.

What to do if you smell gas

Knowing where the lever is that turns off the gas supply is also essential. If you smell gas, extinguish all naked flames, open the windows and phone for help immediately. Don't switch on electrical switches – even lights, which may cause a spark. If you need to go into the basement, use a battery torch.

The nationwide emergency telephone number for gas is 0800 111 999. It doesn't matter which company you buy your gas from. Write the number on a label by your gas meter.

Gas appliances must have air ventilation, which is provided when they are fitted. Take care not to block or obstruct these vents with furnishings. Fitting a carbon monoxide detector may also help save your life if a gas appliance malfunctions and releases poisonous gas into your home.

Electrical safety

Knowing a little about the electrical supply may also save your life and at the very least make your home safer. If, when light bulbs and fuses blow, you normally leave the repair to someone else, you are creating a potential hazard. In the darkness you may slip and fall – one of the commonest of all household accidents – which can even be fatal. Keep at hand a supply of all the different types of light bulbs used in your home and restock when your supply runs low.

It's useful to learn how to replace a fuse or reset the trip switch at your electricity consumer unit in case the lights or sockets fail. If the electricity goes off, check with your neighbours or look and see if other homes have lights on. If no one has power, there is a supply problem so telephone your supplier. If it's just your home, there is probably a problem at the fuse box. Electricity can kill, so you should always treat it with the utmost respect, but you can safely change bulbs and fuses.

If you don't know how to fit a plug, get someone to show you. All new appliances come with a factory-fitted plug.

Replacing a fuse

☞ There are two kinds of fuses: those that protect individual appliances and those that protect whole circuits from overloading.

☞ Fuses that protect appliances are usually fitted in the plug, but sometimes they may be in a separate box marked 'fuse' (washing machines, central heating boilers, water pumps and electric showers have these).

☞ When appliances suddenly stop working, it's worth checking the fuse. For example, the plug fuse in an electric lamp can sometimes blow when the light bulb blows.

☞ Most modern and factory-fitted plugs don't have to be unscrewed to replace the fuse. The fuse is inside a flip-open cover on the face with the pins. The most common fuse ratings are 3A and 13A, which specify the amount of protection the fuse offers. Radios and lamps that consume little power have 3A fuses, while washing machines and dishwashers require 13A protection. Electric cookers have a 30A fuse and a special circuit.

☞ Never replace a fuse with one of a higher rating. For example, never replace a 3A fuse with a 13A one, as you may damage the appliance and make it unsafe.

Replacing a light bulb

- ☞ Before you change a light bulb, always check that the light is switched off at the wall socket or, if it's a portable fitting, that the plug is removed from the wall.

- ☞ Bulbs and fittings get very hot while in use. Switch off and wait for them to cool before touching.

- ☞ When changing a bulb, never exceed the maximum rating for the fitting or shade. This is marked on all new shades and fittings. Common limits are 60W and 100W. The rating is to protect the shade or fitting from overheating.

- ☞ If the old bulb has blown and shattered the glass, leaving the metal bayonet inside the fitting, turn off the circuit at the mains isolator. Push a cork into the socket and then use it to twist out the broken fitting.

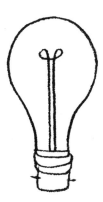

What to do when all the lights, sockets or both fail

- Check your neighbours have normal supply. If they don't either, it is a local fault so telephone your supplier.

- If only your property is without power, check your consumer unit or fuse box.

- If all the lights fail, check at the consumer unit that the trip switch labelled 'lights' has not moved into the off position. If it has, reset it. If the switch fails to reset, there is a more serious problem and you should consult a qualified electrician. If the consumer unit continues to 'trip', you should also seek professional help. Try and establish what caused the switch to 'trip' – did one of the light bulbs blow?

- A modern sealed consumer unit doesn't have any fuses to change. Each circuit is protected by a trip switch. These are labelled according to the circuits they protect: lights, sockets, cooker and heating.

- Older-style fuse boxes have individual removable blocks containing wire fuses. These are more difficult to handle. Turn off the mains at the master switch before removing any of the fuse blocks.

- If the blocks aren't labelled, which is not uncommon, you will have to remove each in turn and examine to see if the wire stretched between the two terminals is still intact.

- You must always replace the wire fuse with one of the same rating (just as with plug fuses). The three ratings at the fuse box are 5A, 15A and 30A. Keep some fuse wire at the fuse box. It is sold with the three sizes wrapped around a card, each clearly labelled.

- When you discover the fuse block that has blown, extend a new length of wire between the two terminals. Look at another fuse block to check you have done this correctly.

- Replace the fuse block and then switch the mains switch back on. If the fuse blows repeatedly, there is a more serious problem and you must call a qualified electrician immediately.

Types of light bulbs

There are a number of different types and styles. They fall into the following categories:

- Bayonet fitting
- Edison screw
- Low-voltage halogen
- Mains-voltage halogen
- Reflector spot light
- Fluorescent tube

Bayonet cap (BC type) fittings push into place, and then take a half twist so that the two side pins locate into the grooves of the light fitting.

Edison screw (ES type) bulbs are for threaded light fittings. There are smaller versions of both the Edison screw and bayonet cap fittings. These are labelled SBC and SES.

Low-voltage bulbs are used with circuits that include a transformer to reduce the current. The bulbs locate into the fittings via two small protruding pins.

Mains-voltage halogen bulbs also fit via two small protruding pins, but the transformer is built into the bulb.

Reflector spot light bulbs have screw fittings.

Fluorescent tubes clip into sprung-steel catches. These fittings also require starter motors. If the bulb is slow in lighting, or only glows at the ends, the starter motor may need replacing. It is a capsule-shaped object usually located on the edge of the fitting.

Emergency telephone numbers

Even once you know how to turn off the water, gas and electricity, you may still need professional help in an emergency, so keep handy telephone numbers for a plumber, electrician and a CORGI engineer (Council for Registered Gas Installers).

First-aid kit

Keep a well-stocked home first-aid kit on hand to deal with any falls, burns, stings or mishaps. You can buy a ready-made first-aid kit or assemble one yourself. Keep everything in a clean, clearly identified waterproof container. Check the contents regularly and replace anything that goes out of date.

CONTENTS FOR A HOME FIRST-AID KIT
- ✚ Assorted adhesive plasters, bandages, gauze, adhesive tape and a pair of blunt-ended scissors.
- ✚ Antiseptic wipes and cream.
- ✚ Eye wash, cup and eye pad.
- ✚ Tweezers for splinter removal.
- ✚ Pain relievers and fever reducers – aspirin, paracetamol and ibuprofen.
- ✚ Hydrocortisone cream for insect bites.
- ✚ Antihistamine for allergic reactions.
- ✚ Thermometer.

Be energy wise

Think carefully about how much energy you use in your home, for the sake of both the environment and your pocket. There are plenty of ways in which you can cut energy consumption – some of them don't cost anything.

Things you can do straightaway, without spending a penny, include completely switching off appliances such as televisions, videos and computers rather than leaving them on standby, which still uses up to 60 percent of the power they consume in use. Turn off the lights when you leave a room and draw the curtains at dusk during the winter to retain heat. Don't fill kettles or baths to the brim – only use the water you need. Turning down room thermostats – even by just 1 percent – can also produce significant savings on your heating bills, in some cases by as much as 10 percent.

Some of the things that require a little outlay are worth considering during maintenance and alterations to your home. Energy-efficient light bulbs quickly recover their additional cost, and a new energy-efficient condensing gas boiler can produce savings of up to 30 percent if your existing boiler is more than 15 years old.

Safety and stepladders

Many jobs around the home require the use of stepladders, whether for changing a light bulb, hanging curtains or washing walls. Treat stepladders with respect as they are a very common cause of accidents.

Safety first when using stepladders

- ✚ Always follow the manufacturer's safety instructions.
- ✚ Always open stepladders fully – never attempt to use them leaning against a wall.
- ✚ Always use on level ground and ensure all four feet make contact with the floor.
- ✚ Keep hands free for holding rails – place buckets and tools on the platform before climbing, wear a tool belt or have tools passed to you.
- ✚ Only one person should ever stand on a stepladder at one time.
- ✚ Never stand a stepladder on top of something else, such as a table – it may topple over.
- ✚ Only use special three-way ladders on stairways.

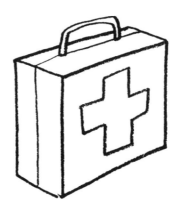

Fire and smoke detectors

One other emergency you should give serious consideration to is what to do in the event of fire. The installation and maintenance of smoke detectors is the most important precaution you can take. These are mandatory in new properties, and should be fitted on every floor.

✚ Test smoke detectors every month – do it on the same day every month so you remember.

✚ Replace the batteries in smoke detectors once a year. Do it on your birthday – you'll remember you've done it and it might save your life.

Prevention is the best precaution against fire. Smouldering cigarettes are a common cause, so never smoke in bed and ensure cigarette stubs are fully extinguished. If an electrical appliance emits smoke, switch it off and unplug it immediately. Don't reuse it until the appliance has been professionally tested.

Fire extinguishers and fire blankets are useful to have on standby. If you don't manage to put out a fire quickly (in less than 10 seconds) you should evacuate everyone and call the fire brigade. Fire can take hold and spread with alarming speed.

Discuss with everyone in your household, especially children, what to do in the event of fire, and how to escape safely from bedrooms. Never go back into a burning building. The effects of smoke inhalation can be serious so be careful when opening doors and seal gaps under doors with a wet towel. If you're stranded upstairs, open the windows and shout 'Fire!' to alert neighbours and passers-by. When locking front doors and upstairs windows, always make sure the keys can be found quickly if there is a fire.

A basic tool kit

Now you have all the essential services covered, there are still some do-it-yourself skills that are useful to master. The best way to learn is by watching someone else – so next time you ask for help, professional or otherwise, don't just vanish and make the tea. Watch what they do, the tools they use, and consider whether you could do it yourself next time.

There are surprisingly few basic skills required: measuring, hammering in nails, driving in screws, sawing and drilling holes. Most of us acquire some of these skills when assembling flat-packed furniture. If you become proficient in these basic skills, you will be able to fit and maintain a huge number of things, from smoke detectors to blinds, curtain poles and shelves.

For DIY tasks you should assemble a basic tool kit, just as you have for cleaning tasks. You don't need expensive, professional quality tools for occasional use. You can either buy a tool kit ready assembled or, less expensively, add to the few tools you probably already own. Keep your tools in a box, and if you have small children store it out of their reach and fit a padlock.

Ideas for a tool kit

- Screwdriver – cross head.
- Screwdriver – slotted head.
- Screwdriver – small slotted head for electrical plugs.
- Steel tape measure – 3 or 5 metres with lockable tape.
- Tenon saw – for cutting wood.
- Junior hacksaw – for cutting metal and plastic.
- Pliers – for bending and gripping metal.
- Spanner – for undoing nuts and bolts.
- Hammer – with claw for pulling out nails.
- Craft knife – with fixed or retractable blade.
- Electric drill – corded or cordless, with hammer action.
- Drill bits – HSS (high speed steel) and masonry bits.
- Safety goggles.
- Battery-powered torch.

The electric drill

One item that anyone serious about DIY needs is an electric drill. If you are comfortable using heavy-duty electric kitchen equipment like blenders and juicers you really shouldn't be scared of using a drill. One commonly held fear is of drilling through something dangerous buried in the wall – like a mains cable or water pipe. You can buy inexpensive electronic testers to detect these things before you start.

Always use heavy-duty appliances with a residual current detector (RCD), which provides further protection in the unlikely event you do drill through electric cable.

Practise drilling holes in a scrap piece of wood or brick before making your first attempt, and wear safety goggles and clothing appropriate to the task – nothing that could get caught up in the drill.

Choosing an electric drill

- There is a bewildering choice available, but a modest model is suitable for basic jobs like putting up pictures and mirrors, fixing shelves, blinds and curtain poles.
- Corded drills are cheapest and plug directly into the plug socket. This type usually has a hammer action as standard.
- You will need a hammer action for drilling into walls that are made of brick and plaster. This is selected on the drill by pushing a button or slide control.
- Cordless drills use a rechargeable battery. There is no need to use extension leads to reach plug points.
- You'll need a selection of drill bits. You need different types for drilling into wood, masonry (brick walls) and metal.

Household pests

None of us wants to share our home with pests
that will destroy our property and make us ill.
They're not fussy about where they live; a ready
supply of food is all they need. If you're careless
with cleanliness then flies, moths, and even mice
will soon move in.

Aggie I've had mice. It was a few years back. I was so shocked when I discovered them because they really give me the creeps. I love baking bread and had stocked up with a bulk purchase of flour, which I stored in the basement. One day I noticed a gaping hole in one of the sacks and a pile of droppings. I called the council immediately; I was just thinking I don't care what it costs, I just want the mice out. I had to throw the whole lot out and the council put down some very strong poison and fortunately that was the last I saw of the little devils.

I don't much like fruit flies either. We keep our vegetable peelings for composting, but in the height of summer fruit flies become too much of a nuisance for it to be worthwhile. They seem to be particularly attracted by bananas and pineapples for some reason.

Kim I've never had a pest invasion, but then my home is so clean what would they be coming in for? I suppose I must confess to fruit flies, aren't they persistent? I don't even have fruit on display. I put out a saucer of honey to attract and trap them, and that works very nicely. If I ever had a more serious problem I'd call for the pest control man, the experts know what they're doing.

Harmful health hazards

Many household pests pose a health hazard. Rats, mice and cockroaches all carry and spread diseases, some of which can be potentially fatal. Some people, especially the young, elderly and expectant mothers, are particularly vulnerable to infection.

Regular cleaning and maintenance is the most effective way of preventing infestation from pests. Most of them are simply looking for food and will move on elsewhere if they don't find it. What constitutes 'food' depends on the pest. If you discover an outbreak, remove all access to the 'food' they are seeking (see specific details for each pest) and block access routes by filling or sealing gaps and holes. If the infestation is serious you should seek expert help.

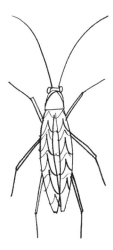

Prevent household pests

- Clear all food away immediately after meals.
- Store perishable food in the fridge or in sealed plastic or glass containers.
- Discard waste food into a covered kitchen bin.
- Empty the kitchen bin regularly.
- Seal rubbish in bags and store outside in a sturdy plastic or metal bin covered with a lid.
- Clear away uneaten pet food.
- Vacuum carpets and upholstery regularly.
- Let fresh air into your home to help eliminate damp.
- Seal cracks in walls, around doors, windows and skirting boards where pests might enter.
- Check cupboards, lofts, cellars and garages regularly.

If you do need to call an exterminator, telephone your local council first and ask if they deal with the type of pest you have. Lots of companies offer pest control services, and they may be able to start work sooner than the council, although they may charge more. Get at least two estimates before you agree to any work and ask the contractor about their code of practice so that you have some redress if the pests persist or the insecticides damage your home. The British Pest Control Association also offers advice to homeowners – www.bpca.org.uk; 0870 6092687.

Ants

Ants are a nuisance but they're harmless. They sometimes come inside in search of food, but their presence doesn't cause the same problems as flies and cockroaches do. You can stop them coming in by sprinkling a line of ant powder across the doorway. If they are persistent, follow their trail outside and put powder around the nest or flood it with a kettle of boiling water.

Bedbugs

Bedbugs are one of the more unpleasant pests, so it's fortunate that they are quite rare. They can be very hard to eliminate, so you'll need to call in a specialist contractor. They like warm, dark conditions and ready access to human or animal blood, so they're at home in sofas and chairs as well as mattresses. Bedbugs don't carry disease, but their bite is painful and irritating so they will disrupt your sleep. Bedbugs can contaminate furniture, laundry and luggage so be wary of buying second-hand goods, which may be infested.

Bees

Bees aren't a pest and many are protected, so it's illegal to exterminate them. They will sting if they're provoked, which is painful and dangerous for anyone who is highly allergic to the venom. Try to lure individual bees out of a window or door, but if your home or garden is invaded by a swarm, contact the local council who will put you in touch with a registered beekeeper.

Some people can suffer from severe allergic reactions to stings from bees, wasps and hornets. Get urgent medical help if any of the following symptoms follow a sting: severe swelling, chest pains or dizziness.

Booklice

Booklice feed on moulds in damp plaster and the glue in book bindings, but they can also get into food cupboards where they eat dry foods such as flour and cereals. They cause real damage only when they're present in large numbers. To prevent infestations keep book shelves well ventilated and store dry foods in sealed plastic or glass containers.

Carpet beetles

Carpet beetles are also known as 'woolly bears' because the newly hatched young have a very hairy coat. They cause considerable damage to carpet, wool, silk and leather because they eat the fibres. If you have an infestation you'll see them walking on the walls and windows as well as in the carpet. Carpet beetles can be difficult to destroy so you may require expert help, but regular cleaning and vacuuming are the most effective prevention from attack.

Cockroaches

Cockroaches are a serious pest. They're more common in warm, wet, tropical climates, which is why you're more likely to see them while abroad on holiday than you are in your kitchen. Cockroaches spread harmful bacteria where they walk and excrete, which can cause serious food poisoning. They nest in warm, dark places under floors or near drains, which makes them difficult to deal with. Cockroach infestations require professional application of pesticide.

Dust mites

Dust mites are microscopic and feed on human and animal skin flakes shed into bedding, carpets and soft furnishings. It's impossible to completely eradicate them, but cleaning does keep them under control. They pose a problem only for people who are allergic to the faeces and cast skin shells. Vacuum all soft furnishings regularly, air rooms and beds to reduce humidity, and launder bedding at 60°C (*see* The healthy home, p. 106).

Fleas

Fleas are usually brought inside by cats and dogs. They feed on dirt and by sucking blood from humans and animals. Their bite is painful and irritating. After sucking blood the female can lay up to twenty eggs, which hatch into new young within two days. Clean pets regularly, fit flea collars and vacuum carpets and soft furnishings to keep control. If you do have a problem, put a flea collar inside the vacuum cleaner to kill any fleas that are sucked inside.

Flies

Flies are attracted to food and smell. They liquefy their food by regurgitating digestive juices and as they do so, they can pass on gastroenteric diseases, which can cause diarrhoea and, in extreme cases, dysentery, typhoid and cholera. A single fly can carry up to two million bacteria on its body. They're fast breeders and females lay hundreds of eggs, usually directly onto food or excrement, which then hatch within twenty-four hours. To discourage flies, keep all food covered and leftovers, including pet food, must be quickly thrown away into a clean, covered bin. Flyscreens and sticky papers are more effective than spray insecticides when it comes to keeping the kitchen clear.

Flour beetles

Flour beetles live in dried foods including flour, cereals, dried fruit and nuts. Infestation can happen before the supplies come into your home because large colonies infest flour mills and bakeries. If you buy food that you discover to be contaminated, return it to the store so other stocks can be checked. Clean cupboards and throw away all affected food. Store new supplies in sealed plastic or glass containers.

Head lice (nits)

Strictly speaking, head lice aren't household pests because they're parasites and can only survive on our scalp. They feed from us and their bites are painful and itchy. Infection spreads rapidly, especially among children. The female lays tiny eggs, which are called nits, at the root of the hair behind the ears; nits can be removed with a nit comb and special shampoo sold by pharmacies.

Mice

Mice will eat almost anything – they'll even gnaw through electric cable. They're highly incontinent, constantly urinating and excreting up to eighty droppings a day, and they breed rapidly – one pair and their offspring can easily become 200 inside a year. Mice harbour parasites that spread diseases to humans, including salmonella, meningitis, encephalitis and tapeworms. If you discover an infestation, lay baits of poison and block all the possible entry points into your home. Cleanliness prevents most rodent infestations; clear away all food and store it in inaccessible containers. If mice do move in, you may require professional help to eradicate them.

Mosquitoes

Mosquitoes are less of a problem in the UK than in tropical countries where they transmit malaria, which can be fatal for humans. Females lay their eggs on stagnant water, so keep water butts and ponds located away from doorways and windows.

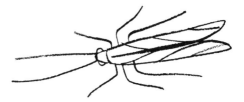

Moths

It's moth larvae that do the damage once the eggs hatch out. The adult female lays her eggs on a ready source of food – often clothing soiled with bacteria, which is why we can find holes in our stored clothes. Moths are less of a problem than they used to be because we use more synthetic fibres and they prefer natural. Always launder clothes and blankets before storing them away. Wrap blankets in sealed bags and lay down with sachets of dried lavender, rosemary and bay leaves, any one of which will deter moths (*see* Caring for clothes and shoes, p. 304).

Rats

Rats are less common in our homes than mice. They thrive in sewers and pose a serious health risk because they are carriers for Weil's disease, which can be fatal for humans. Rats look for easy food, breed rapidly and cause structural damage by gnawing through building materials. They're a health hazard so they must be exterminated by professionals – a service usually provided by the local council.

Silverfish

Silverfish are harmless. They like the damp of kitchens and bathrooms and also feed on the glue in wallpaper paste. Improve ventilation by opening windows or fitting extractor fans in order to reduce the damp.

Wasps

Wasps can give a powerful sting when they're provoked. Remove individual insects by coercing towards open windows, but take care during early autumn when they are at their most docile but still have a ferocious sting. Wasps die naturally with the onset of cold winter weather so destroying nests tends to be considered unnecessary.

Woodlice

These small prehistoric looking armoured creatures aren't pests, although they do look threatening. They much prefer life outside, so pick them up on a piece of paper and put them back in the garden. They make their colonies in damp, dark spots under plant pots and rocks; so don't place these objects close to doorways. If woodlice insist on wandering in, draw a chalk line across the doorway to deter them.

Woodworm

Woodworm bore small round holes and leave powder residue in timber furniture, floors and beams. The presence of fine dust around the holes usually shows that the woodworm is active. Woodworm will spread to other timber so check old and antique furniture carefully before you buy. Treat small infestations with a branded liquid pesticide from a hardware store, but you'll have to call the professionals if joists or floorboards are infected.

The healthy home

We all hope that a clean home will be a healthy home. For some people, though, it doesn't matter how much they clean – an allergy or sensitivity makes using chemicals difficult or unpleasant. But all of us can benefit from improving the environment inside our homes and reducing our exposure to potentially harmful gases and chemicals that are contained in even the most benign-looking everyday products.

Aggie Fortunately I'm not allergic to anything except hyacinth bulbs (which make my skin go itchy). None of us are, in our house, but many of my sons' friends carry those asthma inhalers around. I'm not sure why kids are so allergic to the environment these days. I don't think it's because our homes are cleaner;

although I'm very against those antibacterial sprays you see advertised all the time – to my mind they're just an excuse for not cleaning properly. If you clean and air your home, there's no need for them at all and, more damagingly, they allow harmful bacteria to grow resistant to disinfectant.

Kim I do have a mild eczema. The doctors seem to have ruled out all the things I'm not allergic to, but haven't found out what does cause it. My doctor has even asked me if, perhaps, I'm too clean, please!

Aggie I'm not at all keen on harsh chemical cleaners and I much prefer using materials that are less toxic. It's better for you, better for the environment, better all round really – we've got enough chemicals in our lives already. OK, sometimes you need to use something a bit stronger, but that's usually because you've left the cleaning too long – like inside the oven. I think it's much better to clean frequently without the toxicity.

Kim I agree, if you clean regularly you'll have little use for harsh chemicals. Some of the people we've met though, I'm surprised they weren't very ill; living in all that filth.

Aggie I'm not a trained scientist, but when I take the bacteria samples from the dirt in people's homes the results are uncanny. The lab report identifies the harmful bacteria present and specifies the symptoms they cause in humans. They're nearly always the symptoms the people turn out to be suffering from. Even if you have allergies, there are plenty of natural cleaners and air filters to help you – there really is no excuse.

Chemicals in the home

Throughout the 1960s and 1970s there were significant advances in industrial technology and a huge number of new chemicals in cleaners and manufactured products came into our homes. At the same time, the methods of housing construction were changing too. New homes are better insulated, more energy efficient and built with an increasing number of synthetic materials.

In recent years, some people have begun to wonder why these developments haven't been purely beneficial. We've become aware of the damage our activities are doing to the environment and we've also begun to realize that some of the chemicals in food, furnishings, cosmetics and drugs can have adverse effects on our health.

We don't use lead in pipes or paint any more, and asbestos is banned as a building material because we have discovered they are harmful to our health. Now some people are wondering what the other chemicals in our homes are doing to us. There does appear to be an increase in the number of allergies we're suffering from and a sharp rise in the proportion of children being diagnosed as having asthma.

In Europe, new chemicals added to household products have required safety testing only since 1981. There are 100,000 chemicals in everyday use that were introduced before testing was legally required, and so for many manufacturers it's cheaper to use the old 'untested' chemicals than it is to test new ones. As a result, only 3000 new chemicals have been introduced and tested since 1981, although there are now legislative attempts being made to change this. That's not to say that all chemicals are harmful, just that we're still not aware of their full impact on our health and the environment.

There are some commonsense things that we can all do to control the environment inside our homes – which is after all where we spend a considerable amount of our lives, even if we're only sleeping.

How we live

We've woken up to the importance of a balanced diet and regular exercise for good health, but there are also other things we can do at home to improve our health. If you or anyone in your family suffers from an allergy or sensitivity, you'll be especially aware of the adverse effects some substances and conditions have on our health.

Allergies

An allergen is any substance that, when it is inhaled, eaten or touched, has an adverse effect on our immune system and leads to an allergic reaction. Different people respond to sensitivities in different ways, but common allergies include dust, pollen, bee stings, poison ivy, aspirin, penicillin and nuts.

Most of us have noticed something that doesn't agree with us: metals that turn our skin green, foods that make us sick, or pollen that makes us sneeze. At one time or another, we've all noticed the effect strong chemicals have on our breathing – solvent-based paint when we're decorating or a harsh spray when we're cleaning the oven. If we're aware of the obvious effects, we should open our eyes to the more subtle damage some chemicals may inflict on us.

Humidity

Double-glazed windows leave us snug in winter, but they trap stale air inside our homes and keep the fresh air out. A sealed environment contains more moisture – from our breath, showering, cooking and various appliances, including refrigeration – which leads to condensation. Fresh air from outside contains less moisture, so by opening the windows you decrease the humidity inside your home and limit the opportunity for moulds and mildew to grow. As well as opening windows, it's important to make sure airbricks and ventilation systems are working and kept free from obstructions. Installing a dehumidifier may also improve the air quality, especially for sensitive people or for those who cannot open windows because they are allergic to pollen.

Dust

House dust includes skin scales, hair, pollen, fibres, fingernail fragments, food crumbs and insect parts. It's thought that between 50 and 80 percent of asthmatics may have a reaction to house dust. Another constituent of dust is the house dust mite, which feeds on the dead skin flakes shed by our pets and us. The dust mite also sheds its skin casts and faeces, which some people are allergic to.

If you, or anyone in your home, suffers from a reaction to dust you'll want to remove as much of it as possible. You should also consider carefully whether the furnishings in your home create or store up extra dust. Hard floors hold less dust than carpet; blinds less than curtains; leather upholstery less than fabric and so on.

Dust mites

Dust mites have eight legs and belong to the Pyroglyphidae family of the arachnids – the same class of the animal kingdom as spiders. Fortunately, because of their translucent bodies and tiny size (the male measures only 420 by 240 micrometres), they're invisible to the naked eye. Examining them under a microscope you would see their creamy white outer shell, protruding hairs and a large mouthpart with which they feed voraciously. It's just as well we can't see their fearsome appearance, otherwise we'd never get into bed.

Dust mites feed mainly on human and animal dander – dead skin flakes. They can be present in huge numbers, but it's impossible to eradicate them completely from our homes because they thrive in the same temperature (22–26°C) and humidity range (70–80 percent) as we do. However, we can limit their number by furnishing and cleaning carefully. They live mainly in lounging areas: chairs, sofas, carpets and mattresses – a mattress may contain anything from 100,000 to two million dust mites depending on how old it is and how it has been maintained. Some reports state that as much as 10 percent of the volume of a six-year-old pillow is comprised of dust mites' casts and their faeces. During its three-month life, the female lays between forty and eighty eggs, while the average human sheds between one-half and one gram of skin a day: easily enough to feed thousands of dust mites for several months. Fortunately, for most of us, dust mites aren't harmful.

How to control dust mites

The simplest way to reduce the number of dust mites in your home is to reduce the heat and humidity and remove dust. Airing bedding rapidly reduces humidity, and dust mites can't survive temperatures below 16°C or above 60°C, so laundering bedding at 60°C or putting a child's soft toy in the freezer will effectively kill them. Doctors may also recommend that severely allergic sufferers seal duvets, pillows and mattresses in mite-proof protective covers, although these extra measures are unnecessary for most of us. Additional measures include removing dust with a damp cloth and cutting down the number of soft furnishings.

Vacuuming regularly with a HEPA filter vacuum cleaner (*see* Equipping your home, p. 58) also effectively removes dust mites and their faeces, but note that a thorough vacuuming once a week is more effective than daily light vacuuming, which stirs additional dust into the air.

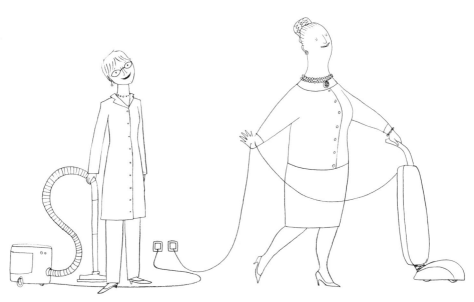

Gases inside our homes

VOCs (volatile organic compounds) are another pollutant in our homes. These are gases that are emitted from many substances at room temperature and pass into the air. In other words, they're volatile, which is how they take their name. They're largely derived from petrochemicals and contain carbon, which is why they're termed organic. They include formaldehyde (which is used as glue in building materials and furniture and is present in tobacco smoke), phenol (an ingredient in disinfectant, fabric treatments and paint) and organochlorines (which include pesticides, cleaning products and solvents).

Many of the products in our homes seep or release gases slowly over time, but we're not yet fully aware of the effect they have on our bodies. Concentrations of VOCs have been measured as being ten times as high inside as outside. When you smell fresh paint or a new carpet you're experiencing the effect of VOCs. They're present in lots of innocent-looking everyday items including perfume, hairspray, fabric conditioner, computer printers and art materials. They're also present in lots of branded cleaning products.

You might decide to try to have fewer of these products inside your home – especially if they make you feel unwell, tired or nauseous and you suffer from headaches, skin rash, runny nose, sore throat, weeping eyes or breathing difficulties. When you decorate, choose water-based, rather than solvent-based, paint; wool over entirely synthetic carpet; and real wood over plastics. These are just some of the conscious decisions you can make that will help improve the quality of the air you breathe.

Cleaning without chemicals

The most damaging exposure to chemicals comes from some of the substances we use for decorating, controlling pests and cleaning. You shouldn't stop cleaning just because you think some of the chemicals on the supermarket shelves might be making you sick – you'll soon become ill for other reasons if you stop cleaning altogether. Cleaning is essential to keep harmful bacteria under control and pests at bay.

Most chemicals are safe for everyday use for the majority of people, but some of us discover we have an unhealthy reaction to particular products – a fragrance, detergent or a cleaning fluid that irritates our skin or makes our eyes stream with tears. If you experience any of these reactions, stop using the product that causes them.

If you are especially sensitive to cleaning products, wear gloves to protect your skin and a respiratory face mask to reduce the vapours and dust you breathe in. Wear dedicated clothes and overalls when you're cleaning and remove them when you finish so you're no longer exposed to dust, pollen and chemical residue. Take a shower to remove all traces of dust and dirt from your hair, face and arms before you change into fresh clothes.

Alternative cleaners

As our ancestors discovered hundreds of years ago, there are plenty of things you can find to clean your home without using branded cleaners (*see* Equipping your home, p. 58, and The chemistry of cleaning, p. 116). Here are a few alternative suggestions for the most common cleaning tasks, but others are included throughout the book.

Kitchen

Washing up A tablespoon of borax added to hot water will remove grease from dishes. You can also mix one tablespoon of borax and one of bicarbonate of soda to make your own dishwasher powder.

Descaler Boil a raw potato and solution of washing soda crystals inside your kettle (but not if it has an aluminium interior) to remove limescale. Or fill the kettle with half vinegar and water, leave overnight and then rinse.

Deodorizer Sprinkling over a little borax or bicarbonate of soda will help neutralize odours from rubbish bins.

Scouring powder To make your own scouring powder, mix a cup of borax, bicarbonate of soda and cooking salt together.

Floor cleaner A solution of washing soda crystals and warm water will cut through grease on vinyl and tiled floors.

Bathroom

Baths, basins and toilets Sprinkle a little borax or bicarbonate of soda powder on to a cloth and use as a scouring powder to clean a porcelain or enamel bathroom.

Toilet limescale Sprinkle washing soda crystals into the toilet and leave overnight to break up limescale.

Shower curtain Wash a mildewed plastic shower curtain in a strong solution of washing soda.

The chemistry of cleaning

Why does cleaning work?

If you've ever wondered why those old-fashioned cleaning remedies actually work, chemistry is the answer. So how does detergent remove grease and bicarbonate of soda eliminate smells? Once you have a grasp of the principles, you'll even be able to devise your own cleaning remedies.

Why is dirt harmful?

A century ago, when there were no antibiotics, housekeepers were extremely concerned about keeping germs at bay, so good home hygiene literally meant the difference between life and death. Today we're not at quite the same risk, but because dirt includes millions of micro-organisms, it can still make us sick.

Of course not all the bacteria in dirt are harmful, but some micro-organisms, including staphylococcus, streptococcus and salmonella, survive on worktops, sinks, toilets and light switches and can cause illnesses such as food poisoning, boils, skin infections, sore throats and pneumonia if they get inside our bodies.

As the name suggests, micro-organisms can't be seen with the naked eye. They only measure between one and two micrometres (one micrometre equals a millionth of a metre). We can, for example, breathe or swallow a harmful dose of pathogens in just a single airborne water droplet. The presence of pathogenic micro-organisms in the air or on a surface doesn't, however, automatically mean that we'll get sick; they have to get into the body first through our nose, mouth, eyes or a cut in the skin. Whether the dose is sufficient to cause infection depends on the individual, although some people are more at risk than others, for example infants, the elderly, the sick and expectant mothers. In a young child, just a few hundred bacteria might cause salmonella poisoning, but it would take a million to infect a healthy young adult.

Where do all these micro-organisms come from? Air, food and water all have the potential to contain harmful bacteria. Some come from our own bodies; they're on our skin and are ejected in coughs, sneezes, saliva and faecal matter. We move bacteria around when we touch things, and walk them in from the street. Our pets, insects and pests all contribute more.

What does 'clean' mean?

Regular cleaning keeps concentrations of bacteria under control and reduces the risk of catching an infectious or fatal dose. When a surface is 'clean', we're really saying that micro-organisms are at safe levels – there are insufficient to cause us harm. The rooms where pathogenic bacteria have the greatest potential to infect us are the kitchen, bathroom and toilet, so these are the rooms that must be cleaned and disinfected most. Because while we clean we're removing harmful bacteria, it's essential to replace cloths and mops frequently, otherwise dirty cloths spread harmful bacteria around. Leave mops to air-dry after use because bacteria flourish in the wet. Just as bacteria thrive in the wet, so do mould and mildew. The spores are airborne so it's impossible to eradicate them completely, but they can be kept under control.

Keeping clean

- Regular hand washing minimizes the spread of harmful bacteria.
- Acids, alkalis, detergents, soaps and solvents chemically neutralize or break up dirt for removal on cloths or in water.
- Physical removal of dirt is just as important as chemical. Scrubbing, sweeping and vacuuming all detach bacteria from surfaces.
- Disinfectant kills bacteria.
- Drying surfaces prevents bacteria returning rapidly – bacteria multiply faster in damp conditions.
- Use clean, dry cloths, mops and buckets to prevent spreading bacteria around.

How does cleaning work?

Cleaning involves both chemical and physical action to get rid of dirt. The physical actions of scrubbing, sweeping and vacuuming all remove bacteria from surfaces. Abrasive ingredients such as silica are added to some cleaners to help rub away more dirt (powdered cleaners contain coarse particles, cream cleaners contain finer particles). We also use abrasive implements to scrub, which include coarse cloths and nylon scourers.

Cleaning also involves bringing together chemical substances that will react with, and break down or neutralize, unwanted dirt molecules so that they can be removed from surfaces – often in a solution of something else. Water or solvents are what we use to do this.

Cleaning chemistry

Acids and alkalis

Chemicals are divided into acids and alkalis. If, when a substance is dissolved in water, it has a pH value above seven, it is termed an alkali, and below seven an acid. Seven is neutral – the value of water (pH values are a measurement of the activity of the hydrogen ions). When acids and alkalis are added together, they begin to neutralize each other and form water and salts. Because most dirt and body oil is slightly acidic, cleaners tend to be slightly alkaline in order to neutralize the acid. While many cleaners are alkali, bathroom cleaners tend to be mildly acidic because soap scum is an alkali.

Alkalis are good for cleaning acidic, fatty and oily dirt, but they're not recommended for painted surfaces because they can remove the oil from the paint, which causes it to crack. A good example of a strongly alkaline cleaner is washing soda. Bicarbonate of soda is less alkaline and can be safely used to neutralize odours, which are often acidic.

Cleaning purposes of alkalis and acids

Acid	Cleaning purpose	pH value
Hydrochloric acid	This is an ingredient in some liquid toilet cleaners.	0.8
Sulphuric acid	This is an ingredient in some powdered toilet cleaners.	1.1
Lemon juice (citric acid)	The naturally occurring acid in citrus fruits is an environmentally harmless cleaning agent and breaks down limescale deposits and removes tarnish from copper (when combined with sodium chloride – table salt).	2.4
Cola	The acid in cola can settle an upset stomach and remove limescale from a toilet pan.	2.5
Clear vinegar (acetic acid)	The acetic acid in vinegar breaks down calcium carbonate (limescale).	2.9
Tomatoes	Ketchup is acidic and can remove the tarnish (oxidation) from brass.	4.2
Carbonated water	Carbonic acid is added to water, which produces the 'fizz' when carbon dioxide escapes.	5.1
Acid rain	Rainwater is slightly acidic.	5.6
Milk	This has some cleaning uses – it can remove ink from leather and fabric.	6.5

Alkali	Cleaning purpose	pH value
Bicarbonate of soda	Mildly alkaline, this cuts through grease and neutralizes odours. It's also used as a 'buffering agent' because of its ability to reduce alkalinity and acidity by holding, or 'buffering', other materials at a pH value of eight.	8
Borax	Used for bleaching whites and deodorizing.	9.2
Detergents	Laundry detergents are mildly alkaline.	9–11
Hand soap	Soap breaks up oil and grease.	9–10
Washing soda	A degreaser and water softener.	11.8
Household ammonia	Ammonia is a powerful bleach contained in some glass and toilet cleaners.	11.5
Hydrogen peroxide	The bleach in oxygen bleach. It's used, in low volume (3 – 5 percent solution), as an antiseptic, mouthwash and a hair dye and decomposes naturally into oxygen and water.	11.65
Household bleach	Chlorine bleach is the most commonly used household bleach. It harmlessly breaks down to water and salt when exposed to the air.	12.5
Sodium hydroxide (caustic soda)	Used in oven and drain cleaning products.	13

Why water alone won't clean

Water is an essential ingredient in many cleaners, but we usually have to add something else. Water on its own can't shift grease and oil because it has the wrong molecular structure. Chemicals are classified into three categories: polar, non-polar and ionic.

Household acids and alkalis

Polar	Non-polar	Ionic
Water	Oil	Salt
Vinegar	Wax	Bicarbonate of soda
Lemon juice	White spirit	Hydrogen peroxide

Polar and non-polar don't mix, like oil and water, but non-polar substances do. In cleaning these include solvents like white spirit and oil. We need to be aware of ionic compounds too – you'll see them listed as ingredients on the packaging of many cleaning products. The smallest particle in an ionic compound is the positively charged ion. The action of these positively charged ions changes substances. For example, when salt dissolves in water it splits into one positively charged sodium ion and one negatively charged chloride ion. Non-polar chemicals don't dissolve ionic substances because they don't split apart the positively and negatively charged particles.

The chemical reason we have to use soap as well as water in the shower to remove dirt is because our skin is covered in natural grease and oil, which is non-polar. Water is polar and can't dissolve the non-polar grease so we add soap, which is made of natural fats to help break down the grease (*see* Laundry, p. 274).

Home-made cleaners

Home-made cleaners work because they use the same chemistry as branded cleaners. Some branded cleaners even boast that they include traditional ingredients, for example vinegar in glass cleaners or bicarbonate of soda in toothpaste.

The reason our home-made cleaners don't always work as quickly as branded cleaners or require repeated applications (for example when we use vinegar to remove hardened lime from taps) is because we don't have access to the more powerful ingredients that manufacturers use. However, as a result home-made cleaners can be kinder to our skin, respiratory function and to the environment.

Always remember that it is potentially dangerous to mix one branded cleaner with another, or to add any home-made ingredients, because there may be a dangerous chemical reaction or release of toxic gas, such as when you mix chlorine and ammonia bleach. Always completely rinse away the residue of the first cleaner before trying an alternative treatment.

There are some safe home-made cleaners you can mix, but don't mix large quantities because they deteriorate over time, and always label the containers clearly and permanently.

Making your own cleaners

To make	Recipe	Uses
Mildly alkaline liquid cleaner	Mix 4 tablespoons of bicarbonate of soda with 1 litre of warm water.	Suitable for wiping inside the fridge.
Strongly alkaline liquid cleaner	Add half a cup of washing soda crystals to 4 litres of warm water.	This dissolves grease and is an effective cleaner in the kitchen and the bathroom.
Mildly abrasive cream cleaner	Add a few drops of water to bicarbonate of soda to form a paste.	Will remove stains and marks from delicate plastic surfaces, for example inside the fridge.
Strongly alkaline abrasive cream cleaner	Add a few drops of chlorine bleach to bicarbonate of soda and mix to a paste.	Effective at removing grease and soap scum from grout lines in tiles.
Window and glass cleaner (acidic)	Mix clear vinegar and water, half and half.	Window and glass cleaners shouldn't contain any abrasives, which could scratch. Spray and wipe dry; there's no need to rinse.

To make	Recipe	Uses
Limescale remover (acidic)	Soak a rag or paper towel in clear vinegar or lemon juice. Not for use on thinly plated surfaces such as gold taps, which would be stripped. Leave for 1 hour and repeat as necessary.	Limescale deposits dissolve in acetic acid, which vinegar naturally contains, and citric acid.
Drain cleaner	Take 1 cup of bicarbonate of soda and 1 cup of clear vinegar.	Pour the bicarbonate of soda into the drain, and slowly add the vinegar. The mixture effervesces, lifting and breaking up grease.
Deodorizer	Bicarbonate of soda is a mild alkali and works by neutralizing acidic dirt and stains.	Sprinkle the powder to neutralize human odours in soft furnishings and urine odours in cat litter. Sprinkle on dry, leave for 1 hour and vacuum off. Also effectively deodorizes smelly sports shoes or inside of the fridge (put some in an open bowl or on half a lemon).

Children and cleaning

Children present their own special challenges when it comes to keeping your home clean, but in time they can also help out around the house.

Aggie I say get the kids involved as soon as they're walking and can fetch and carry things, as I now wish I'd done. They contribute to the mess so it's only right they should help clear it up. Kids definitely need to learn that they can't just keep getting more and more toys out without putting some away first.

Kim When I was a girl we were lucky if we had a spinning top and a kaleidoscope. My sister Gloria and I used to polish the apple green linoleum in the hallway. We took out the tin of Mansion polish, rubbed a bit on our cloths and worked from each end of the hall floor until we met up in the middle. Then we used to put our dusters on our feet and skate about on it for an hour – my, it shone. We thought we were the bee's knees, me and Gloria, when we did that.

Kids today aren't taught cleaning. I think that's good and bad, after all they're only young once. I don't think it should be 'your job is the hall', but they should tidy their own room and help with the dishes and the table. But cleaning the windows, that's not kids' work.

Aggie My three sisters and I had to help around the house when we were growing up. Although it was a bit annoying at the time, we also knew that we'd rather live in a clean and comfortable home than a mucky, smelly one. Kids like to see a difference, the before and after. When I first started appearing on television my youngest, Ewan, really wanted to clean things after the show because it looked such fun, which was great.

Kim What tickles me is people say I'm a fearsome character, but the kids aren't afraid to talk to me; they see through it. I think you have to lead by example. I'm a very tidy person, so I put things away. I'd start with getting children to put their toys away.

Aggie I think you have to make everything fun if possible. The boys would help me with baking even before they could reach the table. I have photos of them standing on a chair to stir the mixing bowl. Rory is fourteen now and he cooked his first meal for the family recently. He was really proud of it, which is great because there's a lot of cooking competition in our house! The boys do lay the table and peel vegetables, and I can just about get them to put their own stuff in the dishwasher afterwards.

I do have to keep on at the boys to put their laundry in the basket and I make their beds for them. I suppose it's a kind of mothering because I'm away from home a lot. If everything else fails, there's always the pocket money incentive – nothing forthcoming until their rooms are tidy. The boys have done ironing for twenty pence an item, more for a shirt if it's done well. OK, so you have to supervise, but it's nice for them to learn how to do something and make a bit of extra pocket money at the same time.

When can children help too?

Children can help around the home and should be encouraged to do so. Many of us earned our first extra pocket money by helping out with chores, and it's an excellent way to learn invaluable skills for later in life.

Children's toys often include replica cooking sets, vacuum cleaners, and even ironing boards so they can play along with mum. When they're ready, it makes sense to let them help out with some of the real jobs. Inevitably they'll be slow to start with, and may even be more hindrance than help, but teaching children new skills can be very rewarding.

You'll need to explain and demonstrate how to do things step by step because you can't assume a child will know how to do something – even if they've watched you do it hundreds of times before. When they've finished a job, admire and praise their work and talk about the task, possibly suggesting things they might do differently next time.

As a child grows up, and certainly by the time they're aged five, you can set tasks for them to do on their own; such as tidy their toys away. You should also set a deadline: 'before you go out and play' or 'before teatime'. By the time they're six, children should be able to straighten their own bed covers, put their clothes away and lay the table. Lots of children enjoy learning to cook – especially baking. Take their enthusiasm as an opportunity to teach the importance of washing hands and keeping food surfaces clean.

Children coming up to ten years old can manage bigger jobs: vacuuming, emptying the bin, washing the car, cutting the grass and ironing a few of their own clothes. Some of the bigger jobs might earn them extra pocket money, but avoid getting into arguments over regular jobs by encouraging youngsters to schedule the jobs themselves and try things their own way.

Older teenagers should be encouraged to take on more and more of their own responsibilities: sorting their own clothes for laundry, ironing, changing their own bed linen and keeping their bedroom clean. This should become second nature, rather than a special effort that is always rewarded. Your children won't always thank you for this training now, but they may when they finally leave home.

Children and housework

Jobs a five-year-old can do
- Straighten their bed in the morning.
- Put their toys away.
- Put their clothes away.
- Help lay the table.
- Help clear the table.
- Help with baking.
- Learn the importance of hand hygiene in the kitchen.
- Put their dirty clothes in the laundry basket.

Jobs a ten-year-old can do
- Empty the bin.
- Vacuuming.
- Wash the car.
- Cut the grass.
- Iron their shirt.

Jobs a teenager can do
- Change their bed linen.
- Clean their room.
- Sort their laundry.
- Prepare a meal.
- Empty the dishwasher.

Family cleaning duties

The happiest homes are those where everyone helps out and works together as a team; the jobs are shared and no one feels as if they're the only one making a contribution. Domestic harmony isn't always easy to achieve and usually someone has to take overall responsibility, but it's definitely easier if parents set their children a good example. Let children offer to do jobs they don't mind having a go at; there's no point giving them all the jobs you don't like because they'll view cleaning as a punishment.

Avoid supervising or checking up on older children, or even your partner, once you've let them take responsibility for a task – otherwise they'll soon give it back to you. Don't criticize the finished result; instead let the rest of the family notice when things haven't been done properly, so you start to work together as a team. If jobs aren't done to your high standards, ask yourself whether you're aiming too high. It's better to encourage everyone to work together than for you to take on the role of martyr. If, after a determined effort, you're still unable to work as a team, then it may be better to hire some additional help (*see* Hiring domestic help, p. 396).

Creative young artists

A lot of craft activities make quite a lot of mess, but of course you'll want to encourage children to be creative. Paints, crayons, glitter, glue and dough are all great fun for youngsters, but not so much of a joy when it comes to keeping surfaces clean. If you can, restrict these activities to a specific table or even better a playroom, so when there are spills or overenthusiasm, the mess can be contained. Vetting art materials carefully will also limit the potential for permanent damage. Avoid paints and pens that are intended for adults because they can be more difficult, or impossible, to shift from surfaces and fabrics. Most art materials specifically designed for use by children are cleanable. Keep any packaging that has specific clean-up advice or the manufacturer's helpline telephone number.

Remove crayon from painted surfaces by rubbing with milk, hairspray or a little methylated spirits. Allow play dough to harden overnight and then pick or brush out as much as you can with a stiff nail brush. Moisten any residue with warm soapy water and brush out the remainder.

One of the leading art materials manufacturers has suggestions about how to remove all their products from almost every conceivable surface: www.crayola.com/ canwehelp – click on the link for stain removal.

Decorating a child's bedroom or playroom

The decoration in playrooms should be safe and easy to clean. Most paint finishes are wipeable now – even some matt emulsions. Carpet is a less practical floor covering in a play area; instead lay laminated flooring, softened with a washable throw rug (anchored with a non-slip mat underneath) to make surfaces easier to clean up.

Use storage boxes for your child's toys and encourage them to put one toy away before taking out another. Each child could choose their favourite colour box, or use different colours for different activities: soft toys, art and craft, building bricks. Toys can accumulate rapidly, so from time to time help your child choose toys to give away to other children.

Toys and hygiene

A lot of parents worry about how hygienic their child's toys are – especially the ones they take everywhere. Toys can become contaminated with bacteria, which are then picked up by the child via their hands and mouth, but most toys can be washed or sponged clean.

Most soft toys can be machine washed (put them in a pillowcase for protection) or sponged with warm soapy water and gently dried with a hairdryer. Freshen up smelly soft toys by putting them in a paper bag with a little bicarbonate of soda. Gently shake the bag to cover the toy and leave for a couple of hours, then vacuum or shake off the powder. Wash plastic building bricks in a bucket of warm soapy water or sterilizing solution. Rinse in clear water and air dry. Don't put plastic building bricks in the washing machine, dishwasher or microwave because the high temperature may melt them or fade the colour.

Children and household safety

Young children love exploring and will play with anything, so as a parent you'll want them to be safe. Remember to store any harmful chemicals, cleaning products, medicines, sharp tools and knives safely out of their reach. Lots of people store cleaning materials in the cupboard under the kitchen sink, where crawling children can easily get hold of them. Once you have children you'll need to secure the cupboard or find a new home for these potentially harmful substances.

Safety precautions for children

- ✛ Garden and decorating chemicals should be safely locked away.
- ✛ Not all parents like stair gates, but fireguards are an essential safety measure.
- ✛ Fit covers over low-level electricity sockets.
- ✛ Pick up animal droppings from the garden to stop crawling infants from touching or putting them in their mouth.
- ✛ Always supervise when you allow younger children to help cook, iron or use equipment. Keep hot pans and liquids out of their reach.

Living with pets

Most pet owners couldn't imagine life without animals, but they do bring extra cleaning responsibilities. Close proximity to animals, even domesticated ones, combined with careless hygiene, can spread disease and provoke allergies in humans.

Kim I say to everybody: a pet is not compulsory; a pet is a luxury. You've got extra cleaning, extra brushing, and extra vacuuming, so if you're not prepared to do it, don't have one, that's all I can say.

I think my Daisy is worth it. She's sweet, she cuddles up and she's always there with us – she even greets us when we come in. Now some animals will scratch or tear things and rip your curtains. I'll take the extra cleaning, but not the damage. Fortunately Daisy never does any damage, she's a very shy cat; as quiet as a mouse.

Daisy's terribly pampered; she sleeps on washable fur rugs. Once I'd worked out where she likes to sleep, I bought a fur rug for each place and I wash them all every week. There's one on the sofa, the pouffe and upstairs on the bed. She shouldn't go in the bedroom, but I don't have any choice, she sleeps curled up on Pete's side.

Daisy's also very timid. She's ever so fragile, bless her – she came from a refuge. She only goes outside once every few days for about ten minutes. She has a sniff at the bushes and then pushes her nose against the glass to come back inside, so she's terribly clean. I even pay to have her teeth cleaned. You may laugh but I think she should be as clean as us – in fact she smells beautiful. If a home smells of dog or cat, then I'm afraid the animal just isn't clean enough.

That's not to say that there haven't been accidents. Daisy is litter-trained, so she always goes to her tray in the utility room and then I scoop out the soiled litter and flush it down the toilet. I always buy the white litter with deodorizer so I can see when she's been. Recently though she's been terribly ill with a stomach complaint, so she's been vomiting. Not in her litter of course, no, anywhere she chooses – usually on the carpet. When I hear her, I act quickly – that's the secret. I say, 'OK Daisy,' to keep her calm and take a knife to lift off as much as possible. I then use paper towels, a warm, damp cloth and toilet soap to dab out the mark. It always works, but I wouldn't want her to do it too often. It's very important for pets to have regular checkups and innoculations at the vet.

Aggie The boys did have some canaries, but at least they were caged-up in the playroom because birds can pass on diseases. We all had to learn the proper hygiene and wash our hands after touching them, but of course it wasn't long before cleaning out the cage fell to me. I would hose it down outside, but it always seems like a much bigger job than it is. Eventually we only had one bird left, which thankfully has now gone to live somewhere else.

Owning a pet means extra cleaning duties

There are over twenty-two million pets in the UK. We've always enjoyed a close relationship with animals, but pets can also be a source of disease. Diseases transmitted by animals to humans are called zoonoses and can be water or food borne, fungal, protozoan or parasitic. The most serious of these are anthrax, rabies and Weil's disease, although these diseases are very rare.

Pets do, however, commonly carry campylobacter, salmonella, psittacosis (chlamydia), tapeworm, toxoplasmosis and toxocariasis. Toxocariasis can cause blindness in humans. Tests on dog faeces found in British parks found that a quarter were contaminated with the worm eggs that cause it. Reptiles can also pass on salmonella via their faeces, which in one tragic British case proved fatal for a young child.

Things to consider

Before you promise your child a pet, discuss the responsibilities that come with it – regular feeding and cleaning of enclosures and litter trays – not just for a few weeks, but for years. Be prepared to take over these duties when your child loses interest or when concentrating on homework is more important. There are also extra expenses for food, equipment, vet's fees, and sometimes care while you're away on holiday. Animals that aren't confined to cages are also likely to soil carpets and furnishings.

Once you own a pet, discuss the diseases that can be passed on in its faeces, urine, vomit, saliva, and waste food and bedding. Always supervise young children while they're handling, feeding or cleaning animals and make sure everyone understands why they must wash their hands with soap and hot water afterwards. Animals should never be kept in the kitchen because their waste can contain salmonella and other harmful bacteria.

To prevent the spread of infection, domestic pets must be quarantined for six months after any foreign travel – except cats, dogs and ferrets, which have a certificate issued by the government's pet passport scheme. Details at www.defra.gov.uk.

Number of pets in the UK 2000

Cats	8 million
Dogs	6.5 million
Fish	2.26 million
Rabbits	1.3 million
Budgies	1 million
Guinea pigs	0.85 million
Hamsters	0.8 million
Canaries	0.36 million
Other birds	1.81 million

© Crown copyright. Source: Department for Environment, Food and Rural Affairs Zoonoses Report 2002.

Cats and dogs

Owning cats or dogs leads to extra cleaning because they roam outside and bring dirt and bacteria back inside the home. They may also harbour parasites, including fleas. Cats are less house-trained than their owners and may even use their urine to define their territory. Both cats and dogs shed hair and skin that dust mites feed on (*see* The healthy home, p. 106). Their litter trays and food bowls may attract other pests or contain harmful bacteria. Never allow a cat or dog to take food from your table or plates because their saliva may also contain these bacteria. Clear away food bowls quickly to prevent pests such as flies feeding from them and transferring bacteria to surfaces around the home.

Don't keep litter trays and dog baskets in the kitchen; instead use a room where food isn't prepared. Remove faeces and urine immediately and replace litter every couple of days. Launder bedding at least once a week.

Cats can suffer from fleas. Fleas are parasites because they require warmth and blood to survive. They will also live on dogs and bite humans. Powder pesticides and cat collars will prevent fleas, but if your animal is contaminated you'll also need to vacuum soft furnishings thoroughly to remove the eggs. Put a flea collar inside the vacuum cleaner dust collection device to kill any fleas that are picked up, and empty out the dust frequently.

Cats and allergies

If you're allergic to house dust, or asthmatic, sharing your home with a cat may be uncomfortable, but it can be tolerable as long as you do some extra vacuuming and dusting. Cats are known for their cleanliness, but when they lick their fur their saliva forms dry flakes, the protein in which causes an allergic reaction in some people. The dry flakes are so light they easily become airborne and can trigger asthma and other symptoms, including itchy eyes and a runny nose. If you do suffer an allergy to cats or dogs, keep them off your bed and soft furnishings.

Cat urine

Cat urine contains urea and uric acid and it is the complex salt crystals in the uric acid that cause the strong odour. These crystals are insoluble in bleach and disinfectant, which is why they won't remove the strong smell. Soda water does help neutralize the acid, and a strong solution of biological laundry detergent may help break up the proteins in the urine. You may, however, find that a branded enzyme-digester product is more expertly formulated than any home-made remedy, especially if the carpet backing is saturated. Unless you manage to remove the stain completely, as soon as it becomes wet again, even through high air humidity, the salt residue will quickly produce more of the strong ammonia-smelling odour.

Diseases pets can pass to humans

Cats

The main risk from cats is toxoplasmosis from the protozoan parasite Toxoplasma, which is contained in cat faeces and litter trays. It can produce flu-like symptoms in us, but pregnant women should take extra care as it can also cause miscarriage or deformity of the unborn foetus. Always dispose of cat litter regularly and carefully – never into the kitchen bin.

Dogs

Dogs can pass on fungal infections such as ringworm, but the main risk is toxocariasis, which is caused by roundworms and their eggs, which are often present in dog faeces. Toxocariasis produces symptoms including chronic abdominal pain, skin rash and loss of vision. Dog owners are advised to worm their pet and make sure children wash their hands after touching them. Parents should supervise very young children to make sure they don't put dog faeces in their mouths or touch their face or mouth while their hands are contaminated.

Birds and reptiles

Unless they roam freely, which some do, the risk from birds and reptiles is more easily contained, but nonetheless still serious. The main health hazard is from salmonella. The most important precautions against infection are to ensure that hands are thoroughly washed after any contact. Birds and reptiles, as with all animals, should be housed away from kitchens and food and their equipment should never be washed or cleaned in the kitchen sink.

The popularity of reptiles as pets has increased, but the Chief Medical Officer was forced to issue a special bulletin warning to the owners of snakes, lizards and terrapins about the risk of catching salmonella from their pets. Nine out of ten reptiles shed salmonella in their faeces, which can be fatal. Young children are most at risk, as are the elderly, pregnant women and those with damaged immune systems.

Children under five shouldn't handle reptiles and older children should always be supervised. Always wash hands with hot soapy water afterwards and never touch or clean reptiles while eating or drinking. Reptiles shouldn't be kept or allowed to roam in the kitchen and their bowls, cages and equipment should never be washed in the sink. If you use the bath to wash equipment, it should be disinfected afterwards, but preferably equipment should be cleaned outside.

Rodents, hamsters and guinea pigs
Rodents can also pass salmonella into their faeces. To avoid the risk of infection, always teach children to wash their hands with hot water and soap after handling or touching the animals, their bedding material or waste. This should be sufficient to prevent cross-contamination. Always wrap used bedding and waste material in newspaper, seal in a bag and dispose of in an outside bin.

Tropical fish
Tropical fish can also pass salmonella to humans. Always wash hands with hot soapy water after handling fish and never clean their equipment in the kitchen sink.

Birds
Birds are the source of psittacosis (chlamydia), which produces flu-like symptoms or respiratory problems in humans. In the year 2000, there were half a dozen cases in Britain, which were traced back to pet shops. Clean bird cages outside whenever possible, and if you do release your birds inside the house, clean up any soiling immediately. Always wash hands after handling birds.

- Always wash hands after touching, feeding or cleaning pets and their equipment.
- The kitchen isn't a suitable room to house or feed any pets.
- Never let pets contaminate any surface where food is prepared.
- Never clean pets' cages or equipment in the kitchen sink. Use the bath and disinfect afterwards or, better still, wash outside.
- Pets should be properly immunized and immediately taken to the vet if they look unwell.
- Take pets outside – even in their cages – for a few hours a day to help improve their health and reduce smells.
- Clean and disinfect pet enclosures regularly.
- Launder all washable pet bedding once a week.
- Floor surfaces contaminated by pets that roam outside should be disinfected frequently.
- Protect soft furnishings from cat and dog hair and soiling with washable covers.
- Faeces, urine and vomit should always be cleaned up and flushed away immediately.
- Completely empty litter trays into an outside bin at least every other day.
- Don't put pet faeces in the kitchen bin – flush them down the toilet.
- Bathe dogs regularly and brush to remove excess dander.

Extra cleaning advice when living with animals

- Vacuum carpets and soft furnishings regularly.
- Sprinkle bicarbonate of soda on to carpets and soft furnishings, leave for an hour to neutralize odours, and then vacuum away.
- Sprinkle bicarbonate of soda into pet litter to deodorize it.
- Wipe dog and cat dishes with a thin film of vegetable oil to make cleaning easier and add oil to the animal's diet, which helps reduce dry-skin dander.
- Spraying dried urine stains with a strong solution of clear vinegar may help neutralize odours.
- Don't use ammonia to clean where cats have sprayed because the smell encourages them to reoffend. Spraying vinegar on fresh cat spray may warn them off.
- Gather pet hairs from soft furnishings with a rolled chamois leather, a rubber glove or a clean rubber-soled shoe. Cover soft furnishings with washable throws if cats and dogs share sofas and chairs.
- Special pet and animal vacuum cleaners have extra features to help remove pet hair and usually include a HEPA filter (*see* Equipping your home, p. 58), which retains more dust inside the machine.

Kim's housekeeping tales:
Brentwood, Los Angeles

Finding a job in Hollywood was harder than expected. I still didn't have a Green Card and so employers were worried that you would skip off; they wouldn't even look at your references! On other occasions I would turn up to interviews with agencies wearing my long painted nails, make-up and jewellery and they would take one look at me and decide I didn't look like a cleaner. They thought I looked too glamorous – ha! Look what they missed out on. After a while I did find a job with a Hollywood executive. Of all the houses I've cleaned, this was probably the most expensive, in a very starry part of Los Angeles.

There was a big staff: a cook, six maids and a nanny for the children. The house wasn't elaborate, but there was a Picasso painting on the wall, which would have paid for several more houses. You couldn't go near it for fear of setting the alarms off; it was wired directly to the security company. Of course I didn't dare touch and anyway the art expert came in and took it away for cleaning.

I started work at 7.00 am every morning, and it was mayhem with kids running around and people dropping in the whole time. I found it very difficult working with so many other staff. People become very territorial about 'their area' and 'their jobs', which isn't really surprising, but I can't be doing with it. Ever afterwards I've made sure it's just Pete and I when we take housekeeping jobs. The other thing is you're all living on top of each other. We had a tiny room at the top of the house.

All the surfaces in that house shone. There was a huge marble hall to mop. There was a special cleaner, which you put a couple of capfuls of into your bucket of warm water. I like to mop with a cotton string mop; you can't beat them. You can't use bleach with a sponge or synthetic mop because they disintegrate.

You certainly don't do a floor that size on your hands and knees, I can tell you.

There was glass everywhere. Huge windows and lots of glass tables with ornaments, trophies and awards on them. You have to be very careful with ornaments on furniture because they can scratch the surface very badly. I used to go to the glass cutters and get tops made to cover some of the furniture in these homes.

The owner also had a beach house in Malibu, which we'd go and look after at the weekend. This man did a lot of entertaining let me tell you, and despite there being a full-time cook, I had to help out too because you had to wait on these people hand and foot. On many occasions you wouldn't finish until 11.30 pm.

Sadly this wasn't the Hollywood life I'd dreamt about, so it wasn't long before we were on a plane back to New York. Even to this day there's a stigma about this work; 'she's only a cleaner, you know'. Well I've been a cleaner and I know what it feels like, it's damned hard work.

Room by room

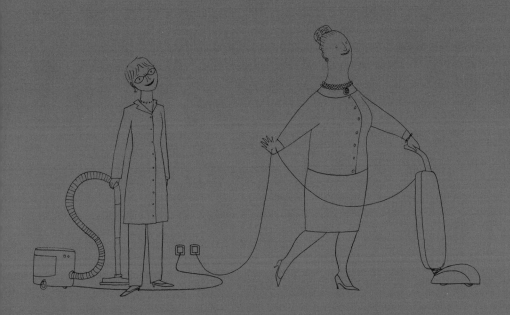

The kitchen

The kitchen is the engine room of the home and, like any engine, it needs regular and loving maintenance to keep it running smoothly. This is where we prepare and often eat our meals, do our laundry and deal with our rubbish, so good hygiene and safety is absolutely essential.

Aggie Keeping the kitchen clean should go without saying. Anything that comes into contact with food that is going into your mouth must be clean. I absolutely love to cook, so I have a large open-plan kitchen, which is definitely the most used room in my house and where I spend most of my time. There's no TV or computer in here, the focus is on the large table where we eat all our family meals and do plenty of entertaining. When we planned the kitchen, there were two things that I just had to have: a waste disposal and filtered water on tap. The waste disposal is a godsend; it doesn't clog up or smell, probably because plenty of lemons go into it and occasionally some hot water and soda crystals to keep it fresh.

Kim This is a brand-new house and the kitchen is all mod cons; the units are a light beech with long steel handles, topped off with dark granite, which I love because it has such a wonderful shine. You have to look after granite, mind, although it's not as delicate as marble. Nonetheless I always protect the work top with a metal trivet that has rubber feet whenever I'm taking pots from the oven. Once a week, or even twice, I take everything off all the surfaces and give them a good wash down, then buff the granite up to a high shine with window cleaning spray.

I've also got one of those new stainless steel sinks that has another bowl the size of a shirt button. I honestly don't know what it's for, but it looks posh. I wouldn't want to go back to those old butler sinks, you're always worried about chipping or scratching them, and the glaze crazes. I always stand a matching grey plastic washing-up bowl in the sink for doing the dishes so that they're cushioned nicely. Some people let all the dregs get trapped under their bowl; don't do that, lift up your bowl, please.

I find scouring powder works very well on stainless steel, but I do these things without thinking. I'm not spending hours on jobs, they're done in two minutes, you really can achieve a great deal if you try, you know.

Aggie I actually quite like washing up by hand and am always happy to do the big things that won't fit in the dishwasher, rather than storing up a second load. I prefer not to use a plastic bowl in the sink. I have a fitted double bowl and rinse under hot running water, and then I usually air dry unless I need to get rid of the clutter immediately. I love restoring order to the kitchen, leaving it gleaming. Once it's done, I can't wait to get stuck into some more cooking or baking.

Kim I always hand wash glassware – it's really not meant to go in the dishwasher – and if I've only used a cup and a plate, I'll wash them by hand too – well you're not going to run the machine for that are you? I put on the dishwasher at the end of the day, and I always put in my dish brush and cloth on the top rack too so that they come out nice and fresh.

Aggie I sort through all my food cupboards regularly and give the fridge a good clean out on a Saturday before restocking it. Any leftovers that can't be used for lunch go out, even though I hate throwing food away. Fish and meat I'm very cautious about, and I let my nose be the judge of whether they are as fresh as the use-by date is telling me. Most of the weekly shop is delivered to the door after I order online. I've been doing the shopping like this for about eighteen months now, and it means that the chilled and frozen food is always stored at the correct temperature between the shop and my home.

Kim Lots of people make a big fuss about cleaning the oven. Let me tell you, my oven is cleaned whenever it's been used. I've got a stainless steel gas hob and an electric oven, which I think is a wonderful combination. I always clean the oven while it's still warm. I go over it with washing-up liquid and an old towel; the roughness really helps shift the grease. You don't want grease to build up in your oven: this way it only takes two minutes and you've saved yourself a big, horrible job later. The stainless steel is easy – just a quick wipe over and buff dry.

Aggie I have three chopping boards, all of them wood. A fresh board for each task is the safest way when it comes to food hygiene. I scrub them clean with wire wool pads and plenty of hot soapy water. I never put anything wood in the dishwasher. I'm also fastidious about constantly changing over all the cloths in the kitchen, which drives my family crazy because they know the answer to the question, 'Where's the washing-up cloth?' is always going to be, 'In the washing machine.'

Kim Don't forget the floor; I do my stone floor at least twice a week. I actually prefer to do it on my hands and knees. I have a separate red bucket for the kitchen – I always think of red for danger, because there's so much going on in here. For me, it's easier to get out a bucket and an old towelling cloth than all that messing about with mops. But do get out the vacuum or sweep the floor first; otherwise you'll end up in a hell of a mess with all those crumbs and hairs on your cloth. I always use warm water and washing-up liquid, wring the cloth out nice and tight, and then leave the floor to dry for quarter of an hour while I go and do something else. Occasionally I add a couple of drops of bleach to my bucket to kill the bacteria.

Kitchen safety and food hygiene

It's essential that food is safely stored and prepared in a clean environment. Lack of cleanliness and poor quality food hygiene can quickly lead to sickness and food poisoning, so this is one room where regular cleaning is essential. Always wash your hands before starting any food preparation, and make sure all surfaces, utensils and cloths are scrupulously clean. Restaurant and commercial kitchens are regularly inspected, whereas hygiene in your own kitchen is entirely up to you.

There are a number of things you should do automatically, which will contribute to the overall cleanliness and hygiene of your kitchen. Each of these is covered in detail over the following pages, but here is a checklist of the main points:

○ Wash hands.
○ Keep work surfaces clean and free from clutter.
○ Don't use the kitchen sink for other cleaning tasks, such as floor washing or shoe cleaning.
○ Follow safe food storage and cooking procedures.
○ Wash up after every meal.
○ Use a covered bin for kitchen rubbish and empty outside regularly.
○ Sweep or vacuum and wash the floor frequently.
○ Don't sort dirty laundry on food preparation surfaces.
○ Keep pets away from the kitchen.
○ Never wipe the floor with your washing-up cloth.
○ Keep separate towels for hands and dishes.

How hygiene works

Good kitchen hygiene is essential to prevent harmful build-up of bacteria and pathogens. Bacteria are everywhere: in most foods, on our skin and within our bodies, but in excessive concentrations they can be extremely harmful. Raw meat and fish carry a high risk of contamination, but cooking kills bacteria and refrigeration normally controls further growth, which is also why hot food must be cooked thoroughly, and chilled food mustn't be left out in the warm. Dirty dishes should be washed immediately after meals to stop bacteria multiplying on their surface, and to deter flies and insects that may spread the bacteria to other surfaces.

How to wash hands

One of the most important things is to wash and dry your hands before starting any work in the kitchen. In commercial kitchens and hospitals, where good hygiene really matters, workers are routinely shown how to wash their hands, but no one teaches us how important it is in our own homes.

Washing hands with soap and hot water removes pathogens and faecal matter from the surface of the skin and under the nails. You should always wash your hands after every visit to the toilet, and before preparing any food. Always wash them again after handling raw meat, fish and poultry and before touching anything else, including cooking implements. You should also wash hands after feeding or touching pets, coughing, sneezing and handling rubbish. As soon as children are old enough, you should teach them the importance of washing their hands after each of these activities.

If possible wash your hands away from the kitchen sink, in the utility room, cloakroom or bathroom, to prevent contaminating the sink where you wash food. Take off all your rings and jewellery and leave them off while preparing food. It doesn't matter whether you use liquid or tablet soap, but don't refill liquid soap bottles because they can become contaminated with bacteria. Bacteria won't grow on tablet soap provided it is left on a drainage block to dry after use.

Lather up the soap and rub the surfaces of the hands together vigorously for at least twenty seconds. Tests have shown that using running warm water is more hygienic than a bowl filled with water. Interlace the fingers and wash each finger and thumb separately by inserting between the curled index finger and thumb of the other hand. Don't forget your fingertips and nails. Tests have shown that if you scrub with a nailbrush you will remove 350 times more micro-organisms than washing without a brush. Incidentally, you are more likely to recontaminate your hands from touching a dirty door handle than from sharing a nailbrush. When you have soaped and rinsed, you need to dry your hands thoroughly. A dedicated hand towel or disposable paper towel is safest, never a towel used for dishes. Don't dry your hands on your apron because you may recontaminate them, and don't leave them wet, because moisture encourages further bacterial growth.

Food safety

Always follow the storage, 'use-by' and cooking advice labels on all food packaging for meat, fish, precooked dishes and those that contain raw ingredients.

Storing and preparing raw meat

Raw meat must be kept refrigerated and then cooked before the 'use-by' date printed on the packaging. It should be stored in sealed containers at the bottom of the fridge, so that any juice or blood that leaks from the packaging doesn't drip on to other foods. You can also freeze raw meat following the instructions on the label. Defrost in the microwave for immediate cooking, or inside the fridge, but not at room temperature where it may become overwarm. Take care that the juices don't contaminate food and surfaces. Once meat has been defrosted it must be cooked and eaten within two days.

Some people like to wash raw meat under the cold tap, but this can splash harmful bacteria on to other surfaces, bacteria that would in any case be killed by cooking. All hands, utensils and chopping boards that come into contact with raw meat must be washed immediately with hot soapy water, and then dried, preferably with a disposable paper towel. Always use separate chopping boards for raw meats and other foods to stop cross-contamination between foods – especially among those that won't be cooked, such as salad tomatoes and lettuce leaves. When the surface of the chopping board becomes damaged and difficult to clean, it should be replaced with a new one. There is a debate as to whether wood or plastic boards are more hygienic, but there is no reliable proof as to which is safer. It is, however, undeniable that washing with hot soapy water after each and every use is essential.

Cooking raw meat

Only joints of meat or steaks should be eaten rare or with pink bits. Frying raw steaks and joints over high heat kills bacteria and safely seals the inside, the colour of the meat visibly changing as it seals.

Other meat, especially chicken, turkey, all burgers, sausages, kebabs and rolled joints, must be cooked right through to kill harmful bacteria, which are present throughout the meat. When cooking burgers, chicken or sausages, cut into the middle of the meat and make sure there are no pink bits. For a roast chicken, push a skewer or sharp knife into the flesh and legs to ensure the juices run clear before serving.

Heating food

Cooked food must be piping hot before it can be eaten safely. Stir food from time to time during cooking, and test pies and other dishes are hot by cutting into them – steam should come out. Check large dishes of food in several places.

Chilling and reheating food

Once food has been cooked, if it is to be served or reheated later, allow it to cool at room temperature for between one and two hours and then store in the refrigerator. Never put hot food straight into the fridge as it will raise the internal temperature and may spoil other food. Once refrigerated, leftover cooked food should be eaten within two days or thrown away. When you reheat cooked food it must be piping hot all the way through. Cooked food shouldn't be reheated more than once, and not at all if the instructions on prepackaged food warn against it.

Refrigerating chilled food

Chilled food must be kept refrigerated. Chilling controls the growth of bacteria, which can be harmful at high concentrations. It's a good idea to use insulated bags with ice packs to transport chilled food home from the shops, because it can quickly heat up in the car, especially during warm weather. When you're cooking and preparing meals with chilled ingredients, always return them to the fridge as soon as you have finished with them. If you're serving chilled food, including salads, party food and desserts, don't leave them standing out of the fridge for more than two hours. Throw away any food that stands out for more than two hours, and never rechill it.

Work surface safety

It's essential to wipe down all work surfaces before starting any food preparation otherwise bacteria can spread to food and may cause illness. If food is spilt on to work surfaces during preparation, especially juices from raw meat or uncooked egg, wipe it up straightaway.

Disinfecting food preparation surfaces

All food preparation surfaces must be cleaned before and after every meal. Warm soapy water – a few drops of washing-up liquid are more than adequate – and a coarse dish cloth are sufficient to remove most bacteria. The friction created by rubbing with the cloth helps physically remove bacteria that cling to the surface. From time to time you should also disinfect surfaces, but wipe away any dirt and spills first because they can neutralize the effect of the disinfectant.

To disinfect a work surface, add a few drops of household chlorine bleach to some warm soapy water. Wear rubber gloves to protect your skin and to enable you to use hotter water. Thoroughly rub the cloth over the entire surface, refreshing the cloth in the water and wringing out tightly. Chlorine bleach is a safe household disinfectant because it quickly evaporates, breaking down into salt and water, and doesn't leave any antibacterial agents behind, which microbes may become resistant to over time. Leave the surface damp for a couple of minutes to let the bleach do its work and then, if it hasn't air-dried, buff off with disposable paper towel.

Kitchen cloth safety

Cloths are the real unseen enemy in the kitchen. Bacteria can multiply on them rapidly in the warm, moist conditions. Bacteria from cloths can then be spread to hands, dishes and surfaces. Even if a cloth doesn't look dirty, it may be contaminated. Use paper towel for drying hands and wiping up meat juice spills to reduce the risk of cross-contamination. Change the dish cloth, drying towel (tea towel) and hand-drying towel every day for fresh ones.

CHECKLIST: FOOD SAFETY

Before you start

- O Wash hands before starting work and after touching raw meat, fish and poultry or rubbish.
- O Wipe down work surfaces before preparing food.

Cooking

- O Check freshly cooked and reheated food is hot all the way through.
- O Cook poultry, burgers and sausages right through until all the flesh changes colour.
- O Wash chopping boards with hot soapy water immediately after every use.

Refrigerating

- O Chilled food must be kept refrigerated or disposed of after two hours.
- O Raw meat must be refrigerated in sealed containers at the bottom of the fridge to prevent juices contaminating other food.
- O Store cooked food in the fridge and eat within two days.
- O Don't leave chilled ingredients out for longer than necessary when preparing dishes.
- O Don't put opened tinned foods into the fridge; transfer the contents first.

Food storage

- Check stored food regularly and stick to 'use-by' dates.
- Keep bagged goods like flour, rice, pasta and biscuits in airtight glass or plastic containers to protect from pests.
- Store new supplies at the backs of cupboard shelves and move older stocks to the front.
- Don't let fruit and vegetables overripen – they attract fruit flies. One item of rotting fruit speeds up the decline of all the other fruit.

Kitchen safety

As well as keeping your kitchen clean and hygienic, you need to ensure it is a safe space to work in. There are plenty of potential hazards from burns, scalds, electric shock, cuts, falls and chemicals used for cleaning. Common sense is the best safeguard against accidents, but there are some extra precautions you can take:

- Always turn pan handles in from the edge of the stove during cooking to prevent catching, or young hands pulling them. Use a stoveguard.
- Store sharp knives in a block or a drawer.
- Never leave oil to fry unattended.
- Carry plates to hot pans, not hot pans to plates.
- Mop up spills immediately to avoid slips and falls.
- Guard against fire – have an extinguisher or fire blanket ready.
- Don't store cleaning chemicals where young children can access them.

Planning kitchen layout and storage

The ideal kitchen layout is widely considered to be the 'work triangle' with the sink, cooker and refrigerator located at each of the three imaginary points. It's not essential to conform to this rule, but it does produce the optimum distance between each of the three main task areas.

Despite having to cope with a wide range of activities, the kitchen must be kept free from clutter. Cooking produces lots of grease, which quickly covers every surface, so you need to be able to clean quickly and easily, which is difficult, or even impossible, if surfaces are covered with rarely used gadgets and appliances; tidy these into cupboards or dispose of them. It can be awkward to wipe away the greasy film left on the tops of cupboards, so cover them with lining paper and refresh with clean paper from time to time. Open shelves may look good in the kitchen showroom, but they create a lot of extra cleaning.

When you're deciding where to put things, it's a good idea to store heavier items such as plates and pans in the lower cupboards and drawers so that they're easier to handle and less likely to drop. Drawers are ideal for pans because you don't need to take out those at the front to access the ones at the back as you do with cupboards. Try and store cooking utensils near the stove, and drinks things near the kettle, to use the space most efficiently. All kitchens tend to collect loose odds and ends, such as pens, batteries and so on, so keep them all together in a dedicated drawer.

Don't forget to clean inside kitchen cupboards and drawers from time to time. Remove all the contents, vacuum out the crumbs and wipe over with hot soapy water, making sure all the surfaces are dry before you put everything back. It's much easier to clean one every week as you go along, rather than try and do them all at once in a mammoth blitz.

Choosing the right kitchen appliances

Equipping a kitchen is a major investment so you'll want the appliances you choose to give pleasure and satisfaction. When deciding which model to buy, find out how it works; whether it does more or less than you want; how easy it is to clean; and how much energy it uses.

Things to consider:

○ Do you like the design and finish? Is it the right size?
○ Does it do more or less than you need? Don't pay for features you'll never use.
○ How easy is it to clean?
○ Look for self-cleaning ovens and frost-free refrigeration.
○ Look at the energy rating. A more expensive model may consume less electricity and cost less in the long run.
○ Once you've found an appliance you want to buy, enter the model number and the word 'review' into an internet search engine to find out how previous buyers rate it; and the best price available.

Clean the outside of appliances too

The importance of cleaning inside the oven and fridge is obvious, but don't forget to keep the cabinets and handles clean too, because bacteria can breed here just as easily and transfer to your hands while you're preparing food. To clean your appliances:

O Wipe the outside cabinet regularly with warm soapy water, and dry with a soft cloth or disposable kitchen paper.
O Remove heavier grease deposits on white painted steel, vinyl and enamelled surfaces with a mild solution of washing soda.
O Use a plastic spatula to scrape away heavy grease deposits.
O Don't use anything abrasive on stainless steel surfaces; instead wipe with a cloth dipped in warm soapy water and buff dry.
O Clean glass panels and shelves with a half-and-half mix of clear vinegar and water (keep some ready-mixed in a clearly labelled spray bottle).

The cooker

Cookers burn gas or electricity, or a combination of both, and there are also some built-in solid fuel cooking ranges available. There are arguments for and against gas and electricity; but gas hobs and fan-assisted electric ovens are generally considered most versatile because they give the greatest control over temperature and cooking speed. Cookers can be either built into fitted units or freestanding. Features to look for include self-cleaning ovens and digital timers.

The oven

Cleaning the oven must rate as one of the worst jobs in the home; no wonder some specialist companies now offer to come and clean it for you. Ovens end up most heavily soiled when grease is baked on during repeated use without any cleaning. The best way to avoid lengthy and difficult cleaning, and having to use caustic chemicals, is to wipe down the interior and door with warm soapy water every time you cook. You can also line the bottom of the oven with foil to catch spills, but change this regularly or it will become difficult to remove. Some ovens have self-cleaning liners and the latest pyrolytic-cleaning models have a super-heated cleaning cycle at 500°C, which burns any residue into a fine ash that is then easily wiped away.

Cleaning a really dirty oven is more of a challenge. You have a choice to make between the gentle and the highly toxic approach, but neither is quick or easy. If you use a caustic chemical cleaner, always wear protective clothing, protect the floor, and ventilate the room by opening the windows and door.

Cleaning the oven safely

✛ Open the windows before using chemical oven cleaners.

✛ Take removable trays outside for cleaning.

✛ Wear a respiratory mask, thick rubber gloves and protective clothes when using chemical oven cleaners.

✛ Always turn off an electric oven at the isolator wall switch before cleaning.

✛ Follow the manufacturer's instructions for self-cleaning ovens or you may permanently damage them.

✛ If you're using a branded oven cleaner, always follow the instructions and never mix with any other cleaner – you could produce poisonous gas or damage the oven.

✛ Caustic chemicals are not suitable for use by expectant mothers or when young children and pets are present.

Non-caustic method of cleaning the oven

The non-toxic method is to coat all the interior surfaces with a thick paste of bicarbonate of soda and a few drops of water. Leave this to soak for several hours or, better still, overnight. You will then have to scrub the residue off with warm water and a scouring pad. This method requires plenty of elbow grease and residue can be tricky to shift. On the plus side, you won't be using any harsh chemicals, so it's suitable for asthma and allergy sufferers, if you are pregnant, or have young children and pets present.

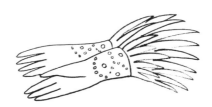

Caustic method of cleaning the oven

An effective, but caustic, method of cleaning all the removable trays
and racks is with a solution of dilute ammonia bleach. You should wear
a respiratory face mask, thick rubber gloves and protective clothes
and footwear and work outside.

Fill a spray bottle with a solution of ammonia bleach and water.
Mark the bottle with indelible pen to warn that it contains ammonia;
you'll also need a plastic bin bag. Remove all the oven shelves and
racks and take them outside. Spray each of the racks with ammonia
and drop them into the bin bag. Once all the racks are done, tie the
bag and leave to soak for a couple of hours.

Spray the inside walls of the oven with the ammonia solution,
taking care to protect the floor around the cooker with thick plastic
sheets and ensuring people and pets won't be harmed.

After two hours, reopen the bag (wearing protective clothing) and
hose down each of the racks with cold water – don't do this on your
prized lawn. The residue should wash away easily. Rinse out the oven
interior using a cloth and clean water.

Wash each tray with warm soapy water before replacing inside the
oven. Heat the empty oven to ensure it is clean before further use.

Caustic and non-caustic branded cleaners

There are caustic and non-caustic branded oven cleaners available.
The caustic varieties contain sodium hydroxide (caustic soda) or
potassium hydroxide. These are highly corrosive chemicals, with
a strong smell, which can burn the skin and lead to respiratory
problems.

Non-caustic cleaners use very different agents, including alkaline
salts and diethyl-glycol-alkyl-ether. Always follow the manufacturer's
instructions and ensure the oven is free from any chemical residue
before use.

The grill

Grill pans either have their own slot (usually gas) or are housed within the oven compartment (usually electric). They are generally either polished steel or have a coated finish. You can avoid heavy soiling, and therefore scouring, by lining the pan with aluminium foil or brushing the surface with vegetable oil. Avoid using harsh scourers on grill pans. Soak heavily soiled pans in a solution of hot water and biological laundry detergent, and then use a washing-up brush or scrunched-up aluminium foil.

The hob

There are three main styles of hobs. Electric hobs have either ceramic glass surfaces or individual hotplates, and gas hobs have burners.

A ceramic hob

Ceramic hobs require special care to avoid scratching and etching. Check the bottoms of pans are clean, and don't scrape them across the surface. Sugar and sugar-based spills must be wiped off as soon as possible or they will crystallize on cooling and pit the glass surface. Scrape off burnt spills with a special plastic hob scraper (from kitchen shops). Use the manufacturer's recommended cleaner-conditioner to maintain the surface as directed – this usually contains citric acid and shouldn't be mixed with any other cleaner.

Electric hotplates

Wipe the steel or vitreous enamel surface around the hotplates with
a soft cloth and washing-up liquid. Stubborn deposits may require a
little cream cleaner, but be careful not to scratch the finish – especially
if it's stainless steel. Wipe hotplates over with cream cleaner or a paste
of water and bicarbonate of soda. Stubborn marks can be rubbed with
a nylon scourer or heated up to carbonize and then brushed away.
The hotplates won't rust if they are heated up briefly to dry.

A gas hob

Gas hobs require pan stands over the gas burners. The stands can
go into the dishwasher, or soak heavily soiled accessories in a bucket
of hot water and biological laundry detergent. The gas burners can
be dismantled and each part scrubbed with a nylon pad and cream
cleaner or a paste of bicarbonate of soda and water. Wipe the steel or
vitreous enamel surfaces around the hotplates with a soft cloth and
washing-up liquid.

The cooker hood

The humble cooker hood has become quite a design statement recently. Its function is to remove steam, grease and fumes coming directly from the hob, either by recirculating air through a charcoal filter or by pumping air outside via a tube and vent. There is also a disposable paper or washable mesh filter. Charcoal and paper filters require regular replacement. The washable metal filter is the main thing that requires cleaning as it gets very greasy. The easiest way to do this is to put it into the dishwasher where it will get a good hot wash and come out dry. Alternatively scrub with a brush and hot soapy water, and dry.

The fridge

Fridges are available with an icebox; as a 'larder' model; without a frozen food compartment; or as a combined fridge and freezer. Frost-free models, which never require defrosting, are also available.

Locate your fridge and freezer away from the cooker and any radiators to improve their efficiency. Frozen food should only be stored in ice-making compartments in accordance with the manufacturer's star rating – usually between twenty-four hours and one week. The fridge should operate between 4–5°C at the top and 1°C in the lowest section of the fridge. Use the top shelf for yoghurt, butter and chilled food; the bottom for fish, raw meat and poultry. If your fridge doesn't have a temperature display, buy an inexpensive fridge thermometer from the supermarket to check it's working safely.

Defrosting the fridge

Defrost the fridge whenever there's a build-up of ice inside on the back panel or around the icebox; it won't work safely if it is frozen up. Unplug the appliance and store all the food in an insulated cool bag with ice-packs while the fridge defrosts. You should aim to have the fridge completely defrosted and repacked within two hours.

Pull the fridge away from the wall and vacuum the cooling elements with the dusting brush attachment, then wipe with a soft cloth wrung out in warm soapy water. Removing the dust will help the fridge work more efficiently, which saves on electricity and prolongs its life.

Speed up the thaw by standing a bowl of hot steaming water in the bottom and leaving the door open. While you're waiting, remove all the shelves and trays, wash them in warm soapy water, rinse and dry. Once the ice inside the fridge has melted, wipe the interior surfaces with a mild solution of bicarbonate of soda (two teaspoons to one litre of warm water). Rub any stubborn marks with a stronger paste of bicarbonate of soda and water or white toothpaste, which you can also use on the rubber door-seal with the aid of an old toothbrush. Once you've finished cleaning, keep the fridge smelling fresh by sprinkling a teaspoon of bicarbonate of soda on to half a lemon, or wrap freshly ground coffee in a muslin bag and place it inside.

The freezer

Unless you have a frost-free model (well worth investing in) you'll have to defrost every few months as ice accumulates. You can avoid rapid ice build-up by opening the door as few times as possible, and shutting it again quickly; the ice is formed by water vapour in the air becoming frozen. Don't buy a bigger freezer than you need – cooling empty space is inefficient – fill the gaps with loaves of bread or rolled-up clean towels.

Defrosting the freezer
Unplug the freezer and store the contents in an insulated cool bag or wrap them in a plastic bag and put them inside a quilt or sleeping bag. Stand bowls of steaming water on the shelves and lay towels at the base to catch the dripping water as the ice thaws. Use a plastic spatula to scrape away the ice, but never use anything metal because you may pierce the cooling elements or permanently scratch the appliance.

Once the ice has thawed, wipe the interior surfaces with a solution of bicarbonate of soda (two teaspoons to one litre of warm water) or warm water with a few drops of washing-up liquid added.

The kitchen sink

The kitchen sink is used to wash and prepare food and clean utensils, so it must be kept clean. Wipe down the sink before and after every use and disinfect at least once a week, taking care to make sure that there are no food particles trapped in the waste or overflow where micro-organisms can breed. To disinfect, fill the sink with warm water and a capful of household chlorine bleach. Let the water flood into the overflow, and scrub with an old toothbrush. Release the water and scrub the waste and plug clean.

Don't do dirty jobs in, over or around the kitchen sink; it must be kept hygienic at all times. Use a bucket for washing floors or presoaking laundry and empty the water into a basin or preferably down the toilet or an outside drain. You may wish to protect the surface of the sink by using a separate plastic bowl for washing vegetables and dishes, but always wipe the bottom of the bowl afterwards to remove grease and grit.

Taps

Kitchen taps usually have a chrome finish because this is the most durable. It won't rust, but it will scratch, and limescale can collect. Use a non-abrasive cleaner and polish with a soft cloth to bring up the shine. Remove limescale deposits with vinegar, lemon juice or a branded descaling product.

If your taps have an unusual finish, such as brushed nickel, always follow the manufacturer's care advice or you may invalidate the warranty. Such finishes are often lacquered to protect the metal, so don't use anything abrasive that will remove or damage the lacquer. If you don't have specific care advice, wipe with warm soapy water and buff dry with a soft cloth.

Cleaning the kitchen sink

Acrylic
Treat acrylic sinks with care and avoid scratches, which will make cleaning less effective. Hot pans will leave a shiny mark on matt finishes. Remove watermarks by rubbing with vinegar and polish out slight scratches with metal polish or a car bodywork rubbing compound. Remove discolouring by filling with a mild solution of bleach and soaking for 5–15 minutes.

Porcelain
The common type is the 'butler's sink', and the main threat of damage is cracking, chipping or crazing of the glaze. Use a plastic bowl or mat to protect the surface from scratches and clean with warm soapy water or a cream cleaner.

Corian®
Corian® can withstand boiling water, but the manufacturer recommends running the cold tap when pouring boiling water into the sink.

Enamel
Don't use chlorine bleach or abrasive scourers to clean enamel because they make the surface dull, scratched and difficult to clean. Wipe with warm soapy water and buff dry for regular maintenance. Remove stains by rubbing gently with a paste of borax and lemon juice, or bicarbonate of soda and hydrogen peroxide bleach.

Stainless steel
This does scratch during everyday use, but it doesn't affect the usefulness of the surface. Warm soapy water is an adequate daily cleaner, but cream cleaner or a paste of bicarbonate of soda will remove heavy soiling or rusty marks picked up from other metal objects. Remove limescale deposits with vinegar, lemon juice or a branded limescale remover.

Unblocking the sink

Prevention is much better than cure, so don't pour cooking fat straight into the sink because when it meets the cold water in the U-bend, it may block the sink. Instead, pour fat into a disposable plastic bottle and then, once full, throw the bottle into the bin. Keep the drain clear by flushing soda crystals and boiling water down the plughole once a week.

If waste water is slow to drain away, or won't drain at all, then unfortunately you have a blockage. If it's not a physical blockage (an object that has flushed down the drain and is obstructing the pipe) then grease and fat are probably the problem and can be shifted with one of the following methods. There are also several branded products that use strong chemicals to do a similar job, but as they are expensive and toxic you may prefer to try one of these remedies first. If you use a plunger as well, it will help force the blockage through the pipe.

◊ First try pouring boiling water directly down the plughole. You'll have to wait until the waste water has seeped away or scoop it out into a bucket. Boiling water may dissolve and dislodge some of the grease. Use a plunger to force the hot water through the pipe.

◊ If boiling water alone fails, try adding some grease shifting agents. Tip a cup of bicarbonate of soda over the plughole and then slowly add a cup of clear vinegar. The two ingredients fizz together. Try several applications to shift stubborn blockages.

◊ Alternatively, pour two cups of washing soda crystals over the plughole and then slowly pour in a kettle of boiling water.

If all these remedies fail, make sure the outside drain isn't blocked. Do this by checking whether any other sinks are blocked too, or unscrew the U-bend trap (also called the bottle trap) over a bucket and look for physical obstructions. If the pipe is physically blocked, push a net curtain wire into it to dislodge the obstruction.

The waste disposal unit

For regular maintenance, follow the manufacturer's instructions or sprinkle a little borax into the drain and allow to stand for fifteen minutes to remove smells. Add a sliced lemon or a handful of soda crystals and hot water from time to time to prevent smells and greasing up.

The dishwasher

One in five homes now has a dishwasher and for lots of people they are the one appliance, once considered a luxury, that saves an enormous amount of time. Today they are relatively inexpensive to buy and there are even slimline versions available for tight spaces. Fully-fitted versions, which are completely hidden behind a matching cupboard door, are twice as expensive as freestanding versions, but can make the kitchen look more streamlined.

The dishwasher works like a shower, with fixed water jets and spray arms attacking all exposed surfaces, so check the arms still rotate freely when the dishwasher is loaded. The upper deck is usually designed for delicates, glassware and cups, while the lower level takes the heavy load: plates and pans. Always load glasses, cups, mugs and bowls bottom-up so the water runs off. It's also worth mixing up the cutlery in the basket rather than grouping by type, so that the spoons don't slot together and hide the dirt from the water jets.

Loading a dishwasher is an art in itself so no wonder it's one of the few domestic chores most men can't resist giving advice on, or interfering with; some have even been known to repack the entire contents. What a shame they simply don't offer to do the job in the first place! Some people like to rinse everything before they load. Scraping is sufficient, but remember it's not a waste disposal unit.

Some things shouldn't be put in the dishwasher. When you're buying cookware and crockery check whether it is dishwasher safe. Anything with a printed or painted pattern, gold or silver trim, will fade after repeated washing, so exercise caution with items you are unsure about. Most plastic is safe, but put it in the upper rack so that it's furthest away from the heat of the drying elements. Over time, ordinary drinking glasses can develop a dull white bloom that cannot be removed, so you may prefer to hand wash them.

What not to machine wash

- Lead crystal glassware – it develops a white, dull bloom over time.
- Antique, hand-painted or gold/silver-trimmed china.
- Glued cutlery handles of bone or plastic which will loosen over time.
- Wooden utensils, chopping boards, handles – wood swells when wet and then cracks when it dries.
- You can load silver and stainless steel in the same load, but ensure that they don't touch because the silver will tarnish and may suffer from black marks.

Once the machine is loaded you need to add detergent. Only use a product designed for the purpose. Detergent is available in powder, liquid or tablet form. Some tablets, which are the most expensive option, include all the additives dishwashers need: detergent for washing, salt for water softening and rinse aid to remove water streaks during drying. You should however still add granular salt (not table salt, which may contain other additives) to the water softener to avoid long-term damage to the machine.

Top up the salt reservoir just before running the machine so that any spilt corrosive salt granules are carried away. Always ensure the cap to the salt reservoir is firmly replaced as detergent could ruin the resin softener. Incoming water is pumped through the water softener reservoir. Softening helps the detergent work more efficiently and stops the heating elements and water jets becoming caked in limescale deposits, prolonging the life of the machine.

Most machines have two main wash programmes: 55°C and 65°C (52°C is considered an adequate temperature for hygienic cleaning). The higher temperature isn't suitable for glassware and delicates because it causes rapid wear.

Poor wash problems

If you are suffering from poor wash results, check you're stacking the machine properly, remove and rinse the filters under running water, and make sure you have salt in the water softener (three-in-one tablets alone don't contain sufficient salt for use in hard water areas. You must also top up the water softener reservoir with granular salt).

You can also clean the machine by running it empty with a glassful of distilled vinegar in the upper rack. At the end of the wash programme it will be left full of water. Examine the remaining water; if there are gritty particles in it the filters or spray arms may be blocked. Check both and run repeat cycles with vinegar, to help shift limescale deposits from the water jets, until the remaining water is clear.

CHECKLIST: LOADING THE DISHWASHER

◊ The upper deck is for delicates. Alternate cups and glasses along the rows to stop glasses scratching.

◊ The bottom tray is for heavy-duty items such as plates and pans.

◊ Invert cups, bowls and glasses so that water drains off.

◊ Stack so that the water spray jets can reach on to and into all the surfaces.

◊ Check the spray arms are not obstructed by the load and can rotate freely.

◊ Mix cutlery types in the basket; the same type tend to slot together, trapping residue.

Washing dishes by hand

More people wash dishes by hand than use a dishwasher. All of us still need to wash some items by hand and it's always more economical and green to hand wash a few items than run a half-empty machine. A dishwasher uses four times the water required to fill the kitchen sink, as well as consuming electricity. You may also have to hand wash some dishes when you're entertaining unless you have a large supply of plates and cutlery. It's a good idea to wear rubber gloves to protect your skin from drying and cracking, which can lead to infection, and so that you can use slightly hotter water.

Tips to save washing-up
⬥ Lay a piece of kitchen paper on the microwave turntable to catch spills.
⬥ Line the grill pan and oven tray with aluminium foil before cooking.
⬥ Don't let food burn on to pans during cooking.
⬥ Leave ovenware and pans to soak while you do the dishes.

The correct order for dish washing has been a subject of much debate over the decades, but generally the cleaner, more delicate items go first, and the heavier, dirtier items last. So usually glassware, cups, saucers and cutlery are followed by side and dinner plates, ending with utensils and pans. You'll probably have your own preference, and quite where the cutlery fits in to the sequence is a source of some disagreement, but as you'll probably be refilling the bowl with clean water at some stage, the second half of the wash can be done with clean water anyway.

You can speed up the job with a few moments' preparation. Gather everything together, scrape off any food residue, and line them up in the sequence you plan to wash in. Do the line-up on the opposite side of the drainer next to your sink. If you do this, you won't have to stretch over other items or go and collect them. Fill the really dirty ovenware and pans with a little water and leave them to soak while you do the dishes. Pans may require some hard scrubbing, but presoaking really pays dividends. For really hard to shift deposits, try adding a scoopful of biological washing powder and simmer on the hob for ten minutes, which loosens even the most stubborn food remains.

Start with a clean bowl and a clean and dry drainer because bacteria breed quickly on wet surfaces. Some people prefer to use a plastic bowl because it cushions glasses and crockery from bashing against the hard sides of the sink. Plastic bowls, drainers and cutlery baskets should be scrubbed regularly. If you prefer to stack directly on to a stainless steel drainer, you may want to lay a drying cloth over to protect delicate glassware from chipping or cracking.

Fill the bowl with the hottest water you can stand to use comfortably, and add a few drops of concentrated washing-up liquid. Some of these liquids contain antibacterial agents. These really are unnecessary because the action of the soap, hot water and safe drying will eliminate most bacteria. Increased use of antibacterial cleaners over time makes them less effective when they really are needed because bacteria become more resistant to their action.

Use clean implements: dish cloths, a brush, nylon and wire wool scourers, but remember sponges are less hygienic because they can harbour bacteria in their holes. If you don't have a wire wool scourer handy, a scrunched-up ball of aluminium foil works just as well. To stop soap-filled wire wool scourers going rusty, store them in a plastic bag in the freezer.

Rinse each item after washing to remove the soap, either by running under the tap or by immersing briefly in a second bowl of warm water. Opinion is divided about which method for drying dishes is more hygienic. Some prefer air-drying because there's no opportunity for contamination from dirty, damp towels. However, any risk can be eliminated by using clean dry towels and changing them often. Linen drying cloths are best for glass because they don't leave any fluff behind.

CHECKLIST: WASHING DISHES BY HAND

◊ Collect, scrape and stack all the dishes.

◊ Line dishes up in the sequence they are to be washed.

◊ Soak heavily soiled ovenware and pans by covering with a little water.

◊ Fill the bowl with hot water and a few drops of washing-up liquid.

◊ Wash delicate, less dirty items first; heavier, dirtier items last.

◊ Use clean, dry drying cloths.

Cleaning and polishing pans and utensils

Aluminium pans Boil apple peelings, citrus skin or rhubarb to remove blackness.

Cast iron Remove rust by rubbing with a raw potato.

Copper To restore shine, rub hard with a paste of lemon juice (or distilled white vinegar) and coarse salt.

Chrome A little bicarbonate of soda on a damp cloth will restore shine, but check the durability of the plating in a hidden area first.

Brass In addition to branded cleaner, tomato ketchup, Worcestershire sauce and toothpaste will all remove tarnish from brass.

Non-stick pans Remove stains from non-stick surfaces by boiling a solution of half a cup of bleach and 2 tablespoons bicarbonate of soda for 5 minutes. Then wash, rinse and dry, and rub the surface with kitchen towel and a drop of cooking oil.

Pewter This is delicate and best washed in warm soapy water and dried with a soft cloth; don't put it in the dishwasher. Stubborn marks can be removed with methylated spirits.

Silverware Rubbing with a paste of water and baking soda will remove tarnish. The most dramatic method – but unsuitable for thin plate – is to line a plastic bowl with aluminium foil, add boiling water and a handful of washing soda crystals, dip in the silverware for a few seconds and rinse.

Stainless steel Although 'stainless', it can become dull. Rub with a paste of baking soda and water.

Limescale deposits and blue streaking (caused by heat) can be removed by covering with water and vinegar and simmering until gone. White dots are caused by pitting from salt. They are permanent and can be avoided by adding salt only when liquids are boiling.

Teapots, mugs and cups The tannins in tea cause discoloration. Fill with cold water, add a few drops of chlorine bleach and leave overnight. Rinse thoroughly.

Vases and decanters To remove scum or red wine stains at the bottom, fill with soapy water or distilled white vinegar, add a few grains of uncooked rice and swill. The abrasive action removes the deposits.

The microwave oven

There are two types: those that cook with microwaves only and those that combine microwaves with a conventional heating grill for separate or simultaneous use. Always follow the manufacturer's instructions, and never put anything metal inside unless otherwise stated. Some foods with high fat and sugar content can catch fire, so don't leave the microwave unattended. The removable glass turntable can be washed in the dishwasher, but catch spillages by covering with a square of disposable kitchen paper before you cook.

To clean and remove smells, place several slices of lemon in a bowl of water and cook on high for 2 minutes. The steam loosens the grease and neutralizes odours. Wipe inside the oven walls with kitchen paper or a clean soft cloth.

The coffee maker

Coffee makers are available in several varieties. Filter machines bubble hot water through a filter containing ground coffee into a jug. Cappuccino and espresso machines force water under pressure through ground coffee inside a sealed device. Descale the appliance every eight weeks by half filling the reservoir with clear vinegar and topping up with water, then bubbling through. Repeat with clean water. To clear a blocked cappuccino nozzle, use a pin or immerse in a jug of clean hot water.

The food processor

Soak all the attachments in warm soapy water, and use a brush on sharp or mesh items. Some foods such as carrots may stain plastic fittings; try removing by soaking in a mild solution of bleach or rubbing with vegetable oil, followed by rewashing.

The toaster

Always unplug the toaster before cleaning or attempting to remove bread that has become stuck inside. Empty the crumb tray and turn the toaster upside down over a sheet of newspaper to dislodge crumbs. Scorch marks on the case around the slots will rub away with a paste of bicarbonate of soda and a drop of water or a dab of cream cleaner on a moistened cloth.

The kettle

There is a wide choice of electric kettles available, with models updated frequently. The most common variety is the cordless jug kettle, which has a separate base for the electricity cord. Look for models that have a lockable lid (in case the kettle is knocked over) and a see-through panel so you can see the water level at a glance. Some kettles have built-in water filters or mesh gauze to keep limescale deposits inside the kettle and out of your tea.

In hard water areas, you will need to descale regularly, either with a branded product or half fill with clear vinegar, top up with water and leave to stand overnight. Pour away the contents and wipe around the inside with kitchen paper, refill with clean water and boil. A heavily scaled kettle may require further applications.

Chopping boards

Chopping boards must be thoroughly cleaned with hot soapy water and wiped dry with paper towel after each separate use to prevent cross-contamination between raw fish and meat and vegetables and non-cooked foods. Using separate boards for each type of food will also minimize this risk. Wooden or plastic boards are equally safe, but plastic boards do have the advantage that you can wash them in the dishwasher. Wooden boards will warp, dry and crack in the dishwasher. Eventually the surface will become heavily scored and be more difficult to clean, and so should be replaced.

To remove the smell from a wooden board, rub the surface with dry mustard powder, leave to absorb the smell and then wash and dry, or rub with half a lemon.

Kitchen knives

Store sharp kitchen knives in a wooden block, slatted drawer trays or on a magnetic strip, but never jumbled in a drawer where they will quickly blunt and be more difficult to remove safely. Wash knives individually in warm soapy water, and dry carefully; don't put them in the dishwasher or leave them to soak because the glue in the handle will weaken.

How to sharpen a knife

A sharpening stone or steel is the most effective way of resharpening a flat-bladed knife; serrated knives can't be resharpened. A steel sharpening rod has grooves, which are designed to straighten out the edge of the knife that becomes folded over during use. Hold the sharpening steel rod in one hand as though an extension of the arm. Hold the knife in the other against the steel at a twenty degree angle. Pull the blade up along its entire length against the steel to straighten the edge. Repeat with each side of the knife until it is sharp. The smaller the angle, the finer the cut will be, but twenty degrees is recommended for kitchen use.

Choosing a kitchen floor

Not all flooring types are suitable for kitchens because the surface needs to be frequently washed and disinfected. Non-textured, sealed surfaces are the best choice, while carpets or rugs are entirely inappropriate because they trap dirt and are more difficult to clean properly.

Cleaning the kitchen floor

Food preparation inevitably creates crumbs, splatters and debris, some of which finds its way on to the floor. You should mop up any sizeable spills as soon as they occur using a floor cloth or paper towel, but never the cloth you wipe work surfaces with. However careful you are, the kitchen floor quickly gets dirty and unhygienic, so you should aim to vacuum or sweep it most days and wash it at least a couple of times a week.

Wash any dishes and clear and wipe down all the work surfaces before washing the floor. This is the last job and once complete, the floor should be allowed to air dry without any foot traffic. Sweep or vacuum up all the loose debris, paying special attention to the areas around fitted units and appliances. Hot soapy water plus a few drops of washing-up liquid in hot water is adequate and your choice of mop or cloth (*see* Equipping your home, p. 58) is sufficient for daily cleaning. Never wash the floor taking water directly from the kitchen sink; it's unhygienic. Change the water for a final rinse if the floor is really dirty. Don't overwet the floor, it will take a long time to dry and you may leave dirt behind in the water.

From time to time you may want to get down on your hands and knees and use a scrubbing brush or floor cloth to give the floor a really good clean. Mops are good for daily use, but they don't get into all the corners or shift especially sticky marks. Pull out the freestanding appliances, such as the fridge and cooker, and wash the floor underneath and behind them too. Use a paste of bicarbonate of soda if you need some extra cleaning action to shift ingrained grease. For regular washing hot soapy water is adequate, but from time to time some extra care may be required to maintain the appearance and finish.

Caring for and maintaining kitchen floors

Ceramic tiles	A durable finish, but the greatest difficulty is keeping grout lines clean, so grey grout is more practical than lighter shades. Sweeping and washing is adequate; don't polish as they will become slippery. Grout lines can be scrubbed with a toothbrush and a paste of bleach and bicarbonate of soda. This is a time-consuming job, so it's easier to specify darker grout when laying floors.
Cork	It's porous, so tiles are sealed to prevent water and grease stains. Waterproof varnish may have to be reapplied periodically.
Linoleum	This is still available today, made with natural materials: wood, cork and linseed oil, fixed to a jute backing. Wash without using abrasive cleaners or scourers. Because it is a more absorbent surface than vinyl, it is vulnerable to staining from spillages, especially if not maintained. The manufacturers recommend special products for stripping and then reapplying wax polish to maintain the durability of the surface.
Marble	Don't use anything abrasive on marble, it scratches and becomes dull. Marble can become very slippery, so don't use any polish on floors, especially in heavy traffic areas.
Quarry tiles	They can be sealed or polished. Reapply branded liquid sealant or polish as necessary. Remove white watermarks by rubbing with a mild solution of vinegar.
Stone	Natural stone is a traditional, but expensive, finish, which requires considerable maintenance. Stone is porous so the surface must be sealed to protect it from staining by water, oils, fats and other natural food dyes that may come into contact with it. The sealant is only slightly absorbed, so needs reapplying to ensure the surface remains protected. Stone should be cleaned regularly to avoid the need for harsh cleaning. Light colours will stain easily unless they are adequately sealed with a branded liquid sealant.

Vinyl   Vinyl floor coverings wear well and are easily washed or mopped clean, although they are susceptible to cuts, scoring and scuffing, which can be difficult or impossible to remove. A pencil eraser will remove scuff marks. Rub other marks with cream cleaner or a paste of water and bicarbonate of soda. Liquid polishes are available to add shine, but they often require complete stripping before any reapplication, which is very time consuming.

Wood   Modern wooden flooring materials are usually factory sealed, but only lay boards marked as suitable for kitchens. Wooden floors must be sealed to prevent water penetration. Although wood can be waxed in light traffic areas, varnish is more suitable where water is in regular contact. Once the seal becomes worn, reapply to prevent staining and to ensure washing removes all dirt.

Kitchen work surfaces

If work surfaces are well maintained they're easier to keep clean. Protect from hot pans and dishes, which might scald or melt the finish, and from sharp objects, which might scratch or scar. Always use pot stands to rest items that have come direct from the stove, and a chopping board when cutting with a knife.

Cleaning work surfaces

Corian®
: A man-made material resembling marble or granite. Remove marks with a mildly abrasive cleaner or the manufacturer's maintenance kit. The surface can be professionally refinished.

Granite
: A hard and heavy stone, which is much less porous than marble and therefore highly stain resistant. Take care not to use anything abrasive as the highly polished surface will scratch. There are numerous branded treatments available but their use is unnecessary.

Laminated finishes
: Laminated board is the most popular surface. A thin, but highly durable, synthetic layer is bonded to composite wood board. It will resist heat and water, but not the direct heat from a hot pan. Laminated surfaces are available in smooth and textured finishes; the smooth is easier to wipe clean but will show scratches. Textured surfaces can trap dirt, but do disguise scratches. Rub gently with cream cleaner to remove stubborn marks or use a paste of bicarbonate of soda and a few drops of chlorine bleach to remove tea stains.

Marble
: Not really a suitable kitchen work surface because it's porous, so it stains easily, and the surface is quickly etched by acids in foods, including lemon juice. Wipe up spills quickly and never use anything abrasive when cleaning, which will dull the shine.

Slate	Naturally porous so is usually sealed. Once sealed it is water-proof and can be washed with warm soapy water. It is vulnerable to scratches.
Stainless steel	A fashionable finish for every surface from appliances to splash-backs. It's resistant to both heat and stains, but does scratch easily so it won't maintain the showroom shine unless carefully handled. Clean and maintain in the same way as stainless steel sinks.
Tile	Tiled surfaces are durable, but not practical because the grout lines are difficult to clean. If tiles become chipped, crazed or cracked, they can trap dirt and become unhygienic. Clean using the same method as for bathroom tiles.
Wood	Even hardwood surfaces must be sealed to prevent water penetration, which warps and discolours the wood. However the surface can be resanded and sealed from time to time. Apply Danish oil with a fluff-free cloth in the direction of the grain and redistribute the excess as it dries.

Kitchen waste

A great deal of rubbish gets generated in the kitchen, which is potentially hazardous to health and attractive to pests. As much as possible should be recycled: glass bottles, tins, foil and plastic can all be returned for further use, and organic waste should be composted where practical. Try to avoid bringing home extra packaging when you shop by taking your own reusable bags; select loose vegetables instead of prepacked; cardboard and glass containers in place of plastic; buy larger sizes rather than lots of small packages.

Choosing a bin

The type of bin you use will be based on the amount of space you have available for rubbish collection, and your personal preference. Whichever type you choose, it should have a removable liner so that you can disinfect it easily, and a closely fitting lid so that insects can't get inside (flies like to lay their eggs in rubbish) – swing-top bins are best avoided for this reason. Bins with different compartments are handy for recycling, or you may decide to store your recyclables outside. Line the bin with a plastic bag so that the whole thing can be scooped out for easy disposal.

Using the bin
All food that goes into the bin should be as dry as possible, and wrapped in newspaper if it's likely to smell. Empty the bin frequently and wash and disinfect it every week. Remove the liner, partially fill with hot soapy water and wipe the inside with a disposable cloth. Allow the liner to dry before fitting a fresh bag, finally wiping inside the lid and around the rim.

The bin should be emptied to an outside bin regularly to prevent smells and deter pests. Plastic liner sacks should be tied closed and put into a sturdy plastic or metal bin with a lid to stop foraging animals and pests gaining access to the contents. Weight the handle down with a brick, clip or tie it shut if wind or animals are a problem. Clean the outside bin with hot water and disinfectant from time to time. Wrap broken glass in paper or place in an open sturdy box so that collectors can see any potential danger.

Deodorizing smells

The best way to prevent stale food odours is to ensure that you have adequate ventilation while you're cooking. Open a window, run the extractor fan if you have one, or open the outside door while you're frying or heating lots of pans.

If there is a persistent smell there's probably some other problem, so look for the source of it – bad smells can tell you that bacteria are growing somewhere. Follow the tips on food storage and using the bin, check scraps of rotting food haven't accumulated behind appliances, and replace kitchen cloths. If you smell dampness, look for signs of water seeping from leaky sink plumbing, washing machines or dishwashers and check plaster walls are dry.

Make your own air freshener
If you just want to freshen up by neutralizing odours, then mix up your own simple spray air freshener with 1 teaspoon of bicarbonate of soda and 1 teaspoon of lemon juice in 2 cups of hot water. Put the solution in a spray bottle and use sparingly.

Simmer a pan of water with some orange or lemon peel to fill your kitchen with a fresh, natural scent.

The dining room

Many families are sitting down to fewer meals together, so a separate dining room is becoming less popular. Recently the trend has been for kitchens to become open-plan dining areas by knocking down walls or extending out into the garden.

Kim I wouldn't choose to have one because I don't do a lot of entertaining, but our new house has a huge kitchen-cum-dining room, which would be wasted on any other use. There's a small table, just for two, in the kitchen so I've decided to go to town and furnish the dining room rather grandly with a custom-made solid oak dining table, chairs and sideboard – in fact I had the wood matched exactly with the oak flooring.

Aggie I'm not keen on a separate dining room. For someone like me who loves cooking and entertaining, I'd rather my guests were with me in the kitchen. I was at a dinner party recently and I remember thinking how much trouble it was for the hostess running back and forth with this, that and the next thing. It can be a real challenge keeping everything hot, and I wouldn't have one of those naff trolleys. I'm glad we don't have a dining room, but a big table in the kitchen for everyone to sit around – definitely, that's a must.

The perfect setting

If your home has more than one reception room and eating and entertaining are high on your list of pleasures, you'll probably have a dining room in preference to any other use. If, however, your dining room has to double up as home office or drying room for laundry, then you'll need some self-restraint to avoid clothes and paperwork taking over.

Choosing the right furniture

Look for a table that will seat at least four or six people and extend to accommodate another two. Extension flaps that fold out are easier to use than those that have to be stored separately. Choose a table top that is both practical and decorative. Glass or wood, solid or veneered – it doesn't matter, but entertaining won't be any fun if you're constantly worrying about whether the finish will get spoilt.

When you're buying a new table and chairs, make sure they match up comfortably. Dining chairs with arms (often referred to as carvers) take up more space and only really work at the head of the table. The chairs are likely to suffer spills from time to time, so you'll want to be able to successfully spot treat any fabric – bear this in mind when you select upholstery. Some fabrics, including suede, velvet and silk, are very difficult to clean, while leather is more durable and can more easily be wiped clean with a damp cloth.

Dressing the table

Many people think of tablecloths as 'old fashioned' or only for Christmas and festivities. If you do like a cloth on a wooden table, it's best to lay a heat-resistant pad and waterproof cover underneath. White linen is always used in the finest restaurants and matching linen napkins provide a very posh look.

The alternative to a cloth is placemats. These should be heat resistant, washable and large enough to accommodate a complete setting. The New Year sales are a good time to hunt down table decoration bargains when department stores are shifting surplus stock after the Christmas rush. Candles or small posies of flowers make a perfect centrepiece for a special occasion. Take your inspiration from restaurants and magazines and copy their ideas.

How to lay a place setting

There are formal rules for how to lay a place setting, but they're not complicated to follow because they're based on need. The well-known rule for selecting cutlery is to work from the outside in as each course is served – it's much easier to pick up knives and forks in this way than to have to lift them out from the inside. A place setting shouldn't include anything that won't be required during the meal – this is why restaurant waiters substitute regular knives for fish or steak knives once you've placed your order. If you're serving fish or steak you should lay the appropriate cutlery from the outset if you have it, but regular knives are acceptable. For everyday dining you can just lay the basics and save the full ensemble for special occasions.

A full formal setting has cutlery for each course. Lay a soup spoon to the outside right (but only if soup is to be served); followed by a smaller knife for the first course; and a larger knife for the main course next to the plate (a fish or steak knife may be substituted, depending on the menu). The blades of the knives should all be laid facing in towards the plate.

To the left side, lay the forks with the smaller first course size to the outside and a larger size for the main course closest to the plate. At the top of the setting, lay a dessert spoon and fork with the handles lying in opposing directions. The spoon handle should lie to the right and the fork handle to the left; the spoon should sit above the fork. Once the main course is cleared away, move these down to the vacant sides of the place setting.

Lay a side plate for bread to the left side of the setting. Lay the butter knife vertically on top of the plate. The napkin can then be rolled, folded or placed to the left of the fork, on the side plate or in the centre of the place setting.

If you're serving wine, lay three glasses to the top right above the knives. These can be placed either in a descending line or arranged as a triangle. Place the largest (water) glass furthest away, followed by a red wine glass, which should be larger than the white wine glass. Once the wine has been poured, it's customary to remove the unused white or red wine glasses from each setting.

Some restaurants and hosts lay an empty plate in the middle of the place setting, which the dish containing the first course is set on top of. At the end of the course, both plates are removed. Serve water from a jug rather than a bottle. It's unnecessary to decant wine, but you may prefer to stand the bottles on the side rather than on the table. Condiments should be served from dishes, and lay more than one set if you're serving more than eight guests.

- Place settings are arranged so that diners work inwards through cutlery.
- Knives are laid to the right with soup spoons to the outer edge. The blade edge should face the plate.
- Forks to the left, smallest to the outside.
- For the dessert cutlery, a spoon and fork are placed at the top of the setting with the handles in opposing directions – spoon handle to the right, fork to the left. Move the dessert cutlery to the side of the setting after the main course is cleared.
- Three glasses are laid in a formal setting in descending size; water largest and furthest, then red wine, then white.
- Side plates are placed to the left of the setting. A butter knife is laid vertically on the plate.
- Napkins can be placed to the left of the fork, on the side plate or in the centre of each place setting.
- A serving plate can be laid in the centre of the setting and cleared when the soup or starter course is removed.
- Butter, salt, pepper and any other condiments should be laid at each end of the table. Lay two sets when there are nine or more guests.

The dining room

201

Room by room

The living room

In the past this has been described as the 'withdrawing room' (where guests 'withdrew' after dinner), the 'drawing room', 'parlour', 'sitting room', 'saloon' and 'lounge', but today the description 'living room' is most in vogue. The television may have replaced the piano as the main source of entertainment, but the living room is still the main room for entertaining guests. This is the showpiece of your home so don't let it show you up.

Kim I've decorated in cream, so mine is a very light room. There are two heavy fabric sofas. I think leather is wonderful, but it's not my cup of tea. When you're buying a sofa, look for cushion covers that zip off, they're so much easier to clean. If they machine wash, so much the better. One word of caution though, if you do wash upholstery covers don't dry them in the machine – they might shrink. Try to wash them during the summer, so you can lay them out in the sunshine on a plastic sheet and a towel.

Aggie We have our living room upstairs because there's a slightly larger room above the hall. Because it's upstairs it doesn't really get much use as a living room and it was always kept as our best room – 'no food, no felt tips' has been the rule since it was decorated. Of course it's an adult's prerogative to break rules, so I do take in the occasional glass of wine.

In recent months it's gradually been turned into a practice studio by my teenage son Rory and his mates. Every day they are up there – bass, drums, sax, piano – you name it. The decor is black, white and cream. There are cream blinds, two black leather sofas – fabric would never survive the daily traffic! – and a built-in cupboard that holds the TV, tapes and video games. There's also a huge amp in the corner – when was that smuggled in?

Kim I've got wall-to-wall cream fitted carpet with a beautiful floral tapestry rug, the scatter cushions pick up the flowers. You run the risk of a cold room if you don't accessorize with warm tones. I vacuum the carpet twice a week and once a month I pull out all the furniture. You presume there must be dirt and dust under there, but I never find it. I could probably get away with doing it once every two months. The curtains are deep yellow and I vacuum them once a month too. I do that because, with no smokers here, it means I only need to get them cleaned about every eighteen months.

I'm a TV fanatic; I've got four sets. The one in the living room is huge, like a cinema, a flat panel on a rather nice plinth. I'm trying to combine traditional and modern and I feel I'm getting away with it. I've learnt so much from the television, much more than I knew when I left school. I remove the dust with a fluff-free duster about three times a week. It takes about five seconds as I'm passing by because I always keep a duster in my pocket, which is why cleaning is so simple. If you don't let dirt build up, you don't need to use harsh chemicals. Don't forget the remote control either; I've seen so many filthy ones. Mine never gets dirty; I run my cloth over the whole thing, pressing down each button ever so quickly, one, two, three, four, five there, five seconds and it's done. If you don't do that, it will take you about half an hour poking around with cocktail sticks.

Aggie The centrepiece of the room is a marble-surround fireplace with a charcoal-coloured slate hearth. I love building a fire, and always mix wood and coal – the coal for the heat, the wood for the flame. When it comes to raking out the ashes in the morning, I use my 'companion set' of poker, brush and shovel, although sometimes the ashes are still warm, which is annoying because you have to leave them to cool. I take a few sheets of newspaper to wrap up the ashes, poke out the grate, sweep up and then finish off by wiping the grate with a damp cloth.

I can't bear house plants, so there aren't any; likewise ornaments. To me plants are dust gatherers, just another job, so there's no place for them here – although I do love fresh flowers and there are always some on show.

Kim I love my house plants, but I always take great care about where I put them. I always have Phallanopsis orchids on show in whites and pinks; you can get three months out of them. Lots of people go wrong with plants. If you want a plant for a sunny spot choose one that likes it there, but please, not a shade lover. I never overwater because some plants just need a quick spray every now and again. Plants don't all need watering on the same day week in, week out – you'll drown them. If you look after a plant properly it will give you years of pleasure.

Welcoming and relaxing

The living room is often the first glimpse inside your home your guests have, so this is the room you'll be judged on. Fortunately, despite being one of the most heavily used rooms, it is also one of the easiest to keep clean. There are really only three regular tasks; tidying, dusting and vacuuming.

Tidy up every day

The living room is a magnet for people and clutter and the secret to keeping it in tiptop shape is to tidy up every day. A couple of things left lying around can soon mount up, and you'll quickly be snowed under. Get into the habit of putting books, bags, toys and paperwork back in their proper place as soon as you've finished with them. At the end of every day, spend a couple of minutes picking everything up from the floor and putting things away: games, music, movies and books; empty the wastepaper basket; and plump up the cushions.

In the morning open the window and let some fresh air in. Fresh air helps removes odours, without the need for any assistance from chemical sprays. Spend a moment dusting or running the vacuum over the heavy traffic areas while you're waiting for your favourite TV show to start and you won't even notice the effort.

Dusting

Carpets, soft furnishings and curtains all add to the dust and there's no shortage of surfaces for it to collect on. A soft, lightly dampened cloth is the most effective method of dusting because it gathers and removes rather than swishing it around. Lambswool and microfibre dusters trap more dust than a traditional duster. A long feather duster is a useful backup for reaching cobwebs, but a lambswool duster or damp cloth on a broomstick is more efficient than feather, which doesn't cling on to them quite so effectively. Don't be tempted to use polish or spray every time you dust because they're not necessary to maintain wood; they release unwanted chemicals into your home; and can produce a waxy build-up on the surfaces (*see* Furniture, p. 322).

Tips to do less dusting

- Collect dust in a damp cloth to prevent it becoming airborne and resettling somewhere else.
- Computer and TV screens attract dust – wipe them over with a fabric softener sheet to reduce the static charge.
- Store unnecessary clutter, such as video tapes and DVDs, in cupboards to save having to dust them.
- Display collections behind glass rather than on open shelves.

Lampshades

Lamps and their shades quickly show the dust, but you can keep this to a minimum by regularly using the dusting brush attachment on the vacuum cleaner or with a soft, barely damp cloth.

- Remove dust from lampshades by rolling a barely damp cloth over the surface.
- Flick a very dusty lampshade with a cloth to dislodge dust, but do it outside.
- The easiest way to remove dust from a chandelier is to leave it *in situ* and place a large old towel underneath. Spray liberally with a specialist cleaner. The liquid slowly drips off into the towel, taking all the dust with it.

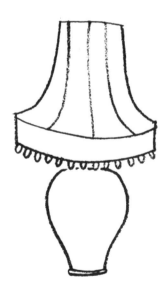

Vacuuming rugs and carpets

The vacuum cleaner is one of the greatest labour-saving devices ever invented. Imagine having to cover all the furniture with sheets and sweep the carpet with a stiff brush as maids once did. Today's vacuum cleaner is a versatile machine that, along with its attachments, can remove a great deal of dust quickly and efficiently. For an increasing number of people who suffer from asthma and respiratory problems (*see* The healthy home, p. 106) completely removing dust, rather than moving it around, has become very important. A vacuum cleaner with a HEPA filter has the highest performance rating for retaining dust in the bag (*see* Equipping your home, p. 58).

Vacuum high traffic areas at least every couple of days to preserve the life of carpets. Dirt falls on to the surface and it's quickly ground deep into the pile, where it becomes much more difficult to remove. Particles of sand and grit rub against the fibres causing tiny cuts, which literally wear the carpet out, as well as leaving it looking dirty.

You should vacuum the heavy traffic areas frequently, but there's no need to vacuum the entire surface so often. However, do pull out furniture from time to time to remove the dust that gathers under tables and chairs. This collected dust is irritating for allergy sufferers and can become a home for fabric pests, such as carpet beetles, which will eat the carpet fibres.

Vacuuming other surfaces

Whether you use an upright or cylinder cleaner, make the most of all the tool attachments as well as the floor head. Use the dusting brush to reach up to picture and dado rails, to the top of shelves, and to gently remove dust from around the air vents of electrical equipment (turn down the suction power first).

Fit the upholstery attachment and vacuum all the upholstered surfaces. Crumbs and grit get ground into the weave of fabrics and then cause fine cuts in the fibres, which result in rapid wear. The fabric strip on the upholstery attachment is designed to remove long trailing hairs. Use the crevice nozzle to suck detritus from the deeper fabric folds and buttoning.

Also, use the upholstery attachment to vacuum the curtains and blinds regularly. Airborne dust particles settle in the folds of the fabric just as they do on any other surface, so vacuum inside them too. Left to accumulate, this dirt becomes difficult to remove – even with laundering or dry cleaning – and leaves the fabric permanently soiled with dirty streaks.

Use the crevice nozzle to vacuum rugs, especially those with fringed edges, and the edges of carpets. When vacuuming a fringed rug, pass the tool outwards over the fringes, working in one direction only to avoid sucking the tassels into the nozzle. The concentrated suction from the nozzle attachment removes dirt from deep in the pile and helps restore the fibres to the upright position. If you do this weekly you will dramatically extend the life of the fibres.

Empty the vacuum cleaner frequently to keep it working efficiently. Some bags can be reused by emptying outside with care, but the walls of bags fitted to HEPA filter machines are designed to absorb the airborne dust passing through the machine and should always be replaced.

- Vacuum heavy traffic areas on carpet regularly to prevent dirt from becoming buried deep in the pile.
- Vacuum under furniture from time to time to remove accumulated dust, which may harbour fabric pests such as carpet beetles.
- Use the flexible hose and attachments to remove dust from picture and dado rails and skirting boards.
- The dusting brush is ideal for sucking dust from around air vents on electrical equipment and the tops of books.
- Use the upholstery attachment to remove crumbs and grit from the surface of furnishing fabrics. The fabric strip is designed to remove long trailing hairs.
- Use the crevice nozzle to suck dirt from deep folds and buttoning in soft furnishings.
- Use the upholstery attachment to remove dust from curtains and blinds. Dust left in fabric folds leads to permanent soiling.
- Use the crevice nozzle to work deep into the pile of rugs and the edges of carpets. This restores the fibres to the upright position and helps extend their life.
- Empty the vacuum cleaner regularly to maintain the efficiency of the machine. The walls of bags fitted to HEPA filter machines help absorb dust and should be replaced when full.

Kim & Aggie   The Cleaning Bible

The fireplace

The fireplace is still the focal point in many living rooms despite competition from flashier and flashier televisions. There's something hypnotic and relaxing about the flickering, dancing flames. If you do burn solid fuel, such as coal or wood, you should take sensible precautions. Don't build the fire unnecessarily high or use flammable liquids to encourage flames, and don't leave it unattended for long periods. When you rake or put more coal on, make sure you immediately extinguish any sparks that fly out and be careful when you lean over that none of your clothing trails near the flames. When there are young children around you should always place a sturdy fireguard in front of the fire.

Run down a real coal or wood fire in plenty of time before going to bed. Use a misting bottle to spray water on the glowing embers to prevent them flaring up or sending out sparks once you've left the room. Place a metal guard in front of the fire.

Always rake ash out from the grate before making up a new fire. Check that the old ashes are fully cold before you remove them. You can keep dust to a minimum by misting the ashes with a little water, which will prevent fine particles becoming airborne. Soot deposits can be scrubbed from brickwork – if water doesn't work there are specialist branded cleaning products from hardware stores that will help shift ingrained soot by leaching it out. If you burn solid fuel regularly, you must have the chimney professionally swept at least once a year. Accumulated soot deposits on the bricks can lead to chimney fires.

Cleaning the fireplace

- Never attempt to clean the hearth or surround while a fire is burning.
- If you burn solid fuel, even the smokeless type, the chimney must be professionally swept at least once a year. Soot deposits can lead to chimney fires.
- Don't wipe ceramic tile surrounds while they're still hot – moisture can cause crazing.
- Remove soot from bricks with a scrubbing brush and warm water with a few drops of washing-up liquid, but not strong detergent, which will leave soap scum on the brick.
- Remove stubborn soot from brick using a specialist cleaner (from hardware stores).
- Scrub a very dirty stone surround with a mild solution of bleach. Test an inconspicuous area first and rinse thoroughly.
- Black grate polish (from hardware stores) is the traditional finish for cast-iron surrounds. Apply as you do shoe polish, but protect surrounding surfaces from splatters.
- Marble is porous and will quickly and permanently absorb stains. Mop up any spillages immediately and wash with a solution of warm water and washing-up liquid, scrubbing with a soft nailbrush if necessary. Never use acid (even lemon juice) to clean marble because it will quickly etch the surface.
- Use a damp cloth to remove soot from cast-iron grates.

Wall coverings

Wall coverings get surprisingly dusty and dirty. Dust can collect on any surface, including walls and ceilings. Open fires and candles produce soot, which darkens paintwork and wallpaper. Even the rising heat from radiators fixes dust to walls, darkening the area above them. As well as the dust, fingerprints and scuffs should be wiped from wall coverings as soon as possible.

Paint

The most durable decoration for walls is washable paint, which is relatively inexpensive, and looks good on any well-prepared plastered wall. If the plaster is imperfect, a lining paper can help disguise the bumps, but badly damaged plaster should be professionally reskimmed. Paint is the easiest finish to clean and repair because it can be washed and touched up without the need to repaint the entire room. Paint is the ideal finish for homes with young children, where fingerprints can often end up around light switches and on walls. Today most paint is wipeable, even some flat emulsions. Spot-remove marks as soon as you notice them, to stop them becoming fixed and spoiling the appearance of the room.

Before you attempt to wash an entire wall surface, vacuum the paint first using the dusting brush attachment. If you don't remove the dust, the dirt will quickly blacken the water and the drips running down the dirty wall will leave streaks, which may be very difficult to remove. A mild solution of washing-up liquid in some warm water is adequate for most surfaces, but you can help shift heavy grease with a solution of washing soda crystals or sugar soap, both of which are strongly alkaline, so test they won't remove the paint in a small inconspicuous area first. Start at the bottom of the wall and work upwards in sections – this way you won't get any streaks that will be hard to remove. Apply the solution with a large, tightly wrung-out sponge or a barely damp soft cloth, taking care not to rub or overwet the surface. Finish by dabbing the wall dry with wads of paper towel or old white towelling. It's much easier if you can work with someone else – one of you washing and the other drying.

Wallpaper

Wallpaper creates a luxurious effect and can help disguise imperfections in uneven plaster, especially when hung over heavy-duty lining paper. All wallpaper can be vacuumed with the dusting brush attachment to remove dust, which helps prevent permanent soiling and keeps the colour bright.

When you decorate, keep the wallpaper care advice label for future reference. Some wallpaper is washable or wipeable, although heavily textured papers are less easy to clean. If you don't have the cleaning information, wipe a small inconspicuous area with a barely damp cloth. If the paper absorbs water, it isn't washable – washable vinyl paper has a protective coated surface. Always vacuum the paper before washing. Mix a solution of warm soapy water with a few drops of washing-up liquid. Apply this with a large, tightly wrung-out sponge or a barely damp soft cloth, taking care not to rub or overwet the surface. Also, take care not to let any drips of water run down the wall because they may leave streaks. Finish by dabbing the wall dry with wads of paper towel or old white towelling. It's easier if you can work with someone else – one washing and one drying.

When you hang wallpaper it is worth fitting switch plates around light switches. These are available in a variety of styles – even transparent plastic. It's also a good idea to keep some spare paper to repair any future damage. The edges of repair patches will be less visible if you tear out a patch rather than cut the edges neatly with scissors. Simply paste the roughly torn patch over any tears or permanent marks.

Textiles

Textile-covered surfaces, such as silk or hessian, should be gently vacuumed to remove dust, which will otherwise become ingrained over time. Spot-clean fabric wall coverings with a solution of mild detergent and absorbent pads, a sponge or a soft-bristled brush.

Use the dusting brush attachment of the vacuum cleaner to remove dust from textured hessian. Take special care at the seams not to lift the edge. Gently pat the surface of very dirty hessian clean with a white, slightly dampened, face cloth or piece of old white towelling.

Wood panelling

Wood panelling shouldn't require too much upkeep. Dust with a soft damp cloth and apply beeswax sparingly once or twice a year. Remove scuff marks by rubbing with a pencil eraser or tackle stubborn marks with a cotton bud moistened with a little white spirit or methylated spirits. Small indentations can add to the character of aged wooden surfaces, but can also be filled or sanded out. Always seek further advice if the wood is antique or valuable.

Caring for pictures and frames

Always take great care when cleaning framed art that isn't protected by glass. Water and chemicals may permanently damage it. Framed pictures and photographs don't require a great deal of regular cleaning – gentle dusting of the frames with a feather duster is sufficient. Don't be tempted to overclean the frames because liquid cleaners may penetrate and damage the artwork. Hang pictures away from direct sunlight, which causes fading, or burning candles, which leave sooty deposits. Condensation and damp walls will also permanently spoil paper and canvas.

Cleaning dirty frames

These methods are good for dirty frames, but are not suitable for valuable artworks:

- Wipe painted frames clean with a barely damp soft cloth and some mild detergent such as washing-up liquid.
- Wipe unpainted wood with a soft cloth lightly dampened with linseed oil.
- Restore shine to tarnished gilt frames with a little turpentine.
- Never spray cleaners directly on to glass that is protecting a picture. It may seep under at the edges and damage the picture. Spray a little cleaner directly on to a cloth or moisten a soft cloth with a little methylated spirits and wipe the glass clean without smears.

Our skin leaves an oily film behind on unprotected paper and canvas so wear cotton gloves if you have to handle artwork. You can dust the surface with a soft paintbrush, working from top to bottom. Valuable oil paintings should be cleaned only by professionals.

Caring for books

The best storage for books is to shelve them upright with the spines facing outwards. The spines should be supported at either side to keep them square otherwise they will distort, which may damage the binding.

Remove books from shelves by reaching in and tipping them outward, rather than pulling at the spines, which may tear away.

Unless books are kept behind glass, they will collect dust. Books stored on open shelves should be dusted from time to time. Remove each volume, hold the covers between thumb and forefinger, and dust the tops of the pages with a soft paintbrush or vacuum with the dusting brush attachment. When packing valuable books away, wrap them in acid-free tissue paper.

Remove the musty smell from an old book by placing it in a bag with scrunched-up newspaper, which will help absorb the dampness and odour.

Video cassette tapes

It's best to fully rewind video tapes for storage because it prevents the exposed tape from becoming damaged and reduces tension between the spools. If the plastic case gets cracked or broken, it also allows for the tape to be lifted into a new housing. Shelve or stack video tapes away from excessive heat, light and dust and away from the video recording heads in the recorder and other magnets (including loudspeakers) that may erase the tape.

Clean the recording and replay heads of video recorders with a cotton bud moistened with methylated spirits. Rub the excess cotton fibres from the cotton bud before you start.

Compact discs and DVDs

All music and video is best protected by its original packaging – this has been true ever since Edison's wax cylinders were sold in cardboard tubes; 78 acetate records were wrapped in paper sleeves; and compact discs were anchored in their specially designed 'jewel cases'. It's always worth handling music and video carefully to prevent grit and greasy fingerprints from damaging the playing surface or dust from getting in the way of playing heads.

CDs and DVDs are laminated with plastic, which can be wiped clean with a soft damp cloth, working from the centre outwards. You can even wash heavily soiled discs in warm soapy water and dry them with a soft cloth. Store CDs in their protective wallets and handle the disc by balancing the rim between your outstretched middle finger and thumb. Avoid leaving CDs and DVDs near direct heat or sunlight where they may distort or warp.

Home entertainment equipment

Dust is the biggest enemy for electrical equipment, which is a problem because the casing also requires ventilation slats to avoid the components overheating during use. The grilles are small to stop fingers and objects touching live components, but they're no obstacle to dust. Vacuum the dust off cabinets using the dusting brush attachment or wipe over with a microfibre cloth. Never use harsh chemical cleaners on the casings of home entertainment or computer equipment. The cleaner leaves a residue which may damage the surface – instead wipe with a barely damp soft cloth. Set your hairdryer to cool and blow the dust away from air vents on electrical equipment, or use a soft paintbrush.

Don't forget to clean remote control keypads because they can become contaminated with germs and harmful bacteria. A quick wipe with a cloth is sufficient if it's done regularly, otherwise rub with a moist antibacterial wipe or a cotton bud dampened with a mild solution of washing-up liquid. Squeeze out all the excess moisture with a towel before rubbing the keys clean. Neat mouthwash will also disinfect remote control keypads. Moisten a cotton pad with a drop and rub the keys free of dirty fingerprints.

Pianos

Pianos are quite fussy about their environment. They require the correct air humidity (50–55 percent) because if the air is too dry or too damp, they quickly go out of tune, the hammer felts become hardened, and the strings may even rust. Installing a humidifier may cut down on visits from the piano tuner. Central heating is an enemy of most wooden furniture and the piano case is no exception – never stand a piano next to a radiator or fire.

Ivory keys on old pianos will yellow over time – newer keys are made from plastic. Keep the lid closed to stop dust getting into the works. The best way to keep a piano in nice condition is to play it regularly.

- Wipe the keys clean with a damp chamois leather.
- Modern veneers and lacquers are sealed and can be wiped clean with a soft dampened cloth.
- Avoid aerosol polishes, which will coat the surface with residue.
- A very mild solution of clear vinegar will remove fingermarks from glossy lacquered cabinets – wipe with a barely moistened soft cloth and buff dry.
- Remove the dust from inside the casing with a vacuum cleaner – or blow it out with a hairdryer with the heat control set to cool.

Curtains and blinds

Curtains and blinds are expensive furnishings, so you'll want to keep them looking their best. Curtains in particular trap a great deal of airborne dust and so you should vacuum them regularly using the upholstery attachment. Pull the curtains closed and vacuum the entire width from top to bottom because dust will settle in the folds and discolour the fabric. The same advice applies to roman blinds where dust gathers in the folds. Even roller blinds will collect dust, especially if they are regularly left fully unrolled.

Some curtains are washable, but refer to the care label first. Always shake the dust from curtains before you wash them. Soak very dirty curtains in a mild solution of warm water and detergent first to loosen up the dust and then wash as advised by the care label.

If there isn't a care label sewn into the fabric, dry cleaning is probably the safest option, especially if the fabric is an upholstery weight and has sewn-in linings. Dry cleaning can prove expensive because cleaners charge by the square metre, so you can keep curtains fresher by taking them down at least once a year, giving them a good shake outside, then hanging them on the washing line to air.

House plants

House plants can bring a flavour of the outdoors inside, but they'll only be happy in the right conditions and centrally heated indoor climates can be fairly inhospitable. The plants we tend to grow indoors are those that require year-round warmth and usually grow outside in tropical climates.

House plants require water, light and warmth, but they're particular about how much of each they like. Low light will produce pale, spindly growth in some plants, while others thrive in it. Overwatering can be just as harmful as no water for some plants. Central heating can make the air too dry so light misting with a water spray may help, but all plants dislike being covered in dust, which clogs the pores in the leaves and leaves them struggling to breathe. You don't have to talk to your plants, although it may help, but they will thrive if you create the right environment.

Large house plants are an expensive purchase so you'll want to provide the right environment to ensure they survive. Always read the care label before you buy, and for very expensive plants ask for advice. If a plant requires plenty of light, but not direct sunlight, it won't do well in a cool shady room. If a plant requires the temperature to be above 15°C, it won't like an unheated conservatory. If a new plant starts to look unwell, diagnose its symptoms. Is the compost too wet or too dry, is there too much or too little light, or is it too close to a radiator? Make adjustments but don't move the plant around too much – plants prefer to acclimatize. However, don't assume it will recover on its own – it probably won't.

Never stand house plants on top of the TV. If water gets inside the set it will cause a serious short circuit. You can remove dust from the plant leaves by wiping with the inside of a banana skin or a soft cloth dipped in a solution of milk and water.

When you're going on holiday for more than a week, stand your house plants together to create a microclimate. Do this in a cool room during summer, or a bright one in winter. If you're going to be away for more than a week, ask a neighbour to water them, or if this isn't possible, create an oasis for them. Line the bath or a bowl with a plastic sheet and two thick newspapers. Spray the newspaper with water until it's saturated but not submerged. Place the plants, without their saucers, directly on top of the newspaper. They should be able to draw up enough water from the paper to survive for a couple of weeks.

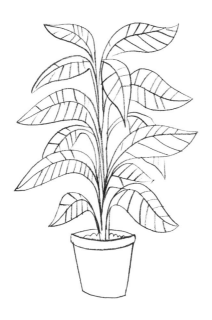

The bathroom

Good hygiene in the bathroom is just as important as in the kitchen. Sparkling sanitary ware and fresh towels don't only provide a touch of sophistication; they're much healthier too.

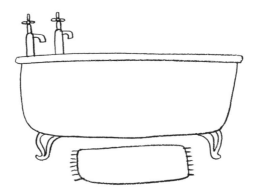

Kim I much prefer taking a bubble bath to a shower. I like a fresh towel for each and every bath, and once I'm dry I'll use the towel to wipe round the inside of the bath and polish the taps. That way there's never any need for harsh cleaners because the limescale never has a chance to build up; hard water is torture. For the shower glass, I'll tell you what I use – half and half vinegar and water. It removes limescale and leaves glass gleaming – it works a treat, it really does. I always use a separate bucket and cleaning cloths in the bathroom – a white bucket for the bathroom, red for the kitchen – you don't want to spread the germs around.

Aggie Vinegar plays a starring role in my bathroom. We live in a hard water area so I always soak the shower head in half water and half vinegar to remove the limescale, but my best tip for removing the hard water deposits that form round the plughole is to rub gently with a pumice stone. Our bath has a shower over it and a glass screen, which is so much better than a plastic curtain – I hate the way they can stick to you! In the summer I'll take two showers a day, one in the morning, and another before bed. I much prefer a quick shower to a bath, but if I do have a soak, I always wash the bath afterwards. That was drummed into me from an early age.

I'm not fussed whether the toilet seat is left up or down. Sharing the bathroom with three boys, I'm very happy for the loo to be left as it's used most often. Matthew trained the boys always to take a sheet of toilet tissue and wipe round the rim when they'd finished, and they've always done it. What more could you ask for?

Kim There's a lot of fuss made about cleaning a toilet; I don't know why. I'll never change my mind about toilet brushes though because in nine out of ten households they're abused. I'll tell you what I do: sprinkle scouring powder around the bowl, rub around, flush, then rub again – don't forget under the rim – and flush. Take a paper towel moistened with a few drops of cleaner, wipe the seat and buff it dry. There, what's all the fuss about?

Aggie I don't like any more stuff lying around than is absolutely necessary. Matthew, the boys and I all use the same shampoo and soap, there are a few cleaning products in the airing cupboard, and that's about it. Oh, and there are the two awards I've won for the TV show – better in the bathroom than on the mantelpiece.

Kim Do you know how to stop your bathroom mirror steaming up? If you rub shaving foam over it and then buff it off, it won't steam up. It doesn't last for ever, but it's a great improvement. Test it out with a steaming kettle and see what I mean.

The height of luxury

Even as recently as a hundred years ago, many houses didn't have an indoor bathroom. All but the richest homes had an outdoor toilet, and baths were taken once a week at the bathhouse or in a tin bath in front of the fire. Today a bathroom is a necessity not a luxury, although they've certainly gone upmarket in recent times with whirlpool baths, walk-in shower enclosures and designer loos.

Hygiene

Despite all the sanitary improvements, harmful bacteria and moulds will readily grow in a warm moist environment, so good hygiene is of paramount importance. Always use separate cleaning cloths and gloves in the bathroom so that there's no opportunity for germs to cross-contaminate with any other room. Wash and thoroughly dry the cloths after every use. Don't leave cloths damp or scrunched up behind the taps because bacteria will flourish.

Good personal hygiene is also essential. Always wash hands after using the toilet and replace hand towels with fresh ones regularly. It's unhealthy to share bath towels because infections, especially skin problems, can spread rapidly. Leave towels to dry thoroughly after use to prevent the growth of bacteria. When the weather is fine, if you have difficulty drying them inside, hang them out on the line. Towels should be washed at least twice a week.

Choosing towels

European towel sizes:

Face cloth	30 x 30 cm (12 x 12 inches)
Guest	40 x 70 cm (16 x 28 inches)
Hand	50 x 80 cm (20 x 32 inches)
Bath	60 x 130 cm (24 x 52 inches)
Bath sheet	80 x 160 cm (32 x 64 inches)

When you're choosing towels, 100 percent cotton has the highest absorbency. Avoid choosing towels with heavy embroidered designs or edging detail, which reduce the drying surface.

Towels are available in a wide variety of colours and designs, but always buy heavily dyed towels from the same batch to ensure colour consistency. Always wash new towels first to remove the fluff and the fabric treatments, which reduce their absorbency, and launder coloured towels together to ensure uniform fading. If you do add fabric conditioner to the wash, take care not to use too much or you'll coat the surface and reduce the absorbency. Thick towels are luxurious to the touch, but they take a long time to dry so may prove an expensive buy if you prefer to use the tumble dryer for your laundry.

Ventilation

It's important to maintain good ventilation in the bathroom, especially where double glazing is fitted. High humidity leads to mould and mildew, which is bad for health, especially for asthma sufferers (*see* The healthy home, p. 106). After bathing or showering, open the window or run the extractor fan to clear the steam. You can also reduce steam by running the cold water into a bath and then adding the hot, which is safer too.

Clutter

Keep bathroom clutter to a minimum; cosmetics, shampoos, cleaning products and bathtime toys can multiply rapidly. Wet plastic bottles provide a breeding ground for bacteria and moulds and sponges, loofahs and toys that are left permanently wet will also soon become mildewed and unhealthy. Have regular culls of all products and use a towel to dry bathtime toys and shampoo bottles.

Bathrooms tend to be on the small side given how much they have to accomplish, so avoid filling the limited space with things that could be kept somewhere else. Laundry baskets, towel stands and occasional chairs all take up valuable space and make cleaning the floor more difficult and arduous.

The toilet

Good toilet hygiene is essential because germs are easily transferred from one person to the next, not only from the bowl but also the flush handle and the seat. If there are several users, the toilet should be cleaned daily with disinfectant, and given a good scrub once a week.

It's important not only to clean the bowl, but under the rim too. Lots of people like to use toilet brushes in order to avoid having to put their hands into the bowl, but there really is no substitute for donning rubber gloves and having a good scrub to get the porcelain clean and shiny. Toilet brushes harbour large quantities of bacteria because they get clogged with debris from the bowl and remain wet. If you insist on using one, soak it in a bucket of water with a few drops of bleach added, wash the container too and leave the whole thing out to dry afterwards. There are now lots of disposable cleaning brushes and pads on the market, but all brushes are an unworthy compromise for strict hygiene.

Sprinkle some scouring powder or disinfectant into the pan and let it soak while you get on with cleaning the bath and basin. You can make up your own scouring powder with borax and bicarbonate of soda, and even make a paste by adding clear vinegar if you need to remove limescale too. Once the cleaner has soaked for a few minutes take a cloth, reserved solely for this use, or paper towel and rub the cleaner around the pan, under the rim and around the seat hinges – you can use an old toothbrush for the tricky bits. You can also gently buff away limescale deposits from porcelain sanitary ware using a pumice stone. Don't dispose of any cloth or towel into the pan as it will block the pipes. Once the whole surface is scrubbed, flush the toilet, swish the clean water around any cleaner that remains, and flush again.

Some people like to put neat bleach into the bowl, which is an effective disinfectant, but don't leave it for more than half an hour before flushing because the bleach can damage the finish of the glaze on the porcelain. There are other homespun remedies for cleaning the toilet pan, most of which utilize acids to remove limescale, or alkalis to neutralize odours. A couple of denture cleaning tablets or a cup of bicarbonate of soda will remove slight stains. Never mix toilet cleaners – they contain harsh chemicals, which may produce toxic reactions or gases if combined.

Don't neglect the seat and flush handle, which can also harbour and transfer harmful bacteria between users. Wash them with warm soapy water and polish plastic seats with a little glass cleaner. Wooden seats are sealed to prevent water penetrating, so you only need to wipe them over with warm soapy water and buff them dry with a soft cloth.

If the toilet is blocked, it's safer to pull out any visible obstruction rather than risk pushing it further into the pipe work where it may become jammed. If the obstruction is past the U-bend of the pan, use a plunger to help shift it. If it refuses to budge, you may have to uncouple the toilet from the soil pipe – a job for a plumber if you're not too confident in your DIY skills.

The bidet

Clean the bidet in the same way as a toilet, paying attention to under the rim. The bidet is easier to clean because you have access to clean running water while you're working. Dry the bowl and rim with a dry cloth or tissue when you've finished.

The basin

The basin and tap handles must be cleaned regularly because they come into contact with hands contaminated after using the toilet. A cream, powder or liquid cleaner is suitable for most surfaces. Once a week, work cleaner into the drainer, the overflow and around the base of the taps where limescale can form. Use an old toothbrush to get into awkward places. You can avoid limescale deposits by drying the basin and taps with a towel.

Remove hardened limescale deposits from taps with vinegar, but not gold-plated taps. If the deposit is stubborn, soak a piece of paper towel or tissue in vinegar, wrap it around the tap, then cover with a plastic bag and secure with an elastic band. Leave it for an hour or so and then check on its progress, but don't leave it overnight because the acetic acid could etch the finish, even on chrome taps.

Polish taps to a high shine with a soft cloth; even a dab of white toothpaste will help buff them and is safe to use on all finishes. Don't forget to clean the plug and chain too; once again a toothbrush is ideal. If you have a concealed waste stopper, unscrew the cover from time to time and soak the waste filter in a solution of bleach, scrubbing away any debris with a toothbrush.

The bath

It's much easier to get into the habit of cleaning and drying the bath after every use than having to scrub it after repeated use. Never use anything abrasive on an acrylic or plastic bath because the surface will scratch and become harder to clean. Acrylic or plastic finishes show stains and won't take much scrubbing before they etch like a skating rink. Enamelled steel or cast-iron baths are more durable, but will still scratch and discolour if mistreated.

To remove stains from an enamel bath, make a paste of bicarbonate of soda with a few drops of water and rub on to the surface with a cork. To remove mild rust marks on a steel bath, rub with salt and lemon juice and rinse.

To clean a very dirty bath, fill it with warm water and add a couple of scoops of biological washing detergent, then leave to soak overnight. For regular use, wash high gloss surfaces with a mild solution of washing-up liquid and buff dry with a towel.

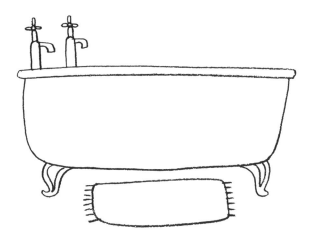

A shower over the bath

If you have a shower over the bath, you should line the bath surface with a non-slip mat for safety. You need to lift the mat and clean the bath surface after every shower to avoid a build-up of soap scum and limescale underneath. Don't forget to wash or soak the mat too. Fill the bath with warm soapy water and scrub with a soft brush. Some mats are also machine washable.

If your bath doubles up as a shower, you'll either have a glass screen or plastic curtain. Glass is smart, but requires lots of cleaning and polishing, although it dries quickly and mould is less likely to grow. Alternatively, a plastic curtain will go in the washing machine and can be rehung to dry. To prevent mildew forming on a plastic curtain, wipe it down with a strong solution of vinegar and put it in the washing machine with the dirty towels once or twice a month.

A shower enclosure

A shower uses less water than a bath and less energy to heat the water, although power showers dispense a great volume of water in a very short time. The shower enclosure is usually made of glass, tile or plastic. Single sheet surfaces such as glass and plastic are the easiest to keep clean because, unlike tile, there are no grout lines to collect scum and mildew. Where surfaces join up, sealant is used to close the gaps. This usually contains a fungicide, but may blacken over time if mildew and mould get a hold, which is possible if the area is constantly left wet.

The moisture left behind on the surfaces is the biggest problem because it quickly promotes mould and mildew. You can reduce this problem by drying the surfaces with a squeegee; leaving the extractor fan running; and leaving the enclosure door slightly open; all of which will speed up the evaporation of water. You can remove soap scum and limescale deposits by spraying the surfaces with a solution of half clear vinegar and half water.

Tile grout lines are slightly absorbent and hold on to soap scum and mildew which is unattractive and unhygienic. Scrub grout lines clean with a powder cleanser and a toothbrush; make your own cleaner by mixing a paste of bicarbonate of soda with a few drops of bleach or vinegar. You can restore the shine to tiles with a little vinegar or window cleaner, and then buff dry with a soft cloth.

Mirrors

Mirrors quickly show splashes in the bathroom and mist over when condensation is heavy; avoid wiping them when they're misted up to prevent smears. There's no need to use chemical spray cleaners for regular cleaning, just buff with a microfibre cloth or mix half vinegar and half water in a spray bottle. Vinegar will also cut through a stubborn build-up of hairspray, especially if you rub with some scrunched-up newspaper.

Toothbrush and soap containers

Lots of us prefer to stand wet toothbrushes handle-down in a mug or container, but these damp conditions collect bacteria very quickly. Wash tooth mugs frequently – the dishwasher is very effective. Soap dishes are a perfectly hygienic way of allowing soap tablets to air-dry, but only if the drainer is kept clean and dry.

Floors

Vacuum and wash the bathroom floor regularly. Vinyl, stone and tile floors, although slippery if wet, are much more hygienic than carpet or rugs, which stay damp, harbour germs and encourage mould. Use a bathmat after showering or bathing to keep the floor dry and avoid slipping. Keep the floor as free from clutter as possible so that all the nooks and crannies around pipe work and sanitary ware are easily accessible. Pour the waste water from floor washing into the toilet, not the hand basin.

Bathroom safety

✚ Never leave young children unattended in the bath or leave the door open while the bath is running.

✚ Fix medicine cabinets out of reach of young children, or preferably keep locked.

✚ Keep the floor as dry as possible to avoid the risk of slipping.

✚ Use a non-slip mat when showering in the bath.

✚ Fit side grab rails over the bath to assist very young and old users.

The bedrooms

The bedrooms should be aired regularly, kept free from clutter and, above all, be comfortable. The centre of attention must surely be the bed because we all need a proper night's sleep.

Kim My bed can never be soft enough. On top of the mattress I lay not one, but two, feather-filled continental quilts. I told you, I like it soft, and there are six goose down pillows on top of that. The quilts are a size larger than the mattress, so they tuck in underneath. I prefer them to mattress toppers, which tend to drift in my opinion. The mattress and divan are covered in beautiful yellow brocade, which I dust off with a rough towelling face cloth every time I change the linen; it's too fragile to vacuum. When it comes to bed linen, I always buy white or cream, 100 percent cotton. It's no dearer and you can do miracles with it. I like a good thread count and percales don't bobble up, unlike some synthetic mix linens. Don't skimp on sheets, they'll last you a lifetime – I've had some of mine for over ten years.

Aggie Our bedroom is decorated in very calm colours. I don't like there to be any clutter at all, and I even keep the furniture to a minimum (yes, we do have a bed!). For me the bedroom's somewhere I go to sleep rather than to relax; I've certainly never had any trouble sleeping. When the boys were younger we all used to lie on the bed and watch TV, but now it's rarely turned on; and whenever it is I fall straight to sleep. Sometimes I'll go up to bed early, especially if there are clean sheets waiting, but early nights are fatal because I'll be awake again at 3.00 am. I don't need much sleep.

The bed gets changed once a week with fresh white bed linen. I don't use fitted sheets – in fact, I positively enjoy doing hospital corners. My mother taught me when I was a child and even inspected to see they were done right! I use a down duvet and three sizes of pillows, the square ones, then the normal size and some small ones. I don't like to be cool, not even in summer, I like to be warm at all times, so in the winter we even have an electric underblanket!

Kim Don't store your white sheets in the heated airing cupboard – they go yellow. I have a straw hamper near a radiator so that they can breathe a bit. If you put a couple of cushions on top it looks very nice. I always wash my duvets in the washing machine – I've got one with an extra large drum. Put them in the tumble dryer along with a couple of tennis balls to stop the feathers clumping. These days you can only get yellow balls, so test they're colour fast first, which they do tend to be. Rub the surface hard with a damp cloth and if no colour comes off, they're fine to go in the dryer. If the colour comes off, weight them down in some salty cold water to fast-dye them.

Aggie Apart from changing the bed linen and controlling the clutter, the other big job in the bedroom is dusting. I think a damp cloth is the best way to pick it up, followed by a good vacuuming once a week. The bedroom must be kept fresh. I don't like sleeping with the windows open because I hate draughty bedrooms, but I always open them up in the morning, fold back the duvet and let the fresh air come in.

Kim Airing the bed is very important. I always have an oversheet under the duvet. During the day I have a very generous turndown with at least three feet of undersheet showing. Open the window too – just an inch mind, I don't want all the dust, flies and bugs coming in. Close the door and let the room have a good air for at least a couple of hours.

I've never liked dressing tables. I find them a bit 'Barbara Cartland' and although I've always loved bold jewellery, I never wear any indoors; I take it all off the moment I come in. I have an armoire in the bedroom with drawers for the costume stuff – the junk jewellery I call it. The pieces that are waiting to go into the safe I rest on a rather lovely stand about fifteen inches tall with silver bars. My Pete, being an ex-bobby, always carries them off and locks them away before bed. I look after my jewels because I've worked hard for them. The chains are forever getting knotted. The best tip is to unpick them with two pins, but don't be lazy and struggle away with your fingernails – you won't do it. Go to the work box and get two pins – it's much quicker and easier.

Furnishing a bedroom

The bedroom should provide plenty of sanctuary, a place to relax and rest, because we spend a third of our lives in bed. It makes sense to spend such a lot of our time cocooned in as much luxury as possible, and there's no doubt that life seems to go more smoothly after a good night's rest.

Those who follow feng shui say it's impossible to achieve serenity if a room is cluttered. They also believe computers, exercise machines and televisions have no place in the bedroom because they stimulate rather than relax. Of course watching TV in bed is something many of us love to do, but you could always compromise and hide it away inside a cabinet as they do in all the best hotels.

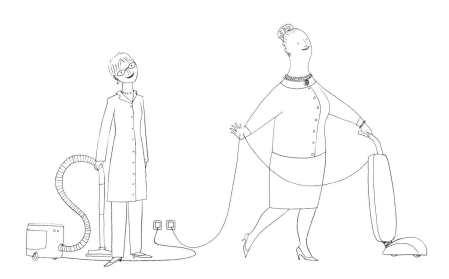

The centrepiece of any bedroom is of course the bed. Our earliest sleeping arrangements were nothing more than a pile of straw on the ground, which was later stuffed into bags. Eventually more sophisticated dwellers filled their bags with feathers and raised them on to platforms to avoid the dirt, vermin and draughts and, lo, the mattress was born. The really wealthy built their beds into grand frames complete with posts and curtains to keep out draughts. Even today they don't come much grander than the four-poster.

In modern times we've experimented with waterbeds and the latest innovation is space-age memory foam, which adapts to our body temperature and weight. People spend a fortune on fully equipped, top-of-the-range kitchens and bathrooms, but it's surprising how little money most of us are prepared to spend on a bed. Only a third of people, in one recent survey by the charity BackCare, said they'd be prepared to pay more than £500, which doesn't make sense when you consider a good bed will last ten years, but clothes that cost a fortune will be consigned to the charity shop after a couple of years.

The most luxurious beds are piled high with pillows and comforters, even the headboards are upholstered, and recently there has even been a trend towards covering mattresses in furnishing fabrics. One word of caution for allergy sufferers: while fitted carpets, full-length curtains and satin throws are cosy, dust mites love these environments too. If you're allergic to them, or suffer from asthma, you'll need to reduce the amount of dust in your home as much as possible. It's impossible to completely eradicate dust mites, but you can reduce their number.

If you're lucky enough to have a separate dressing room you won't need to find space for wardrobes and drawers, but most of us do. Fitted wardrobes with hanging rails, shelves and drawers make the most efficient use of awkward alcoves, but they represent a considerable investment, and you can't take them with you when you move. Modern, off-the-shelf, flat-packed wardrobe systems offer almost the same amount of flexibility, although their components are based on standard dimensions.

Let the air in

The best thing that you can do to keep the bedroom healthy is to let plenty of outside air in, even in the winter. We all, like it or not, perspire a great deal while we're asleep; the average adult sweats a quarter of a litre of moisture into the bed every night. We also shed a great deal of skin, which, combined with the warm damp environment, creates a perfect feeding and breeding ground for dust mites.

Some people are allergic to dust mite faeces (*see* The healthy home, p. 106). Airing the room and the bedding helps remove some of the humidity in which dust mites thrive and reduces their number. Allowing fresh air in also prevents condensation problems, which can lead to mould and mildew, which are harmful to our health. If you have black or green spots growing on the window sills then you already have a condensation problem, and should open the window for at least twenty minutes every day to help cure it.

Once you've opened the window, turn back all the covers on the bed, at least while you shower and dress. After about twenty minutes the air in the room will have been exchanged and the mattress and linens will be fresher and drier. If possible, you should leave the bed open to air for longer than twenty minutes; ideally for a couple of hours.

Controlling clutter

The bedroom won't be restful if it's piled with clutter, but of course there are some things we do need to store here. Most of us own far too many clothes, more than we can ever wear, but hate to part with them. Do sort through your wardrobe and drawers at least every season. Don't feel compelled to tackle all your drawers in one go. Spend ten minutes sorting out just one drawer every morning over a week or so, and they'll soon be in shape.

You should always empty your pockets before hanging or folding clothes. Most of us collect all kinds of things in our pockets by the end of the day, so to prevent these items cluttering up surfaces, and making them more difficult to dust, put them into a bowl or decorative box to sort through later. Display your finest potions and lotions, but find a drawer to hide the everyday stuff away in so that surfaces are easier to dust.

Don't return soiled clothes to drawers and wardrobes. If you can't easily put clothes away at the end of the day, the room will quickly become cluttered, so if lack of clothes storage is a problem, sort through your wardrobe or create additional space by adding rails, shelves, drawers or covered trays that will slide under the bed (*see* Caring for clothes and shoes, p. 304).

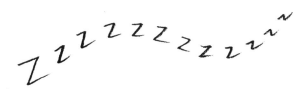

The bed

A restful night's sleep brings tremendous benefits to our mood and our health, so it's essential to invest in a good quality mattress. There's a difference between choosing a bed and a mattress. The mattress provides the direct cushioned support for the body, while the bed frame supports the mattress. Choose a style of bed you like and then, before you buy the frame, research the options for a mattress. Divan beds include their own upholstered base and can be fitted with a headboard.

The wider your bed the better, so if your room will accommodate a larger bed, then upgrade. A traditional UK double size is just 1.35 metres (4 feet 6 inches), less than a single bed allowance for each adult, but do check that your new bed will fit through any narrow stairwells or door openings.

Five tips for better sleep

- Avoid heavy meals, stimulants (coffee, alcohol, nicotine) and exercise before bed.
- Establish a regular routine for bedtime. Condition your body clock, relax with a bath, read a few pages of a book, or listen to some gentle music. Avoid watching television, which stimulates the eyes.
- A cool (18–22°C) darkened room is most comfortable. Darkness aids sleep, so fit blackout blinds behind curtains if necessary.
- Sudden noise can disrupt sleep, but some people find a constant low background hum, such as air conditioning, blocks out other noises.
- Invest in a mattress that is comfortable and supportive.

Choosing a mattress

A good quality mattress will last for at least ten years. After that, the springs start to distort and the quality of the support they provide deteriorates. If your sleep is disrupted or uncomfortable or you suffer from a bad back, a new mattress is probably overdue. Down- and synthetic-filled mattress toppers are designed to provide extra warmth and comfort, but are not an alternative to a properly supportive mattress.

Do your research before investing in a new mattress. Discuss your preferences with sales staff and don't be bashful about lying on the display models (with your partner if that's how you will sleep). You may feel self-conscious, but it will be worth it for the many nights of good rest you'll enjoy afterwards if you choose wisely. Many people mistakenly believe that firmer mattresses, often marketed as orthopaedic, are in some way better for you. This isn't necessarily true, so do talk to the experts.

Confusingly the names given to mattress sizes throughout the world are similar, 'king' and 'queen', but the dimensions are different, which is worth remembering when you book a hotel room in America or decide to buy the excellent value sheets while you're there. The European sizes are based on metric measurements and the American on imperial. A UK king size is 1.5 metres (5 feet), but in America this is called a 'queen'. European lengths are a standard 2 metres (6 feet 6 inches), but a UK double is shorter at 1.9 metres (6 feet 3 inches).

If you have the room to manoeuvre around the bed, and still have space to comfortably open the doors and drawers of surrounding furniture, the minimum size mattress you should consider for two adults is a king (1.5 metres/5 feet) width, while double width (1.35 metres/4 feet 6 inches) is fine for one adult.

Mattress sizes

Small single

75 cm x 1.9 m
2'6" x 6'3"

Single
(Twin size in the US)

90 cm x 1.9 m
3' x 6'3"

Small double

1.2 m x 1.9 m
4' x 6'3"

Double
(Full size in the US)

1.35 m x 1.9 m
4'6" x 6'3"

UK king
(Queen size in the US)

1.5 m x 2 m
5' x 6'6"

UK super king
(King in the US)

1.8 m x 2 m
6' x 6'6"

Mattress care

Follow the manufacturer's advice about turning the mattress to significantly extend its life and comfort. Twice a year is the minimum unless it specifies 'no turn' on the label. You can also vacuum the mattress from time to time, although some manufacturers advise against this in case it disturbs the filling. If so, use a barely dampened face cloth to brush off the dust.

Always protect your mattress with a washable cover to keep it clean. Use a waterproof cover if necessary for incontinence or young children because dampness rots a mattress and leads to mildew. Wash this cover frequently and remove any spots or soiling from the mattress cover as soon as possible, using a foamy mix of hand wash laundry detergent or shaving foam. A solution of clear vinegar will help remove the smell of urine, but dab it away with clean water. To remove unpleasant odours from a mattress, sprinkle liberally with bicarbonate of soda, leave for a few hours and then thoroughly vacuum off the powder. Always make sure the mattress is completely dry before remaking with sheets, using a hairdryer if necessary.

Bed linen

The choice between a bed made up with sheets and blankets or covered with a duvet is entirely down to personal preference. Some people like the heavier weight of blankets, while other sleepers prefer the insulation but lightness that a duvet offers.

Polyester and cotton mixed fibre sheets (usually fifty/fifty) offer a non-iron alternative to traditional all-cotton sheets. Fitted sheets also save on ironing, but make sure you buy the correct depth for your mattress otherwise the elasticated corners have an annoying habit of working themselves free. To make up a mattress with a flat sheet, simply stretch and fold the excess corners under the mattress in two large triangular flaps just as you would wrap a parcel – this folding technique is traditionally known as 'hospital corners'.

Duvet covers come with four different types of fastenings: buttons, fabric ties, poppers and zips. Buttons and ties are easier to mend than zips and poppers.

To fit a duvet cover, turn it inside out and hold the corners in line with the duvet corners. Flick the cover down along the length of the duvet and shake. For a large or heavy duvet, lay the cover on the bed with the opening at the bottom. Push each of the two top corners of the duvet into the corners of the cover and pull the cover down along the remainder, fasten and then shake.

Pillowcases are available in several styles. The standard is also known as a 'housewife' and is a simple slip-on cover with an end flap. The Oxford style has a flange around the edge, and 'European' generally refers to a square shape.

A valance is the coordinating decorative cover or skirt for the divan base. The mattress sits on top of it. Valances are available in cotton and polycotton with gathered or box pleats. They don't require laundering every time the bed is changed, but do at least vacuum or wash from time to time.

You'll need at least two sets of bed linen and will probably acquire several because they last for many years. Avoid storing white linens that are unused for long periods in heated cupboards because they will become yellowed, especially along the exposed folds.

Mark the size (king, double, single) on each sheet to save unfolding them when looking for fresh bed linen. Wrap matching sheets and pillowcase sets inside the duvet cover to save time putting together sets.

Thread counts

When you're planning to buy new bed linen, it's worth doing a little research first. When you're confronted with a choice of polycotton or 100 percent Egyptian cotton; the terms 'percale' and 'sateen'; and bewildering thread counts, you may feel in need of a lie down.

Polycotton is simply a mixed fibre of polyester and cotton, usually fifty/fifty. One hundred percent cotton bed linen is often specified as Egyptian cotton. Cotton comes from the fuzzy fibres that surround the seeds of the cotton plant and different types of plants produce different staples of cotton. The longer the staple, the more strength, smoothness and softness the cotton fabric has. Egyptian, Pima and Sea Island cotton have the very longest staples. Pima and Sea Island cotton are mainly used for clothing.

The thread count is the number of vertical (warp) and horizontal (weft) threads in a square inch of fabric. The thread count is often shown on the packaging by adding the two numbers (warp and the weft) together. A good quality cotton sheet starts from 180 threads (the term 'percale' means a thread count of 180 or higher), but thread counts of up to 400 are available. In theory, the higher the thread count the softer the feel of the sheet. This is sometimes described as 'the hand' – a subjective measure of the softness when you run your hand across the surface of the fabric. The quality and staple length of the cotton fibre also contribute to the feel.

There are three basic weaves for textiles: plain, twill and satin. The weave varies by the way the warp crosses the weft. Sateen sheets have a satin weave (the warp threads pass over two weft threads), which gives a sleeker 'hand' and a sheen to the fabric. Sateen sheets have high thread counts, but they also tend to be less durable because the weave is looser.

If you want a long lasting, easy to launder, cotton sheet you won't go far wrong with Egyptian cotton, which has a thread count of between 180 and 240. Feel the 'hand' by running your palm and straightened fingers over the surface, and decide on an acceptable level of comfort for you. Egyptian cotton does vary in quality (it is grown all along the Nile Valley), so don't assume that it is a universal mark for fine cotton.

Blankets

Blankets are still favoured by some people. All-wool is the most luxurious, but synthetic fibres and wool mixes are available. Woollen blankets should be aired and rested from time to time to allow the fibres to recover. Store them in bags with a moth repellent (dry bay leaves, lavender and cedar wood will all repel moths). Launder or dry-clean blankets from time to time, stretch back into shape whilst damp and line dry.

Electric underblankets are a matter of personal taste, but always check that the cables are in good condition. They should be replaced every few years for added safety.

Duvets

Duvets were widely used in Europe, especially Scandinavia, long before they became popular in the UK. They're also known as continental quilts (in Australia they are called a 'doona', originally a brand name that has now become the generic term). The word 'duvet' comes from the French for down, although duvets are no longer exclusively filled with down and feather – today synthetic fillings are equally popular. There is no evidence that dust mites are more at home in feather-filled duvets, but synthetic fillings are often marketed as hypoallergenic. For allergy sufferers, duvets have the advantage over blankets that they can be sealed inside dust mite-proof covers.

The warmth of a duvet is measured by its tog rating. The tog is a measurement of thermal resistance, mainly used for textiles, which was devised in the 1960s by the Manchester-based Shirley Institute (a research foundation founded in 1920 by the British Cotton Research Association). A typical duvet tog rating is 13.5 tog for the winter and a 4.5 tog for summer. Some duvets combine a 9.0 tog with a 4.5 tog, which can be used separately in summer or spring and then fastened together to provide the warmest combination during the depths of winter.

When you're buying a duvet, your first consideration should be the filling. Feather and down (usually from geese or ducks) are traditionally used because they're lightweight and provide excellent thermal insulation. Down is a slightly superior insulator over feather because it has more filaments, which gives it an excellent 'lofting' quality – in other words, it traps more air. Down is also softer than feather because feathers have a tougher spine (although down is not, as some people mistakenly believe, a description for newly grown feathers).

Goose is the warmest and softest widely available down filling, and Siberian goose the most expensive. Often manufacturers mix down and feathers to reduce the cost but to be described as 'down filled', the duvet should have at least 51 percent down. The softest and rarest of all downs is from the eider duck. The eider uses its down to line its nest and this is then collected up by hand for use in the most luxurious and expensive quilts, which sell for hundreds of pounds. Regular duck down duvet fillings are usually less expensive than goose.

Whatever filling you decide on, you also need to pay attention to the composition and construction of the cover. A 100 percent cotton down-proof fabric will stop the feathers shedding or poking through the cover. Some covers also claim to prevent dust mites getting through the fabric. A box type construction ensures that the feathers remain in separate pockets, while the channel type designs tend to cause the feathers to fall to the bottom, so they need more shaking to restore the bulk.

Some people raise an ethical objection to down and feather because it's a by-product of farming, or taken from live birds. There are plenty of synthetic alternatives to natural fillings, which tend to be less expensive and are easier to wash and dry.

Buying a duvet

- Select your preferred filling – down, feather or synthetic.
- Down is lighter, warmer and more expensive than feather.
- Synthetic fillings are easier to wash and dry and less expensive.
- Choose a tog rating (13.5 tog for winter, 9.0 tog for spring/autumn and 4.5 tog for summer).
- Look for a box construction to keep the filling in place.
- Check that covers are down-proof or dust mite-proof as appropriate.

Duvet care

Both feather and synthetic filled duvets should be regularly aired and laundered. Spot-clean soiling in the same way as a mattress. There's no need to wash feather more than once a year and it must be thoroughly dry before reuse. Because of the bulk, a domestic washing machine drum may not be sufficiently large to accommodate a king, or even a double size, duvet, so a trip to the laundrette may be the only option. Avoid chemically dry-cleaning duvets because the solvent leaves a residue on the feathers.

Pillows

Pillows are available with down, feather and synthetic fillings, ranging in support from soft to firm. As with duvets, down is the softest and considered the most luxurious. Combinations of down and feather are more common and less expensive, but do look carefully at the composition. Duck feather and down may have as little as 10 percent down, but duck down and feather should have at least 51 percent down. Duck feather is cheapest; followed by duck feather and down; duck down and feather; then goose feather; goose feather and down; and finally pure goose down – although it's rare to find a pillow that is 100 percent down. Check that the cover is down-proof to prevent the spines of the feathers poking through.

Pillows are also available with synthetic fillings, which are often described as hypoallergenic and are easier to wash and dry. There are also memory foam pillows available, which are designed to complement the latest space-age mattresses.

Always fit a protective cover beneath the pillowcase to protect from soiling. Pillows should also be machine washed with detergent, but without fabric conditioner, and then tumble-dried. Add some tennis balls to the dryer (if yellow, check they're colourfast first) to prevent the feathers from clumping.

If you karate chop a pillow in half lengthways with your whole forearm, it's much easier to stuff into the pillowcase.

Making up the bed

- Change linen once a week; twice in hot weather.
- Turn the mattress at least twice a year, turning lengthways and widthways.
- Always protect the mattress with a cover – waterproof if necessary.
- Use a fitted or flat sheet over the mattress cover.
- For flat sheets, fold under at the corners as if wrapping a gift.
- Some people prefer a top sheet underneath a duvet cover.
- Two blankets are an alternative to a duvet.
- Always cover pillows in protective cases.
- Wash pillows regularly.
- Wash duvets in preference to dry-cleaning. Use the larger laundrette machines if necessary.

Headboards

Headboards are available in a variety of finishes: wood, veneer, upholstered fabric and vinyl. Even polished wood collects a lot of dust. The pillows should prevent the head from touching the board or it will become soiled. Vacuum or wipe all headboards when the bed is changed. Soiling on fabric can be spot cleaned in the same way as the mattress.

Under the bed storage

Don't use the space under the bed as a dumping ground, although it can provide invaluable extra storage. Divan sets sometimes include drawers, either at the sides or the end, so check which layout will work best for your space when you're choosing a new bed. You can also buy plastic trays with lids. The space under the bed gets very dusty, so pull everything out once a month and vacuum thoroughly, which will ensure that moths and carpet beetles don't move in, and dust mites are kept under control.

Lighting and lampshades

Light fittings can get very dusty, especially bedside lamps and shades. Always unplug lamps at the socket before cleaning. Wipe the base over with a towelling cloth or a dampened duster at least once a week. Vacuum fabric and paper shades using the dusting brush attachment. Another method is to remove the shade and roll a barely dampened cloth over the surface, gathering the dust. Take care not to get the metal frame wet, which may rust. If the dust proves stubborn, take the shade outside and give it a sharp flick with a duster. When you replace the shade, don't forget to wipe the bulb too.

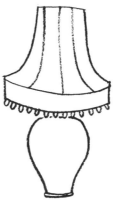

Mirrors

The bedroom is definitely a place for a full-length mirror. If you don't want a mirror in full view, fix one to the back of the door or behind the wardrobe door. Mirrors can become coated with a thin residue of hairspray and perfume, but a solution of half clear vinegar and half water will cut through it. If the mirror is coated, you'll have to rub harder – a microfibre cloth or scrunched-up newspaper is ideal, and coffee filter papers work well too because they don't leave any flecks of paper behind.

Caring for jewellery

Most people keep their jewellery in the bedroom, which burglars know too. If you have valuable or sentimental pieces and you decide to keep them at home, fit a concealed floor or wall safe, but locking them in a drawer won't deter a burglar. Remember to insure your jewels for what they are really worth – jewellers give appraisals for insurance value – and itemize high-risk items on your home contents policy. It's also worth taking photographs to help with their recovery should the worst happen.

When you're getting dressed, put your jewellery on last because it can snag clothes. Cosmetics and perfume can also damage pearls and metals. You should store pieces of jewellery individually in a soft case to prevent tangles and scratches; chains are especially prone to knotting.

Looking after jewellery

○ To unknot a chain, work the knot free with two pins (using a magnifying glass if you are far-sighted). It's much easier than using your fingernails.

○ If jewellery leaves marks on your skin, it may be caused by tarnish or an allergic reaction. Clean the item and then paint the metal with a thin coat of clear nail polish.

○ The best care for pearls is to wear them as often as possible because the natural oils in skin prevent them from drying out and cracking.

○ Examine precious pieces of jewellery every few months to make sure the stones and clasps are secure. Always have any necessary repairs made by a jeweller – repairs are a lot less expensive than a replacement if a clasp breaks loose.

Most stones, except the porous ones – coral, emeralds, jade, jet, lapis lazuli and opals – can be washed clean with a mild solution of washing-up liquid and warm water and a soft brush. Always wash jewellery in a small bowl, never in the sink where there's the risk of it disappearing down the plughole. Wipe other pieces with a chamois leather. Care for the softer stones by wiping them with a soft cloth and a drop of baby oil once a week.

The hall, stairs and floors

It's very easy for the hall to become a dumping ground for shoes, bags and keys. This is the first place to wage war on clutter because it sets the tone for your home.

Kim I always remove my shoes on the mat outside and come inside in stocking feet. I put my shoes upside down on the floor and my slippers are waiting on the mat just inside the door. There's a rug across the wooden boards and a lovely cream stair carpet, which wouldn't be practical for children, but that isn't something I have to worry about.

Aggie Shoes off is the rule for everyone who comes into our house. The shoes all get piled up in the hall and front room; there can be quite a few when Rory is holding band practice! The most important thing is to have a big, thick doormat. I have one at the front and another along the entire width of the sliding doors that lead out on to the garden from the kitchen. I like the coconut type best and they're very satisfying to shake out.

Kim I like to pick up the outside coconut mat about once a month, bang it against the wall and then roll it up like a sausage with the bristles outermost, so all the dirt falls out. It's not easy mind, you have to be feeling strong. Coconut mats also vacuum very well.

Another thing – don't have a bowl in the hall for the keys. It's very ill advised from a security point of view. I've seen it on TV – burglars fishing through the letter box, so my keys are stored safely in a drawer.

Aggie I have a position at the foot and the top of the stairs for everything that has to go up and down. I get very upset if people don't take things up with them because there's so much traffic in our house.

Kim What I do is, I put everything I bring down during the day back on the stairs when I've finished with it. You go up and you bring down a book, and then another thing: well that's OK the first day and the second day, but by the end of the week, if you don't take things back you'll be in a mess. I gather everything up and go round putting things away before I go to bed.

Aggie We have a carpet runner up the middle of the stairs, which is the style I prefer, but it does mean that the surrounding paint needs a lot of maintenance. The banister is untreated mahogany, so every now and again I run a damp cloth over it and I'm always shocked at the filth that comes off, it's indescribable what the mucky paws leave behind.

Kim It's really terribly easy to clean a wooden floor, and aren't they popular these days? I wet a yellow duster in warm water, wring it out tight and tie the four corners over the head of a soft broom. Then I wipe the head in the direction of the grain, reverse the duster and do it again, and that's it. Once a week is enough, but then I don't wear my shoes indoors.

Cluttered hallways

It's very tempting to drop everything just inside the hallway when you arrive home. Coat racks and pegs quickly collect forgotten bags and jackets, so try to cull the contents regularly and unpack shopping bags as soon as you arrive home, otherwise the entrance to your home will resemble a waiting room.

Don't leave your car keys anywhere near the door, such as on a shelf or in a bowl, where they could be hooked through the letter box by a thief – it's a favourite trick. Put car keys where they won't be found by any burglar.

Halfway upstairs

There's always an endless stream of stuff that has to be carried upstairs. Tireless trips up and down can be saved by gathering a pile of things near, but not obstructing, the foot of the stairs for trips you would otherwise make empty-handed. Encourage everyone in your house to help carry the load upstairs. Put a basket at the foot of the stairs from where everyone can reclaim their clutter.

Use a thick doormat

Lay mats inside and outside the front door – a thick one for the mud outside and another inside – but don't rely on the mats to do all the work. If you decide to make your home a 'no shoes' zone, you'll be in good company, your carpets will last years longer, and you'll save on cleaning. There really is no good reason to wear outdoor shoes inside your home. You'll need to provide inexpensive slippers for your guests – not a big investment to more than double the life of your carpet.

Stairs

Stairs should always be well lit – most stairway falls are avoidable. Never try to carry things on your own that two people could carry more safely and don't carry things that may trip you, such as trailing laundry. Refix loose carpet as soon as possible. Never use a conventional stepladder to work at height on stairways; a three-way ladder is safer.

Flooring

Flooring materials are increasingly diverse as people seek out more unusual and fashionable alternatives. Some floors, such as limestone and marble, are much harder wearing than would ever be required for a home, while other fads are less enduring; sea-grass matting won't go threadbare, but it's almost impossible to shampoo successfully. When you choose a floor covering you should consider its purpose and weigh the foot traffic against the comfort, cost and practicality.

Carpets

Carpet always gives a warm welcome, especially during the colder winter months, which is why traditionally we have laid carpet rather than the wood and tile favoured on the continent. In the hallway, however, carpet can quickly show signs of dirt unless you take some precautions:

- Choose darker shades for carpet in heavy traffic areas.
- Lay a thick coir doormat, which is too broad to step over.
- Establish a 'no shoes zone' rule inside your home.

Regular vacuuming is the best care for carpet. It removes dirt and grit from the pile, which would otherwise rub against and cut the fibres. Vacuum all the carpets at least once a week and more in heavy traffic areas to remove the dirt and lift the pile. From time to time it's worth fitting the nozzle attachment and vacuuming deep into the fibres to restore the pile and remove the deepest dirt. If you vacuum regularly, you'll also increase the length of the intervals between shampooing.

To restore pile flattened by heavy furniture, place an ice cube over the fibres and allow it to melt. After an hour, tease the fibres upright again with the vacuum cleaner nozzle attachment. Alternatively, spray the carpet with a light mist of water and gently tease up the fibres.

Cleaning carpets

Professional steam cleaning applies a small amount of water under pressure, which is then immediately sucked away again. Domestic carpet shampoo machines tend to leave behind more water and sometimes even soap. Once the carpet is dry, new dirt quickly sticks to the soap residue, so a freshly shampooed carpet can soil again rapidly. The same principle holds true for lots of carpet stain spot removal products, so whenever possible, tackle dirty marks with clean water or soda water first.

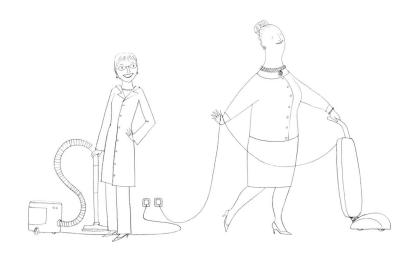

To hand shampoo a wool carpet

- Vacuum the carpet thoroughly to remove loose dirt.
- Test colourfastness in a hidden area.
- Start at the corner furthest from the door to avoid walking on damp carpet.
- Dilute a little wool clothes washing liquid in a spray bottle and lightly mist the carpet, taking care not to overwet it.
- Brush the dampened carpet pile gently with a soft nailbrush.
- Remove the soap and soiling by pressing with pads of white kitchen paper or an old white towel (so as not to transfer dye).
- Remove all traces of soap by patting off with another clean damp towel.
- Lay out a clean dry towel and stand on it to absorb all the remaining moisture from the carpet.

Carpet stains

Always blot or scrape away the excess liquid or substance before tackling the stain, then work from the edge of the stain towards the centre. Only use white paper or a white towel to prevent dye transferring into the carpet and dab, never rub, a stain. The pile will become permanently damaged otherwise and there will always be a mark.

Treating carpet stains

Carpet stain	Treatment
Blood	Dab with cold water. If the stain is removed, stop here. Otherwise, sprinkle with salt and then dab away with clear water.
Chocolate	Scrape away the excess with a knife. Mix a strong solution of biological laundry detergent and brush with a soft nailbrush in the direction of the pile. Dab with clean water to remove soap.
Cigarette burns or scorch marks	Burns can only be disguised. First, carefully remove the burnt fibres with a battery-powered fluff remover, nail scissors or sandpaper. If this looks acceptable, stop here, otherwise you'll need to remove a few fibres from elsewhere and glue them over the bald patch.
Ink	Spray with hairspray and wait until dry. Dab with a strong solution of biological laundry detergent. Dab away soap with clear water.
Make-up	Scrape away excess with a knife. Mix 1 cup of clear vinegar with 2 cups of warm water and dab stain. Dab with clean water.
Nail polish	Dab with a cloth impregnated with a small amount of non-acetate nail polish remover.
Oil	Dab gently with a cloth impregnated with a few drops of liquid lighter fuel.
Red wine	Blot away the excess, and then dab the stain with soda water.
Tea and coffee	Blot away all the excess liquid. Mix 1 teaspoon of washing-up liquid with a cup of warm water and sponge on. Blot again. Mix 1 cup of clear vinegar with 2 cups of warm water and dab again, blot away, and then dab with clean water.
Urine	Mix 1 cup clear vinegar with 2 cups of warm water. Dab the solution and rinse away until the smell is gone. Dab with clean water.

If you're unable to remove a severe stain there is a repair option. Lay an appropriate size plate over the stain and cut around it with a craft knife. Take a carpet remnant, or cut a piece from inside a fitted cupboard or underneath permanent furniture, and cut in the same way. Stretch heavy-duty adhesive tape across the underside of the existing carpet and press on the patch. If the carpet is wool, tease the fibres together at the edges with steam and a soft nailbrush.

Rugs

Unlike fitted carpet, the advantage of a rug is you can pick it up and take it outside. Hang it over a line, gently beat out the dust and leave to air. It's also worth turning rugs from time to time to even out the wear and any fading caused by sunlight.

Remove stains from a rug in the same way as carpet. You can also shampoo a rug by hand or with a machine, but for valuable wool or silk rugs it's better to protect your investment and take it to a professional who will return it clean and dry. When you have to remove a rug for cleaning, or to protect it from party revellers or decorators, roll it carefully with the pile inwards. Don't fold it because you'll crease and damage the pile.

Wood floors

Wood floors are either solid timber or a composite board laminated with a thin veneer of a decorative wood. Some versions are synthetic and use a printed image to resemble a wood finish. The planks are generally factory sealed or are varnished once they have been laid or sanded. Polyurethane varnish is the most common and durable seal, but it will show scratches and can't protect the wood from dents and damage caused by sharp stiletto heels.

It's fashionable to sand and seal wooden floorboards in older properties. The boards can be varnished or sealed with liquid wax. Reapply wax when it can no longer be buffed to a shine. Apply with a floor polisher or two traditional string mops – apply with one and buff with the other.

Vacuum a wood floor with the dusting brush attachment so as not to scratch the surface, and take care the cleaner's wheels don't scratch either. Microfibre mops are ideal for removing dust from wood floors. The soft cloth head is in direct contact with the floor so it traps all the dust, unlike sweeping.

Sealed wood will withstand a little moisture, so after sweeping or vacuuming wipe clean with a barely damp duster stretched over a broom head. Don't mop waxed wood because watermarks will show where the wax is worn away.

Tiles

Although tile is cold and hard underfoot, it's easy to sweep and mop. Some tiles are glazed and don't need any further protection, but porous unglazed tiles should be sealed to protect from stains. The hallway in Victorian homes was often tiled and many original examples remain in good repair today. Period red terracotta hall and porch tiles were polished to a high shine with Cardinal or Mansion polish, neither of which seems to be produced any longer, although you can buy Tableau red wax polish for a similar period look. You don't have to polish terracotta tiles red; a coat of clear seal will show off the natural patina. Take care not to polish floor tiles until they are slippery – a matt finish is safer underfoot.

Windows

There shouldn't be any necessity to clean windows every week except in rooms where lots of steam collects, for example in the kitchen and bathroom. To clean the inside window glass, you'll want to use less water than if you were cleaning the outside (*see* The outside, p. 342) to avoid wetting carpets and floors. In any case, the interior side of the glass should be considerably less dirty.

You can easily make your own window cleaning spray by mixing half water and half clear vinegar in a spray bottle. Spray a little of the liquid directly on to the glass, starting at the top. Take an old cloth, paper towel or newspaper and wipe across the entire surface. Then take a dry cloth, chamois leather or fresh dry newspaper and buff the glass to a shine. Newsprint does make a mess on your hands or rubber gloves when the ink transfers, but it really does cut through the grime – so no wonder glass has been cleaned with it for decades. Another traditional method is to add a couple of drops of ammonia to water; some branded window cleaners include both ammonia and vinegar.

Kim's housekeeping tales:
Colt's Neck, New Jersey

It was 1986 by the time we arrived back on the east coast of America, and I went to work for a woman and her very rich industrialist husband. I called it the White House because of the way it was decorated: white walls, white furniture and white carpets. It was a beautiful house, with a tree growing up through the middle, yes a tree indoors, and a wooden bridge through it. It was very Californian actually, but a devil to keep clean on your own.

As I said, everything was such a light colour it was extremely hard work. The walls were painted white and even the stripped floorboards were colour-washed white – 'white pickle' finish it's called, which shows up every speck of dirt, so I had to vacuum and wash all the floors every day. In America they think they're always just a few steps ahead of us, and this lady had a central vacuuming system installed when the house was built; it cost $20,000. There were vents all over the place, and you had these big long tubes that plugged into them, with the suction coming from a unit in the basement where all the dirt ended up in a big bag, but honestly it was next to useless. Eventually the lady said to me, 'Well that was a waste of money Kim,' and we got two top-of-the-range portable vacuums, which was much better.

When you work in these homes you quickly learn where everything is kept, so you're responsible for putting things away – all the clothes, everything. Before the lady used to take her suits to the dry-cleaners, I would wrap foil around the delicate buttons to protect them. You have to anticipate everything; you literally do anything and everything. You know their homes better than they do. The lady used to say, 'Oh Kim, I'll never replace you.' Her guests used to walk in and exclaim that you couldn't tell anyone lived there; the place was so spotless.

The lady had a very expensive collection of Lalique glass and tableware, which is highly collectable. It's very intricate so you have to be careful when you're cleaning it. When you're having a Lalique morning, you'd better not be thinking about anything else and don't have a drink and do it, or you'll have no job. Actually, I'd only been working there a few weeks when I knocked a piece off a low table. I just turned around too quickly and caught it. I'm not making excuses; it was broken. My heart was in my mouth when I went to tell the lady. She would have been well within her rights to take it out of my money, but she didn't, thank goodness. I've never broken anything since in any of the homes I've worked in.

The rest of the decorative glass was displayed safely in a cabinet, so it didn't need cleaning more than once every couple of months. She could have had it all out on show catching the dust – she didn't have to spend the time cleaning it. When you're cleaning glass you need to work with 'angel wings' and be ever so gentle. I find it responds well to warm water and a drop of washing-up liquid, but always use a plastic bowl. Take one piece at a time and gently dip it in – like bathing a baby – you don't want to be clanking them against the sink or each other. Washing them isn't the only hazard, there's carrying too; never more than one piece at a time.

The lady's husband had a lot of silver trophies on display, which his horses had won. They were a beggar to clean. It used to take hours with cream polish, which was a devil to get out from the crevices. Then one morning I was polishing away at the kitchen table, with the TV on in the background, and a woman came on and said, 'Never get worried about cleaning silver, let me share a secret'… Now obviously she had my attention. She took a plastic bowl, lined it with foil, and poured in a kettle of hot water and a scoop of Tide washing powder. Then she dipped in each piece of silver, for just a few seconds, and it came out gleaming! I tell you I skipped through the house as I went to fetch the rest of the trophies. I couldn't get them fast enough. It was miraculous. I did every single one in less than half an hour, the old polish even came out of the crevices. A while later I learnt you could do the same trick with soda crystals, so it's not a problem that Tide detergent isn't sold in the UK.

General maintenance

Laundry

There was a time when doing the laundry took all day, but there's no reason for washday blues in our highly automated homes. Even the laundrette offers a service wash, so you don't have to hang around – let the machines do all the work.

Kim When I was young the laundry was quite a chore, I can tell you. To keep whites white you worked hard and there was a lot of boiling things in buckets on top of the stove going on. You would have to rub like the dickens with the soap until the wash was spotless, and it took hours. Today everybody thinks everything is a hard chore. Compared to years ago it is not, I can tell you.

Never let the laundry mount up. Do you know some people only wash when they've got no clothes left to wear? I can't understand that. I wash every day; as soon as my clothes come off they go straight into the washer. I can't stand having dirty laundry around. If you don't sort, you'll ruin so many clothes. I can't tell you the number of people I've seen in the laundrette over the years washing all their clothes together until they turn grey.

Aggie I know this sounds daft, but I love washing, I love sorting clothes and I love ironing; I just love everything about it. I like loading up the machine, taking it out again, and I even get pleasure from hanging it up. When we get back from a family camping trip, I can't wait to get stuck in. I tip out all the bags, sort everything into piles and spend the rest of the day working through it all.

What works for me is to wash as soon as I have a full load. I don't think half loads are economical, or a good use of time. I automatically sort laundry into whites, lights, darks and coloureds and then do whichever there's most of, but I don't wash every single day. I prefer powder detergent because it's easier to measure. I've never used fabric conditioner because I don't like the heavy perfume, and anyway I actually like stiff towels!

Kim I like the powder best, although I use liquid for hand washing. I do use fabric conditioner, but not for lingerie because it spoils the elastic. I don't like my towels over soft, or over rough. They may like showing soft towels in the adverts, but they just don't absorb; it's all trial and error. I do tumble dry, but not shirts, they go straight on to rubber hangers because they can't slip off. When I was working in Eaton Square, the lady had these special rubber hangers from Germany, so I ordered some too and

I can tell you they last a lifetime. If you do use a tumble dryer, be sure to clean all your filters or you'll be wasting your time, and your electricity.

Aggie I dry all the laundry either out on the line or on a clothes airer in the conservatory. I'd never used a tumble dryer until I was filming in America and my apartment had a dryer. It seems that in Los Angeles they tumble dry everything even with all that Californian sunshine available! When everything's dry, I fold it into a basket ready for ironing. Most people hate ironing, not me. The best tip is to buy the broadest board you can get your hands on. Usually I iron in the kitchen with the radio on. I set the minute minder on the cooker for thirty minutes and then stop when the alarm sounds. I can get tons done in that short amount of time – at least a couple of machine loads.

Kim Of all the chores, ironing is the one I like the least. I fold everything into my ironing basket and do it once a week. Mind you there are only two of us in this house and we don't want for clothes. Years ago I saw an ironing system from Switzerland at The Ideal Home Exhibition. The woman who demonstrated it told me, 'When you've ironed with this you'll never use anything else.' It cost £400, but she was right – all the big houses have them – and the ironing is done in no time. The top-of-the-range model even has an inflatable ironing board cover, but that's unnecessary in my opinion.

It pays to look after your clothes

The excitement of having something new to wear quickly fades if it loses its original colour, shape or feel. By following the care labels attached to all garments, storing them carefully and carrying out a little maintenance, they'll stay looking like new for much longer.

Ten ways to make laundry easier

- Always read care labels.
- Wash clothes quickly before dirt becomes ingrained.
- Treat stains when they happen.
- Sort laundry into whites, lights, brights, darks and delicates.
- Empty pockets and fasten zips and buttons before washing.
- Don't overload the machine.
- Use the correct amount of detergent.
- Select the wash programme appropriate for the most delicate garment in each wash.
- Fold clothes as soon as they're dry to prevent creasing.
- It's much easier to iron clothes and linens whilst damp.

No more washday blues

The days when women spent the whole of Monday hand washing the week's laundry are fortunately long gone now that most homes have a washing machine. Doing the laundry is unlikely to rate as a favourite pastime, but everyone loves putting on clean clothes.

It's much easier to dress in the morning if the majority of your wardrobe is freshly laundered, ironed and ready to wear. It's no good owning a large wardrobe if most of it is lying crumpled on the floor or in the laundry basket. Get into the habit of automatically adding dirty clothes to the laundry basket and encourage others in your household to do the same by leaving laundry baskets in several locations.

When you buy clothes, avoid things that have to be hand washed or dry-cleaned, especially if you struggle to get round to these jobs. Many of the clothes left on the racks at sale time are dry-clean only and the cost of all that professional cleaning can wipe out any saving. You should do hand washing regularly because if these clothes languish in the laundry basket, there's little point in owning them.

Dirty clothes are best collected in containers that allow air to circulate – so baskets and cloth bags are better than plastic. Never put wet or damp towels or clothes straight into the laundry basket, otherwise the entire contents may become mildewed and possibly permanently stained. To keep your laundry basket smelling fresh, line the bottom with a fabric conditioner sheet designed for use in tumble dryers or add a sachet of dried lavender.

Sorting the laundry

If you sort dirty clothes into different categories as they collect you'll save a lot of time and be able to see in an instant which load you should run next. If you don't have the space to store laundry by category, empty the entire basket and sort into heaps, according to colour and delicacy. Always wash clothes of similar colour and delicacy together. New clothes always advise this (to guard against colour runs), but applying this rule throughout the life of the garment will help preserve colour crispness. If you mix all the colours in every load, your whole wardrobe will quickly take on a greyish appearance.

Sort laundry into:
Whites – don't mix whites with any other shade because they will quickly discolour.
Lights – striped whites, off whites, beige and pastels.
Darks – blacks, blues and browns.
Brights – reds, yellows, oranges, fluorescents.
Delicates – fine linens, woollens, silk and lingerie.

Get into the habit of turning dark clothes inside out to preserve their colour, and emptying pockets. Do this every time you add something to the basket rather than have to sort through the whole load later. Always make repairs before clothes go into the wash, otherwise the vigorous action of the machine may make the damage worse. Check that buttons are firmly attached; if not, remove or resew them. Fasten zips to help clothes keep their shape and avoid them snagging on other items.

Colourfastness

Reds and pinks often bleed colour during the first few washes, so you should wash them separately or with the same colours. To test for colourfastness, wet a small hidden patch of the garment and press an old white cloth against it (a handkerchief or an old face cloth). If the dye transfers, the item isn't colourfast. If you're unsure about whether to continue washing an item separately, put an old white cloth into the machine with it. If the cloth picks up dye, the garment is still bleeding dye. Turning dark clothes inside out helps preserve their colour.

Delicates and net laundry bags

Most lingerie will last longer and look better if you hand wash or machine wash it on the gentle or delicates cycle. Invest in a net laundry bag, which you can find in the haberdashery or cleaning department, and zip your delicates inside. Net laundry bags prevent stockings, tights, lacy and embroidered items from fraying, fading, tearing and snagging.

Using laundry bags is also a good tip if you spend a lot of time sorting clothes or underwear for children. Collect each child's laundry separately and zip inside its own bag once sorted. It can go into the dryer like this too, so there's no need to pair up all those endless socks. You can use a pillowcase pinned at the flap if you don't have zipped mesh bags.

- Add soiled garments to the laundry at the end of each day.
- Sort laundry as it collects.
- Empty pockets and fasten zips before adding clothes to the laundry basket.
- Turn dark garments inside out to preserve the colour.
- Store soiled clothes in a basket or cloth bag to allow air to circulate.
- Never add wet or damp items to laundry. Dry wet items first, otherwise they'll mildew the entire basket.
- Place a fabric softener sheet in the bottom of your laundry basket for a fresher fragrance.
- Avoid mixing fluff generators (towels, sweatshirts) with fluff absorbers (corduroy, blacks). Turn fluff collectors inside out.

Linens and towels

Bed linen and towels must also be washed at least once a week. Try to get into the habit of changing bed linen and towels on fixed days – say bed linen on Friday in time for the weekend and the towels on Mondays and Thursdays. Wash the clothes on the other days depending on which you have most of: lights, whites, darks or brights.

Care labels

Textile and clothing manufacturers sew care labels into their products. These small labels, illustrated with the international Textile Care Symbols, provide invaluable advice as to how the item should be cleaned. These care symbols are used throughout the world. If they look more like hieroglyphics, you haven't studied them closely enough because they cram a great deal of useful information into a tiny space.

Four groups of symbols explain how each garment should be washed (washtub), bleached (triangle), dried (square), pressed (iron with dots) or dry-cleaned (circle), and whether any of these processes is unsuitable (crossed out).

The laundry care symbols have been in use for forty years. To celebrate, Morphy Richards commissioned a survey from YouGov that found that nine out of ten people don't understand the symbols. Only one in ten identified the symbol for do not dry-clean, but eighteen- to twenty-nine-year-old women identified the most symbols correctly.

Kim & Aggie   The Cleaning Bible

Laundry symbols

Washing

95 High temperature and maximum wash/spin cycles to ensure whiteness for white cotton and linen without special finishes.

60 Vigorous washing at a temperature that maintains colour. Suitable for cotton, linen or viscose.

50 Reduced machine action and lower temperature for synthetics. Cold rinse and short spin minimize creasing. Suitable for polyester/cotton mixes, nylon, polyester, cotton and viscose items with special finishes; cotton and acrylic.

40 Cottons. Wash at a low temperature to prevent colour run. Suitable for cotton, linen or viscose where colours are fast at 40° but not 60°.

40 Gentle wash and spin to preserve colour and shape and minimize creasing. Suitable for acrylics, acetates and polyester/wool blends.

40 Reduced machine action preserves colour, shape and size of machine-washable woollens. Suitable for wool and wool mixed with other fibres such as silk, but only if the label says machine wash.

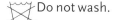 Hand wash only (unless your machine has a special hand wash programme). Suitable for wool, silk, cashmere and delicate fabrics.

Do not wash.

Bleaching

Fabric may be bleached with chlorine (household bleach). Suitable for whites.

No bleach.

Drying

May be tumble-dried. Dots within the circle indicate the appropriate heat setting: two dots for high, one for low.

Line-dry after short spin.

Drip drying is recommended with garment soaking wet. Recommended for shirts with easy-iron finishes.

Dry flat. Recommended for knitwear.

Ironing

Suitable for ironing. Three dots is hot, suitable for cotton, linen and viscose.

Two dots are for a warm iron, suitable for polyester mixtures, wool and silk.

One dot is for the lowest heat iron, suitable for acrylic, nylon and polyester.

Do not iron. This symbol is found on some synthetics.

Dry-cleaning

Dry-clean. The letter indicates the solvent the dry-cleaner is to use. P is the solvent perchloroethylene.

Dry-clean. The underscore specifies an extra delicate process.

Do not dry-clean or press.

Dry-cleaning

There are four main reasons why some garments and fabrics must be dry-cleaned:

- To prevent shrinkage.
- The garment is constructed of different materials, which will shrink at different rates and deform when washed.
- The dye is unstable in a washing solution.
- The surface finish needs special care, for example velvet and suede.

Always dry-clean matching items – parts of an outfit or soft furnishing covers – at the same time in case the colour fades.

If an item is stained, take it to the cleaner within twenty-four to forty-eight hours and explain the cause of the stain so that the appropriate action can be taken.

Some laundrettes have coin-operated dry-cleaning machines. These can be a less expensive alternative way of cleaning large items such as curtains and loose upholstery covers that don't require special treatments. Vacuum or shake off as much dust as possible first, and don't use these machines for delicate items or when the 'P' symbol or any other dry-cleaning letter is underlined, because these items require expert care.

Textile care labels are covered by consumer law, so if the instructions prove incorrect, the manufacturer must replace or repair the garment. This can also mean that the care label may sometimes err on the side of caution and advise dry-cleaning simply because this is the safest option. Equally, the garment manufacturer may not have carried out all the necessary testing so may play it safe and advise dry-cleaning.

You might decide to ignore dry-cleaning advice when something is aged, dirty or stained in a way that dry-cleaning is unlikely to rectify. However, you should never hand wash anything that stipulates dry-cleaning unless you are prepared to accept that it may be ruined as a result.

Loading the washing machine

A great deal of expensive research has been put into developing the modern machine to produce the best wash, so the least we can do is follow the manufacturer's instructions. It's important not to overload the drum and different size items should be loaded alternately. Use the bathroom scales to measure the weight of the load. If it's easier, weigh yourself first and then again with the washing in your arms. Subtract your weight from the total to arrive at the weight of the load.

If you overload the machine, the wash performance will decrease because the garments won't move freely in the detergent; you'll run the risk of flooding; and the machine may become unstable during the spin cycle and attempt to dance across the floor. Make sure all pockets are empty, as stray sharp objects like pens and keys may damage the drum. Always use detergent designed for automatic machines, otherwise suds will flood the room. A handful of washing soda crystals will help reduce suds if you mistakenly put non-automatic detergent in your machine.

CHECKLIST: WASH LOAD WEIGHTS

Item weight
Duvet cover – double 1000–1500 g (2–3 lb)
Duvet cover – single 750–1000 g (1 lb 8 oz–2 lb)
Sheet – double 700–1000 g (1 lb 6 oz–2 lb)
Sheet – single 450–700 g (1 lb–1 lb 6 oz)
Pillowcase 100–200 g (4–7 oz)
Towelling hand towel 150–250 g (5–9 oz)
Towelling bath towel 700–1000 g (1 lb 6 oz–2 lb)
Bathrobe 1000–1500 g (2–3 lb)
Shirt 200–300 g (7–11 oz)
Dress 350–500 g (12 oz–1lb 2 oz)
Jeans 700 g (1 lb 6 oz)
Underwear 50–100 g (2–4 oz)
Tea towel 100 g (4 oz)

How laundry detergent works

Detergent and soap are both antibacterial and remove dirt in warm water. Soap is made from natural fats and alkalis while detergent is synthetic – made from petrochemicals. Detergent was invented in the 1940s during wartime when animal and vegetable fats were in short supply. Previously clothes were washed in soap, but because it forms scum and leaves a film on clothes (just like in the shower), it has now been overtaken by modern chemical detergent. Soap is kinder to the environment because it is derived from a renewable resource (unlike detergent that is from oil) and soap flakes are still used today as a gentle method for washing woollens.

Detergent and soap are both surfactants ('surfactant' is an abbreviation for 'surface-active agent'). Surfactants reduce the surface tension of water, otherwise it would just bead up in droplets (as it does on your skin). The addition of a surface tension breaker helps the water to 'wet' and spread across the fabric surface, soaking the clothes. But that's only half the story.

Surfactant molecules have two parts, which form a long, complicated hydrocarbon chain. One end is attracted to water (hydrophilic) and breaks the surface tension, while the other end is attracted to oil and grease, but hates water (hydrophobic). These molecules wrap their hydrophobic tails around the oil droplets, leaving the oil emulsified. The oil is held trapped in droplets (just as vinegar and oil don't mix in a salad dressing) and can be flushed away in the water. Detergents usually contain more than one type of surfactant designed to work on different stains and fabrics.

Detergents also contain builders, which help the surfactants penetrate clothing fibres more deeply to shift difficult stains. Biological detergents contain enzymes that help break down complex protein and grease-based stains such as blood and grass. Detergents for whites often contain optical brighteners to make the wash appear whiter and brighter.

Detergent and fabric conditioner

Detergent comes in a variety of forms: powder, liquid, powder tablets and gel capsules, some of which even contain fabric conditioner. Powder is the cheapest option and often the most versatile and effective. Liquids are good at lower wash temperatures and are more readily dissolved when hand washing. Some liquids require a special dispenser ball to be placed in the machine drum, but this must be removed before drying. Tablets and capsules are heavily marketed as more convenient for dispensing a measured dose, but they are expensive and don't do the job any better. Detergents labelled for use with colours don't contain bleaching agents, while those designed for whites often contain optical brighteners to make the wash look whiter.

Washing machines use different dispenser devices, but usually the detergent is dispensed from a drawer in front-loading automatics. There are three slots: usually, from left to right, prewash, main wash and final rinse (for fabric conditioner). The water enters the drum through these slots at each stage, taking the detergent with it, although some liquids, tablets and capsules are placed directly in the drum. When adding detergent, always follow the manufacturer's dosing instructions for the water hardness in your area and the degree of soiling of the load.

Modern biological detergents are very sophisticated and contain enzymes, which are good at loosening protein and oil-based stains such as blood, egg and perspiration. Some people find their skin suffers an allergic reaction to these enzymes, even when just tiny amounts of residue remain in a fabric. If you experience this problem, you could switch to non-biological detergent, but these are less effective at removing some stains. If you want the cleaning action of a biological detergent, try running an additional rinse cycle at the end of the wash.

Fabric conditioners are designed to improve softness, reduce static in synthetic fibres, and make ironing easier. Conditioner is available in a wide variety of fragrances, so choose whichever you prefer. You can use a detergent that includes conditioner, but you'll have less control over how much is dispensed. Some textiles, such as towels, don't react well to large doses of fabric conditioner because it coats the fibres and reduces their absorbency.

Laundry troubleshooting

If you follow all the advice on sorting laundry, selecting the correct wash programme, using the correct amount of detergent and drying carefully, you shouldn't have many problems with your wash quality. Loading and emptying the washing machine takes less than ten minutes once you get into the routine.

Problems occur when you take short cuts. When whites go grey the water isn't hot enough or insufficient detergent has been added. When colours run, the laundry hasn't been sorted carefully enough or the wash is too hot.

Common laundry problems

Problem	Possible cause	Prevention/cure
Whites look grey.	Insufficient detergent in hard water area; excessive soiling or load size.	Rewash with the correct detergent dose in the hottest water safe for the fabrics. White linens should be washed at the hottest recommended temperature at least every third wash to preserve whiteness.
Nylon whites look grey or yellow.	Washed with non-whites or bleached with chlorine.	Don't mix white nylons with non-whites or they will become dingy. Chlorine bleach turns nylons yellow. Rewash with a detergent containing oxygen bleach (hydrogen peroxide).
Yellow on white acrylics.	Due to exposure to sun or heat.	Irreversible. Avoid exposure to excessive sun or heat.
Whites have turned yellow.	The sun can leave yellow patches on whites when dried on the line.	Dry whites inside out or in the shade.
Colour runs.	Colour runs are due to incorrect sorting or a wash temperature that is too high.	May not be reversible. Rewash in hottest water safe for the fabric or rewash with a branded run remover.
Dark colours and denim jeans have white streaks after washing, even when using detergent for colours.	Friction in the wash removes dye along creases.	Can be redyed, or rewash with a branded colour run remover. To prevent turn jeans inside out and select a less vigorous wash programme.
Mildew on fabric – black spots, possibly with red and green.	The item has been left damp. Do not leave items damp as mildew forms and can stain.	Difficult to remedy. Attempt soaking for 2 hours in non-chlorine bleach, such as peroxide, then rewash as per care label.

Underarm stains remain, from pale yellow to black in colour.	Some brands of deodorant mixed with perspiration cause staining.	Soak overnight in water containing peroxide bleach. Rinse and wash as the care label advises.
White streaks of powder left on fabric after washing.	The machine is overloaded.	Rewash, reducing the load quantity as directed by the machine manufacturer.
White residue on clothes.	May be mistaken for undissolved detergent, but is caused by mineral deposits in hard water.	More detergent needs to be used. Rewash and use correct quantity.
Holes appear in wool and silk clothes, especially at the seams.	Biological powder, which contains enzymes, has been used.	Irreversible. Enzymes attack wool and silk. A special gentle detergent must be used.
Woollens have shrunk or surfaces have gone 'felt-like'.	The fibres have tightened in the wash. The wash temperature is too high or the drum action too vigorous.	Only wash woollens on the wool cycle. Shrinkage is almost impossible to remedy, but try rewashing and stretching back into shape whilst damp. Dry flat.
Synthetic garments are badly creased, even after ironing and further washing.	Excessive wash temperature or drying heat has caused damage. Synthetics are very sensitive to heat.	Irreversible. The fibres have become permanently damaged. Always wash and dry synthetics as directed on the care label.
Fabric torn or small holes have appeared.	Item may have been trapped in door seal or caught on other sharp items such as zips and fastenings. An existing hole may have grown bigger in the wash. Has bleach been used?	Load the machine carefully. Fasten zips and buttons. Wash delicate items in a laundry net or pillowcase. Dilute bleach before contact with fabrics.
Towels are hard and flat.	Insufficient detergent can cause mineral build up in hard water areas. Drying on radiators can also cause this.	Use more detergent. Add a small amount of fabric conditioner or tumble dry to restore fluffiness.

Washing machine and dryer maintenance

Make friends with your washing machine and it will repay you.
Pamper it every now and again by removing fluff and stray coins from
the filter and it won't flood the floor. Rinse out the detergent drawer
to stop it getting clogged and mouldy so that the machine performs
with optimum efficiency. Use a toothbrush to dislodge any detergent
clogged in the drawer recess. From time to time, run the washing
machine empty at a high wash temperature with some washing soda
crystals or clear vinegar. This will help remove limescale deposits and
stop mildew and scum building up on the rubber door seal, which can
stain clothes and make the machine smell. A new door seal is a costly
repair, so it's worth doing this just to save the expense. After every
wash, leave the door open to help prevent mould and stagnant smells
building up inside the machine, and to extend the life of the door seal.

Remove fluff from your dryer frequently, using a soft brush if
necessary. If your dryer is the non-condensing type, and needs external
ventilation via a tube, make sure you provide this otherwise the
condensation will damage your health, and your home, by causing
mould and mildew.

Washing machine

○ Follow the manufacturer's loading instructions for maximum load weights.

○ Remove all sharp objects from pockets.

○ Only use low suds detergent suitable for automatic machines.

○ Rinse out the detergent dispenser tray frequently. Use a toothbrush to remove deposits.

○ Remove fluff and stray items from the filter regularly.

○ Run the machine empty with washing soda crystals or distilled clear vinegar in the dispenser drawer from time to time to remove limescale deposits and prevent the door seal from becoming mildewed and damaged.

○ Leave the door open after each wash to air the machine and stop mildew.

Dryer

○ Remove fluff from dryers after each cycle. Use a soft brush if necessary.

○ Ensure suitable ventilation for non-condensing dryers.

Hand washing

Most sensitive modern fabrics can be machine washed on the delicates or 'hand wash' programme. However, there will be times when you don't have enough laundry to justify running the machine; you may need something washed more quickly; or because hand washing is advised by the care label.

For hygiene reasons, laundry is best washed away from the kitchen sink. Use the utility room, bathroom or a separate plastic bowl. Wear rubber gloves if you have sensitive skin, but make sure you don't run the water too hot as a result.

Detergents designed for hand washing are gentler and produce more foam than is suitable for an automatic washing machine, but always ensure the detergent is fully mixed with water before adding any garments. Wash just one item at a time, starting with the whitest or lightest colours, and continuing through to the dark items last. Attend to any spot staining first. If the fabric is durable, a soft nailbrush and some toilet soap are ideal for removing ingrained grime from cuffs and collars. Unless you're presoaking to remove heavy soiling or staining (which can be done in a bucket) don't leave the garments sitting in water for any length of time. If you are presoaking, then soak the whole garment, not just the stain, in case the dye fades.

Gently knead the water through the fabric, softly squeezing but never wringing or stretching. After a few minutes, when you're confident the soap has done its work, gently squeeze the excess water from the garment and set it to one side. If items lose dye keep them separately and change the wash water. Once all the garments are washed (it's too tiring to do more than half a dozen items in one go, unless you're doing underwear), it's time to rinse. You can use tepid or cold water. Add each item in the same order as before and agitate. Rinse until no further soap is left in the water and it remains clear. You can pour a little fabric conditioner into the final rinse, but make sure it's fully diluted before returning any clothes.

Finally, squeeze out as much water as you can. If excess dye has come from any of the garments during the washing process, spin-dry them separately to prevent dye transfer. If the garment is too fragile to spin-dry or will stretch with drip-drying, such as some silks and woollens, roll in a towel, squeeze out all the moisture, then reshape and dry flat on another towel.

CHECKLIST: HOW TO HAND WASH

- Don't do too many items at once and wash delicate items separately.
- Dissolve or dilute the detergent before adding the clothes.
- Check the water temperature is not too hot. If you're wearing rubber gloves, use your elbow.
- Gently knead and squeeze the soap through the garment for a few minutes.
- Don't leave the clothes standing in water, unless you're presoaking heavily soiled items.
- When presoaking, always submerge the whole garment, not just the stain, in case the dye fades.
- If excess dye leaks from a garment, change the water and set the garment aside from the others to avoid spoiling them.
- Squeeze excess soapy water from each garment, but never wring.
- Rinse each garment until no further soap comes out, and the water remains completely clear.
- When adding fabric conditioner to the final rinse, make sure it's fully diluted before putting in the clothes.
- Squeeze out excess water and drip-dry, spin-dry or dry flat, depending on the garment and fabric.

Drying

Spin-drying

Most machine wash programmes select the appropriate spin speed. Lower speeds help prevent creasing and reduce the need for ironing. Hand washed garments can also be spun-dry, but refer to the care label and select an appropriate low spin-speed and, if in doubt, drip-dry. Don't spin white and coloured garments together in case the dye transfers.

Line drying

By far the most efficient and environmentally friendly way to dry laundry is outside on a washing line. Even in the city, the air freshens everything up and the breeze helps the creases drop out, making ironing easier. Use a plastic-coated washing line and wipe the entire length over with a clean damp cloth before you put any of your precious washing where the birds have recently perched. Use clean clothes pegs and a prop to keep the load off the ground. The sun's strong rays can bleach out colour, so peg your strongly dyed and darker items in the shade or they will fade.

When you peg clothes out on the line, help them keep their shape by hanging correctly. Generally, clothes for the top half of the body hang upside down, and for the bottom half the correct way up.

- Shirts by the tail.
- T-shirts by the hem.
- Trousers by the waistband.
- Skirts by the waist.

Clip a clothes peg to the bottom of each of the pleats on a skirt to reduce creasing and the need for pressing. Clip pegs to the bottom of lighter articles, such as tights, to prevent them blowing around the washing line.

Some garments keep their shape better if you hang them to dry on a hanger, but only use plastic or rubber hangers because wire and wood will leave marks. Peg the hook of the hanger to the clothesline to prevent it being blown off.

On a very bright day, take care the sun doesn't fade your wash or yellow your whites. Rainwater won't hurt your washing, but the smell of next door's barbecue will; so keep a watchful eye out, and bring it in if necessary. If you have young children, put the washing line or rotary dryer away when they're not in use and explain why they're not toys.

Drying flat

Some garments, like woollens and knitwear, should be dried flat rather than hung, which would stretch them out of shape. Reshape woollens gently by hand and lay them on a white or colourfast towel to dry naturally. You can also buy special mesh drying racks, which lie over the bath.

Tumble drying

If you don't have access to any outside space, there are two alternatives to line drying. You can use a tumble dryer or air-dry on racks. Tumble drying swallows up unsightly laundry quickly, but also eats electricity and puts additional wear into clothes (all that fluff has to come from somewhere). Dryers tend to take smaller loads than washing machines so you may need to dry a load in two batches.

Clothes will dry more quickly if you mix large items with small, but don't mix colours. Always reshape and remove creases before you add damp clothes to the dryer otherwise you'll bake them in. Refer to the care label for the correct heat setting – if the dryer is too hot some fibres may shrink or melt. Tumble drying will make towels softer and fluffier, but only at a cost.

If you want to tumble dry something more quickly, add a dry bath towel. If you overdry the load and find it has baked-in wrinkles, add a wet bath towel and run the machine again.

Air-drying on racks

If you have the space, air-drying on racks is a good alternative to line drying, but don't drape clothes directly on to radiators because you'll cause condensation, mould and mildew. Reshape each item while it's still damp to make ironing easier, and space them out so that the air circulates. Open a window while you're drying washing to prevent condensation, which is bad for your health.

Ironing

Ironing ranks high as one of the least favourite household chores, and many people would happily never iron again. You could decide never to iron again by paying someone else to do it for you; investing in non-iron polycotton bedding; or carefully reshaping your clothes while damp.

How to do less ironing
- Use fabric conditioner in the final rinse.
- Select lower spin speeds.
- Reshape clothes while damp.
- Use cooler and shorter tumble drying cycles.
- Dry shirts, skirts, dresses and jackets on clothes hangers.
- Fold garments carefully when dry to reduce creasing.
- Iron garments while still damp – it's much easier and quicker.

The alternative to no-ironing is to follow the maxim that works so well when applied to all the other chores around the home – 'do a little and often'. Pressed clothes do look better and freshly ironed sheets and duvet covers are far more inviting.

To make time spent ironing pass more quickly, listen to the radio or your favourite music and set a time limit of thirty minutes. If you have a dedicated place or a utility room, ironing becomes much less of a burden because you can leave the board ready and waiting, and start and stop as, and when, you have a few minutes spare. It's much easier to iron for ten or twenty minutes than two hours at a stretch. An entire load can be ironed in very little time with practice.

Set the ironing board at a comfortable height and plug in the iron, using an extension cable if necessary so that the flex runs freely. Have everything else you need close at hand: a flat surface for pressed items; water to top up steam irons; a pressing cloth; water spray bottle; and lint (fluff) remover are all invaluable. Keep a roller lint remover and battery-operated pilling shaver handy because removing any bobbling will improve the appearance of your clothes.

Sort the ironing into categories. With experience you'll quickly identify the fabrics (acrylic, nylon, polyester) that require a cool iron; press these first. Increase the temperature to warm (polyester mixtures, wool and silk), and finally to hot (cotton, linen). Ironing in this sequence will save you having to wait for the iron to cool down. Do iron tea towels, dishcloths and handkerchiefs as the heat helps sterilize them.

Pressing

To avoid making fabric and seams shiny, iron clothes on the reverse side or use a pressing cloth (a linen tea towel or unstitched pillowcase is ideal). Iron again on the outer side only if you have to. Smooth the seams and hems flat by hand and press by lowering the iron down with a light touch. Don't run the iron backwards and forwards repeatedly unless absolutely necessary. Don't iron over zips or press fastenings because you'll leave a shiny mark and scratch the iron sole plate.

How to press trousers

- Turn the trousers inside out.
- Lay the trouser pockets on the shaped end of the board and press them flat.
- Iron the seat of the pants and then the front pocket area.
- Press the waistband.
- If no front crease is required, press the legs flat from seam to seam while the trousers are still inside out.
- If a front crease is required, turn the trousers the correct way about.
- Align the inside seams of each leg and lay lengthways on the board.
- With a pressing cloth, press the bottom of each leg. Repeat up to the seat and to below the front pockets, or up to the waistband if pleated.

How to press a shirt or blouse

- Iron the inside of the cuffs first and then the outside if necessary. Iron the outside of each sleeve, starting with the cuff opening side.
- Press each shoulder over the shaped end of the board.
- Iron the collar, the underside first. Only repeat on the inside (the visible side) if necessary to avoid shining the fabric.
- Press the first front panel, straightening the hem (and pocket) by hand.
- Go around, not over, the buttons (most irons have grooves in the sole plate to make this easier).
- Reposition the shirt over the board and continue over the back and around to the next front panel.
- Store on a hanger when finished. Fasten the top two and middle buttons to maintain the fabric shape.

How to press a sheet and duvet cover

◿ Save time by folding the sheet or duvet cover in half with the corners aligned.
◿ Use the hottest steam setting if possible (check the care label).
◿ Use the entire length of the board and press from the fold towards the edges.
◿ Keep the pressed section off the floor by placing a chair on the other side of the board.
◿ The reverse side should only require brief pressing, if at all.

How to press a pillowcase

◿ Stretch into shape.
◿ Iron the inside flap.
◿ Place the closed end on the board and drape the flap end in front of you. Press the closed end, working out towards the corners.
◿ Work back towards the opening end.
◿ Fold lengthways into thirds or quarters, but don't press in creases.

If an item is overdried or creased, dampen it with a water spray or use a damp pressing cloth. Make your own fragranced ironing spray by adding a few drops of an essential oil such as lavender oil (from aromatherapy shops) to a spray bottle filled with water.

Once pressed, either hang or fold each item as appropriate (*see* Caring for clothes and shoes, p. 304). As a guide, hang more formal clothes such as dresses, shirts and trousers, but fold T-shirts, jeans and sweatshirts. Note how items are folded in shops and copy them. Fold T-shirt sleeves in to the rear and then over so that each meets in the middle of the back. Fold up from the bottom either in half or thirds, according to preference or the depth of your wardrobe's shelves or drawers. Jeans should be folded into thirds, bringing the bottom to above the knee and the waistband over. Never return any items that are still damp to wardrobes or drawers; leave them to fully dry first.

Maintaining your iron

An iron needs to be comfortable for use over extended periods. There is a bewildering choice available, so ask around your friends which brand they have and whether it works well. Don't buy an iron for the packaging; handle it first and check the weight and comfort of the grip. Resist choosing an iron that is too light because a weightier model will assist with the pressing.

It's worth investing in a good quality steam iron, preferably one that can be filled with tap water (because you won't need to buy supplies of distilled or ionized water). If you worry about leaving the iron switched on when you go out, choose a model with an automatic cutoff. Some models have a built-in water spray feature, but using a separate spray bottle or damp pressing cloth is more effective.

The water reservoir of a steam iron must be kept free of limescale deposits as the manufacturer recommends, which is why only distilled water can be used in some models. You can flush the reservoir of some models with a solution of white vinegar, but check the handbook first because it will destroy the mechanism of some self-cleaning irons.

Keep the sole plate clean and free from scratches by wiping and then polishing with a soft damp cloth (when the iron is switched off and cool). If the sole plate picks up burnt-on sticky residue, don't scrape or scour it off. Instead, heat it up to the warm setting and rub with a tightly stretched, dampened, loose weave cotton cloth or towel. If residue remains, rub with white toothpaste or bicarbonate of soda and a coarse damp cloth.

Caring for clothes and shoes

We all love buying them and wearing them for the very first time, but what happens after that? If it's all downhill after the first outing, here's how to keep your clothes looking their best.

Kim I have plenty of wardrobe and drawer space. There are separate drawers for lingerie, bras, briefs, stockings, hair ornaments, hair scrunchies, outdoor scarves, day scarves and gloves. Finally, there are drawers for all the things you shouldn't hang: T-shirts, jeans and knitwear.

Aggie I definitely have too many clothes, despite frequent culls; perhaps I need another wardrobe? I do like to care for my clothes; I know exactly what I like to fold or hang and where everything is. I hang suits, jackets, coats, skirts and shirts and fold jeans, blouses, jumpers and cardigans. I do have quite a few cashmere things now, which I store separately in lavender-impregnated plastic bags to keep the moths out. I also scatter opened soaps around, which is something my mother does. I have no idea whether it works, but I don't have any moth holes. I also hang cedar blocks to deter the moths, which are quite an extravagance but it all seems to work.

Kim I'm very fastidious about my clothes. I always hang my suits to air on a hanger before they go back in the wardrobe. I'll take a careful look too – are there any spots that need to be removed, is the suit still in shape, or does it need dry-cleaning? I cover them all in plastic bags for storage – I buy them on a roll – before they go back on to the rail. Because it's difficult to tell one dark suit from another once it's protected by plastic, I hang a luggage tag over the hook with a brief description, ' navy pinstripe, never creases' or 'navy with buttons on the pockets'. If I ever saw a moth, everything would be out and I'd clean the wardrobe from top to bottom, but I don't think I've ever had one; I'm very careful.

Aggie I do switch over my summer and winter wardrobes, which is always a good excuse for a clear-out. My sisters are the main beneficiaries of my frequent wardrobe clearances; they normally go away laden with all my unwanted extra work clothes. My shoe collection has grown too, so now I store them in canvas hangers with individual compartments. I like suede shoes, but I've given up buying light colours because they are impossible to keep pristine. I use a soft nailbrush to lift the nap, and if you steam them over the kettle it helps get some of the marks out.

Kim As you'll know by now, I can't abide clutter, but you're probably also thinking, 'What is she hiding?' I'll tell you what dear, shoes. Oh dear, I must have over a hundred and fifty pairs. They're all in the original boxes with marker pen labels on the outside so I can easily see what they are. They're grouped into evening shoes, black business shoes and summer sandals, all in neat stacks. It got so bad Pete marched me in there and forced me to go through them. Do you know I took out twenty-two pairs, never been worn, still in their wrapping! It's very naughty. He carried them right out to the car, told me, 'They're not coming back in you know,' and drove them straight down to Oxfam. I'll tell you a secret though; I've replaced every single pair.

Aggie When it comes to packing to go on holiday, I like to start a week early. I set the suitcases up in the spare room and as the clothes come out of the laundry, I put them straight in. I've got packing down to a minimalist art. In fact I'm probably guilty of taking too little; there was one time when I even forgot the boys' pyjamas, but that's another story. Basically, I try and pack as neatly as possible so I don't have to re-iron anything. I roll my skirts and dresses and wrap the shoes in cotton bags. I'm very careful with toiletries – especially anything that might leak like nail polish remover. My real travel essentials are my favourite nail scissors, which I've owned for about twenty-five years and go everywhere with me; a Swiss army knife; and, if I know I'm going to be doing any cooking, I even take my own paring knife with me. It can all be a bit of a nightmare at airport security!

Too many clothes

Just a hundred years ago most working people could only afford a suit of work clothes and Sunday best; no wonder antique wardrobes are so small. Even as recently as sixty years ago, the government ran magazine adverts urging women to 'make do and mend' to reduce pressure on wartime resources, while today, in contrast, we have an outfit for every occasion, season and activity. Too many clothes, even though they may no longer fit or be fashionable, is the problem facing most people.

Declutter your wardrobe

Plan in advance to have a big sort out and make it an excuse to invest in some matching shapely wooden clothes hangers. You only need to buy good wooden coat hangers once in your life, so why wait when you can get the full benefit now? Pick hangers that have broad, gently shaped shoulders, with grooves for hanging straps and a grip strip for trousers on the rail, because these are the most practical and versatile design. Wooden wishbone clothes hangers (so called because of their shape) are often advertised as special bulk buys in newspapers, or look out for bins of them in department stores at sale time. You may also decide to invest in some trouser hangers (the clamp-type design) and a few padded hangers for your very special delicate garments. Once you're suitably equipped, you'll finally be ready to dispose of all those horrible wire hangers, which come back from the dry-cleaners and ruin the shape of your clothes. Buy some white, acid-free tissue and lining paper and a roll of plastic bags. Acid-free tissue paper has a certified neutral pH of 7 and it won't discolour garments (or tarnish metal and jewellery). You can buy five hundred sheets for less than £10 by mail order via the internet. Get out a spare suitcase, put on your favourite music and you're ready to start reorganizing your wardrobe.

Start by taking everything off the rail and laying it on the bed. Next, remove all the shoes and clutter piled up at the bottom of the wardrobe and empty any shelves or drawers. Vacuum inside and wipe all the interior surfaces with a clean soft cloth and warm soapy water. Don't skip the cleaning unless your wardrobe is already spotless because it's important to leave everything smelling fresh.

Next, pick up each garment from the bed and take a hard look at it. Discard anything you haven't worn for more than two years. Start a charity shop bag; decide which friend would look good in it; or create a pile of clothes to sell, though anything you pass on must be clean and in good condition. Clothes that are soiled or damaged should be sent for rag or rubbish. Old clothes are a good source of rags, especially T-shirts, but cut off any buttons or zips that might scratch when you're polishing.

Examine any clothes that can't be worn because they need to be repaired or altered. Ask yourself if you'll ever do them; are they even worth the time or expense? If the answer is yes, then organize to have them done now, even better today, otherwise put them into the rag bag or pass-on pile.

If you think you lack the ruthlessness, or just don't know where to start with this grand clearance, then invite a friend round (whose taste you trust) to help you. Model all the clothes you're unsure about and you'll soon know from their reaction whether your wardrobe really is incomplete without that kilt.

Rehang each item you decide to keep on one of your smart new hangers. You'll be amazed how many things you'd forgotten about. Align the hangers with the wishbones curving in harmony, not clashing. Group your clothes together in a way that makes sense to you because a logical layout will help you find and pair up outfits more quickly. Perhaps you'll colour coordinate, or group work and leisure,

Kim & Aggie   The Cleaning Bible

best and everyday wear together. Hang the category you wear most at one end of the rail so they are readily accessible and there's no excuse not to put them away.

Repeat the same process for drawers and shelves. Find new homes for things that get tucked into wardrobes and drawers that shouldn't be there, or create one place and group them all together. Line your drawers with tissue, decorative wallpaper (single rolls from the end of batches are very cheap, even in designer stores) or lining paper.

No more costly mistakes

As you sort through your wardrobe make a mental note of:
- The types of clothes you buy too many of.
- The shops or labels you buy but never actually wear.
- The sale bargains that still have the tags in them.

Try and avoid making these mistakes again in the future, and make a note of the things your wardrobe could do with next time you're shopping for clothes.

Clothes moths

It's not the adult moths that do the damage to your clothes, it's their larvae. The female lays her eggs on fabric, which will provide food when they hatch out. Soiled garments are ideal because they contain a feast of bacteria for the newly hatched larvae, which is when the holes appear in your clothes. Usually by the time you discover the damage, the culprits are long gone. The larvae are so small they can be mistaken for fibres, so rather than try and pick them out, rewash the entire garment to ensure they're all removed.

To help prevent moth damage, never put clothes away into storage that have been worn; they must be washed or dry-cleaned first to remove the soiling. Place a moth deterrent such as cedar blocks, dried bay leaves or lavender inside the wardrobe.

How to keep your clothes looking their best for longer

- Don't crowd clothes. Hang them on the rail with space between so that they can breathe and so won't get crushed and crumpled.
- Have regular clothes culls – adopt a 'one in, one out' rule – to keep your rail slim.
- Invest in matching wooden wishbone clothes hangers. The most versatile hangers have generous shoulder support and grooves to accommodate garments with fabric hooks.
- A few padded hangers will cushion delicates, but they're not suitable for everything.
- Always hang clothes to air before putting them back in wardrobes and drawers.
- Empty all the pockets before hanging or folding clothes.
- Fold woollens because they stretch on hangers.
- Fold jeans because the knees stretch on a hanger.

- Remove spot marks and soiling, by dabbing with a soapy cloth, before putting clothes away.
- Always wash or dry-clean soiled clothes before stains set.

Store your out-of-season clothes away

While you're sorting through your wardrobe you should remove all the clothes that are out of season. The chances are that when you started clearing out, the clothes rail was bulging. Clothes must be allowed to breathe because it stops them from getting creased, crushed, stale and mildewed. Take this opportunity to put the out-of-season clothes to one side ready to pack away.

You can pack away seasonal clothes in a spare suitcase; crates with lids; zip-up plastic bags; or you can also buy special storage bags that hook up to the vacuum cleaner hose to create an airtight seal. Store these on top of the wardrobe, in a spare top cupboard or under the bed. If you're lucky enough to have access to another wardrobe, rotate the contents between the two and hang the in-season clothes in the room where you usually dress.

Fold clothes with care, as if they were new, and wrap them in acid-free tissue paper to prevent creasing. Wrapping things carefully now will keep them fresher. Make sure everything you pack away is clean to deter textile pests such as carpet beetles and moths, and finish off with some dried lavender, bay leaves or cedar blocks to be on the safe side.

Never store anything that is damp or in a place where it can become damp – mildew will rot and permanently stain fabric. If you think your wardrobe may be damp, put a charcoal briquette – the type you would normally burn on the barbecue – in each corner to help absorb the moisture. You may also need to drill some ventilation holes in the back, sides or bottom to increase the air circulation, which will help reduce the dampness.

- Store out-of-season clothes separately, if possible, or pack them away to save wardrobe space.
- Never pack away dirty or soiled clothes; always wash or dry-clean first.
- Don't store clothes in plastic dry-cleaning bags; they trap solvent smells and can turn white clothes yellow.
- Air freshly dry-cleaned clothes to remove solvent odours before returning them to the wardrobe.
- Don't store clothes you know you'll never wear again.
- Don't store clothes that will never fit again.
- Don't store clothes that you hope will come back in fashion because even if they do, the colours and fabrics are always different.
- Give unwanted clothes to friends, family and charity, or sell them.

Repairs and alterations

If you can master sewing on a button and turning up a hem, you'll have the two basic skills necessary to make repairs and alterations to your clothes. Once you have these skills, you can save the time, hassle and expense of professional alterations and you'll be able to do your own repairs quickly and easily whenever and wherever they're needed.

If you notice a button that is loose, snip it off and keep it safe or, better still, sew it back on immediately. It's much easier to resew than to match a button later.

Sewing on a button

- Select a colour thread that matches the thread used to attach the other buttons. Thread the needle and make two small, closely overlapping stitches on the underside of the fabric where the button is to be attached.
- Push the needle through to the side the button is to sit and push the needle through one of the holes in the button.
- Loop the needle through the button and back through the exact same point in the fabric. Don't overtighten the thread at this stage or you'll be unable to fasten the button into the fabric. If you prefer, push a matchstick under the button to keep it raised.
- Repeat by restitching through the same point in the fabric and looping through the button. Either cross the stitches through the button holes or sew in two parallel tramlines, depending on which style matches that used for the remaining buttons.
- Once two pairs of loops are complete, tighten the thread, leaving sufficient slack between the underside of the button and the surface of the fabric for the button to pass through the buttonhole when fastening.
- Once the button is firmly attached, you may loop thread around the threads between the button and the fabric. Pass the needle through the button but not the fabric. Wrap around the threads until tightly wound, and then push through the fabric.
- Finish off with two further small overlapping stitches in the underside of the fabric.
- If the fabric is fragile and might tear, or the strain on the button is considerable (for example with a heavy coat), a button may also be required on the underside in a sandwich effect – if the remaining buttons are attached using this method, the replacement should be too.

The basic sewing kit

- A selection of needle sizes.
- A needle threader – a wonderful, inexpensive accessory.
- Pins and safety pins.
- A thimble.
- A selection of thread: black, white, fawn, brown, grey and blue.
- A small pair of scissors.
- A measuring tape.
- Spare buttons.
- Invisible iron-on mending tape is ideal for repairing pockets and linings.

Turning up a trouser hem

Fabric has to be hemmed otherwise the threads fray and unravel.
To alter the length of garments, for example for a pair of trousers,
once you've cut off the excess fabric you have to make a new hem.

- Pin the trousers to the required length, tucking the excess fabric up
  inside. Remember to check the length when wearing footwear or heels.
- Turn the trousers inside out and measure the excess fabric, ensuring
  both legs are the same length.
- Mark the new length with chalk or a pin.
- Allow sufficient fabric to make a new hem. Copy the existing hem
  measurement plus one centimetre to fold under, or allow five
  centimetres (plus one centimetre to fold under).
- When you are certain you have the correct length evenly pinned or
  tacked with loose running stitches, try the trousers on again just to
  be sure before you cut any excess fabric away. Remember the rule,
  'measure twice, cut once'.
- Keeping the trousers inside out, cut off the excess fabric.
- Fold one centimetre over and press with a warm iron. This is to
  prevent the end of the hem fraying.
- Fold over the remaining five centimetres and press.
- Select a thread that matches the fabric.
- Thread the needle and anchor the new hem at the side seam with
  two small overlapping stitches.
- Make small running stitches along the hem edge, catching just a
  single thread of the fabric so that the stitches remain invisible from
  the finished side of the trousers.
- Finish off by anchoring the thread with two small overlapping stitches.

Shoes

You should be as equally ruthless with sorting your shoes as sorting your clothes. Try them on and make a mental note of the styles you have too many of and colours you don't wear, and discard any that you haven't worn for more than two years, are uncomfortable or broken. If you own shoes that you've never worn because they don't fit or are impossible to walk in, pass them on and try to avoid making the same mistake again. You can send shoes that still have further wear in them to recycling collection points.

Always store your shoes together in pairs in their boxes, on racks or in canvas hanging compartments, which you can buy in department stores or via mail order. Shoeboxes are ideal because they don't cost anything extra and they're an exact fit for the contents. Most shops will offer you the box and if they don't, ask if they have a spare one. If you do store shoes in boxes and the original labels don't identify the contents clearly, take a digital or Polaroid photo and stick it on the outside of the box to give you complete control over your wardrobe at a glance.

Don't wear the same shoes every day if you can avoid it because they will quickly lose their shape and rot inside. Shoes must be allowed to air-dry before they're reworn or put away. They absorb a lot of moisture from our feet during the day, which if they're stored damp, causes them to rot, grow mildewed and smell. Don't put wet shoes near direct heat because the leather will dry and crack; instead pack them with absorbent kitchen towel and leave to dry naturally. Shoe trees or wads of tissue paper will help shoes recover their shape during drying and storage.

Get into the habit of wiping clean or polishing shoes before you put them away again. You're much less likely to choose the scuffed and dirty pair when you open your wardrobe. You can remove the white salt stains picked up during the winter from leather shoes by wiping them with a mild solution of clear vinegar. You can help remove odours by sprinkling bicarbonate of soda inside smelly shoes, leaving overnight, and then shaking or vacuuming out.

CHECKLIST: CARING FOR SHOES

- Don't wear the same shoes every day – allow them to air before wearing again.
- If you need to wear the same shoes every day, as part of a uniform for example, have another identical pair and wear them on alternate days.
- Sprinkle bicarbonate of soda inside smelly shoes to absorb the odour overnight and then shake or vacuum out.
- Stuff wet shoes with paper kitchen towel to absorb moisture and preserve their shape. Leave them to dry naturally – never near direct heat.
- Never put shoes away unaired – they will mildew, rot and smell.
- Clean shoes with a soft damp cloth or wax polish before putting them away. Polish nourishes the leather and stops it drying out and cracking.
- Never clean shoes over the kitchen sink or on work surfaces where you prepare food – work over a sheet of newspaper.
- Have shoes resoled and heeled before they become permanently damaged.

317

How to choose a suitcase

There are some upscale hotels where your personal butler will pack
or unpack your suitcase for you. Sadly, such decadence isn't available
to all of us, so if you find packing more pain than pleasure, why not
discover how to make opening your luggage a luxury?

Owning a selection of different-sized cases or even a matching set
of luggage is a great advantage because packing works best when you
don't have to cram things in, or have them rolling around in a half-
empty case. A large suitcase for the summer holiday, a medium size
for long weekends and an overnight bag covers all eventualities. Both
hard and soft cases have their advocates, but wheels are essential.
Airline security experts say flashy or expensive luggage attracts thieves,
who hope the contents will prove equally valuable. If you tie a strap
or ribbon around your case or the handle, you'll be amazed how
much easier it is to spot on the airport carousel.

Start packing early

A couple of days before you're going away, make a list of the things
you need to wash and shop for. Packing is much less stressful when
all your clothes are freshly washed and pressed. Don't assume you
can iron things when you arrive at a hotel because the equipment
provided by most hotels isn't up to much.

Lay out on the bed all the clothes you think you'll need. Make piles
of each group of clothes and calculate whether you have sufficient
for each day and event on your trip. Most of us travel with too many
clothes, so at the end of your next trip note how many things you
bring back unworn and adjust accordingly next time.

Do the same with your toiletries. If you travel regularly, look out for small sizes of your favourite products or collect hotel-supplied shampoos and moisturizers. Reuse any small containers by refilling them with your usual products before each new trip. Put toiletries inside a waterproof wash bag, and wrap any larger containers that you have to pack loose in plastic bags ('locking' food storage bags are ideal) to protect your clothes in case of leaks; sun lotion is a frequent culprit of damage.

Now make a pile of the important things that will ensure your trip runs to plan: tickets, passports, driving licence, money and insurance documents. It's a good idea to make a photocopy of your passport and driving licence in case they are lost or stolen – pack these copies in a separate place. Don't forget the other things you may be glad of: music, books, a camera, sunglasses, a corkscrew and a torch.

Finally, lay out your shoes. At least one spare pair is always a good idea, but as shoes don't pack well, try not to take too many. New shoes sometimes come with fabric carry bags; keep these to use when you travel (and look out for the handy shoe bags provided by some hotels along with the laundry bags).

Have a last look over everything you plan to pack. Is there too much, too little, are they the right things, too posh, too casual, too warm, too cool? Check the weather forecast at your destination (www.bbc.co.uk/weather has a worldwide five-day forecast) and adapt accordingly.

If you're travelling by air with a partner, swap one change of clothes each between suitcases so you'll both have something to wear if one of your bags goes missing (most bags are found within forty-eight hours). Put a slip of paper with your name and hotel inside your suitcase, but don't write your home address on the luggage tag during outbound travel because thieves have been known to use this information.

Packing everything into the suitcase

Select the best-size suitcase or bag for the number of things you have laid out. Give it a quick vacuum inside and line it with tissue paper. Lay the largest, flattest garments into the bottom. Fold trousers into three to avoid a crease at the knee or leave the legs dangling out of the case, then fold the legs back over once the other clothes are on top. Place three or four sheets of tissue paper between each layer to stop your clothes getting unnecessarily creased. People who travel a lot, including many top models, believe that packed clothes crease less if you roll, rather than fold, them.

Pack tops next and fill in the gaps with underwear and accessories. Put balled-up socks into the shoes to save on space and prevent your shoes getting crushed. Wrap each pair of shoes inside a separate bag to keep your clothes clean and then put them at the bottom edge of the case (when it's standing upright) so their weight won't bear down on your clothes. Finally, put anything you may need during the journey or as soon as you arrive near the top. Secure the inner contents with the restraining straps if your case has them, and put in a slip of paper with your name and destination so you can find each other again in case of loss.

If you can, unpack and rehang everything as soon as you arrive so that it all remains fresh. Use the tissue paper you packed with to line the drawers and shelves in a hotel. If any of your suits and shirts emerge crumpled, hang them in the bathroom while you run the shower and the steam will make the creases drop out.

- Plan your washing and shopping a couple of days before packing.
- Lay everything you plan to take out on the bed.
- Use a case that won't crush or be too big for your clothes.
- Tie an identifying ribbon or strap to the handle.
- Put your name and destination inside the case.
- Take photocopies of your passport and driving licence in case of loss.
- Pack the largest, flattest garments first.
- Fold or roll all your clothes; it's much easier than re-ironing everything.
- Lay sheets of tissue paper between each layer of clothes.
- Put balled-up socks into shoes to save space and save crushing.
- Put each pair of shoes into a separate bag to stop them squashing each other.
- Collect travel-size toiletries and pack in a waterproof washbag or plastic bags in case they leak.
- Unpack as soon as you arrive to keep everything fresh.
- Hang creased suits in the bathroom and run the shower – the steam will make the creases drop out.

Furniture

If you've searched high and low to find exactly the right piece of furniture, you'll want it to last for many years. With the right care, a good piece of furniture can easily give you a lifetime of enjoyment.

Kim The worst thing you can do for wooden furniture is place it in the sun. If there's an ornament on top, you'll be left with a bleached top and a dark patch. If you stand wooden furniture in front of the radiator, you're doing two things wrong, drying the wood and killing the heat. My best pieces are in the coolest, shadiest part of the room.

Aggie I definitely believe in looking after furniture – it should last a long time. I only buy things I really like, so I want them to last. The oldest piece I have is a Scottish mahogany chest of drawers, which belonged to a great aunt. I polish it twice a year with soft beeswax; you can always see the difference afterwards, which is very satisfying.

Kim I have several pieces of furniture that are very precious to me, like my Georgian mahogany coffee table and bureau. Even when I buy modern pieces, like my beech bedroom suite, I spend a lot of time looking for exactly the right thing.

Aggie The living room has two black leather sofas, which I polish and feed from time to time. A friend brought me some impregnated leather wipes, but they dry out very quickly when you use them on such a large surface, so I've kept those for cleaning my handbags now. The dining chairs are by a Danish designer and they're unlacquered oak. I've found the best way to clean the wood is by wiping with a mild solution of liquid meant for washing woollens, which gets the greasy marks off. The wood does take on its own patina after a while, and I think that's part of the charm of good furniture.

Kim Modern furniture usually has a factory finish to protect the wood so it's very hard wearing and you don't need to do much to look after it. I do polish the antique pieces with beeswax about once every three months. I know how to make up my own wax, but I don't usually bother because you only need such a little on the cloth; I like the creamy stuff best. There's a strong temptation to overpolish wood, but I don't like it when you can see your face reflected in furniture.

I always put coasters on everything out of respect, but make sure they're heatproof, mind. You can get some lovely coasters, but they're not all heatproof. Another good tip, which I always do, is to get the glass cutters to cut you a glass mat the size of a plate or a saucer to stand under house plants and vases to protect furniture tops. It's ever so inexpensive and they'll even do you a nice bevelled edge. If there's ever a mishap, I think a professional polisher is much more use than messing about with mayonnaise and cigarette ash trying to disguise the damage, which is what some people suggest.

Modern wooden furniture

A revolution has taken place in the way furniture is made and supplied today. A century ago, wood was the main material used and every piece was handcrafted and assembled. But by the middle of the Second World War, timber was in short supply. In 1943, the Government's Board of Trade issued a catalogue of thirty standard designs of 'utility furniture', which used just the specified quantity of oak and mahogany, but it was still factory assembled.

Today, the majority of our furniture is sold in flat-packs ready for us to carry home and assemble ourselves. Many materials are finished with synthetic plastic coatings or sealants, which remove the necessity for regular waxing and polishing. Tables and cabinets are often made from uniform panels of medium-density fibreboard coated with a thin layer of real wood or even plastic that resembles wood. The panels are then fixed together at home with metal bolts and wooden pegs.

This mass-produced furniture doesn't require much routine maintenance other than a quick wipe with a barely damp cloth or a little mild soapy water to remove marks. Abrasive cleaners, even cream cleaners, can leave fine scratches on the surface, which spoil the appearance and trap dirt. However, many of us still prefer our furniture to be solid wood rather than plastic, so traditional furniture and antiques remain popular.

Preventing damage to wooden furniture

All furniture, whatever it's constructed from, is at risk from three main forms of attack:

- Environmental (heat, light, humidity).
- Chemical (from ingredients in cleaning materials, food and drink).
- Physical damage (burns, scorches, knocks).

The best way to look after your furniture is to be aware of these risks and to do your best to prevent any damage from occurring in the first place. However, even with the best intentions accidents do occur, only some of which can be easily rectified.

Environmental damage

Wood is at risk from both excessive dampness and dryness. Excess moisture causes wood to swell and warp, while lack of humidity (for example dry, centrally heated air) will cause it to dry out and crack. The best protection is to keep precious wooden furniture away from damp walls and corners or direct heat from radiators. Direct sunlight also bleaches the colour from wood and fabric over time.

Applying wax alone to wooden surfaces won't prevent damage caused by the environment inside the home. You must take direct action to change the conditions. Increase humidity by leaving bowls of water near radiators or using an electric humidifier. Likewise, any source of dampness must be eliminated. Damp is often caused by leaking drainage pipes, breached damp-proof courses or poor ventilation. Precious furniture should be stood away from strong direct light streaming through windows, otherwise fit blinds to shade the room or diffuse the light. In historic stately homes, you'll notice that all these environmental controls are used to preserve precious antique furnishings and fabrics.

Chemical damage

The surfaces and finishes of wooden furniture are at risk from chemical attack by the ingredients in modern cleaning materials and by things that get spilt on them – alcohol in perfume and drinks and natural dyes from food spillages. Even plastic protective mats can transfer dye into wood. Protecting the surface is the best way of preventing damage.

Spread coasters liberally around any surface where liquid from drinks may make contact. If water seeps through the protective finish, it swells and distorts wood, while alcohol in drinks and perfumes penetrates and strips the agents used in French polishing. Acetone in nail varnish remover will also damage many polished surfaces.

Foodstuffs can also damage surfaces. The citric acid in lemon will bleach wood, while strongly acidic dyes in red fruits will penetrate and stain the grain. The best prevention from this form of attack is to cover tables with protective plastic tablecloths (with a soft backing) or placemats and coasters. Vanity or dressing tables can be covered with glass to protect the wood from perfume and nail varnish remover spills.

Physical damage

Physical damage occurs to wood through scratches, knocks, burns and scorches. Dust contains particles that are abrasive, so when objects are slid rather than lifted across highly polished surfaces, the friction causes tiny scratches. An object may also have sharp or rough edges, which cause further damage. This is why it's a good idea to line the base of a lamp or ornament with a piece of felt.

Knocks are caused by collisions with other objects, such as opening doors or vacuum cleaners. These can result in dents and nicks, which often penetrate further than the surface. Deeper dents are impossible to repair except by filling or sanding smooth, but smaller scratches and indentations can be disguised with a little coloured wax.

The most common cause of physical damage is heat, either burns from a flame or scorching heat from a bowl, plate or mug. Prevention is the best precaution. Always use heatproof table pads underneath your tablecloth, trivets and coasters. Damage caused by heat is difficult to repair, but can sometimes be disguised, usually by fine sanding or rubbing away of the damaged wood, then applying dye and polish to the newly exposed surface.

Preventing damage to wooden furniture

Form of attack	Cause	Cure
Excessive humidity or dampness in the atmosphere.	Wood swells and warps when it absorbs moisture.	Remove dampness by improving ventilation, repairing plumbing or drainage leaks and attending to damaged damp-proof courses.
Insufficient humidity.	Central heating removes the moisture from air. Wood dries and cracks when the air is too dry.	Avoid placing furniture close to radiators. Place bowls of water above radiators to humidify the air or fit an electric humidifier.
Sunlight.	Powerful direct natural light causes bleaching of colour from wood and fabric.	Avoid placing furniture in strong direct sunlight, or use blinds to shield or diffuse the light.
Chemicals.	Chemicals in cleaning and beauty products; natural acidity; and dye in foods and drink can damage polished and lacquered finishes.	Protect surfaces from chemical exposure by using coasters, mats, trivets or sheets of glass. Avoid using any cleaning products with undisclosed chemical ingredients.
Knocks and dents.	Collisions with other objects, such as doors, chairs and vacuum cleaners, will result in dents and scrapes.	Physical damage can be repaired only through physical remedy – filling or sanding the surface.
Burns.	Burns caused directly by naked flames such as cigarettes and candles.	The damaged surface must be removed by fine abrasion and the appearance of the newly exposed surface disguised.
Heat scorching.	Both indirect and direct contact with very hot items can scorch the surface or damage polished finishes.	Damage caused in this way is difficult to repair. The surface must either be disguised or refinished.

Regular care for wooden furniture

A quick wipe over with a microfibre, lambswool or barely damp soft cloth is sufficient to remove dust and keep wooden furniture in good condition. It's also a good idea to use a paint brush or vacuum cleaner attachment to remove dust from carvings and mouldings, before it gets trapped and hides the detail.

Wax polish

There is a temptation to over-apply polish, which can quickly lead to a build-up of wax on the surface. This isn't harmful to the furniture, but it takes much more effort to apply and shine polish than simply remove dust. If you apply polish once or twice a year, it's usually sufficient because a coat of wax polish can be re-buffed to a shine many times before another application is necessary.

Wax does protect the surface of wood, to a certain extent, from penetration by liquids and gives it a pleasing appearance and fragrance. Applying wax to wood won't remove dirt or clean it, quite the opposite; it traps dirt to the surface. Dust and dirt should always be removed with a damp cloth before any wax is applied. If you want to remove the old wax layers, wipe with white spirit or turpentine, but there's no need to strip wax other than for improved appearance.

It's important not to change the type of polish you use. Different ingredients, especially silicone oil, which is included in many branded furniture sprays, can react with beeswax polish and a whitish bloom on the surface will be the result. The only remedy if this happens is to remove all the polish with white spirit and rub with a little fine-grain wire wool before applying and building up several new thin coats of wax.

Making your own wax polish

To make your own wax polish, take a tablet of beeswax (from hardware stores) and place it in a heatproof bowl inside a saucepan of water. As the wax melts, add a few drops of essential lemon oil or cedar oil (from aromatherapy shops) and a little turpentine. Allow to cool and then apply the mixture to the wood, working in the direction of the grain, with a soft cloth.

Another way to soften a block of beeswax is to place it in a microwavable bowl in the microwave for 2 minutes on high. Watch it constantly because you don't want to splatter the oven with wax. Once melted, add a few drops of turpentine to keep it soft.

Soak a soft cloth in liquid wax and store it inside a screw-topped jar ready for use.

French polishing

French polishing is a technique, rather than a type of polish. It involves building up several layers of polish to achieve a deep colour, high gloss and a long lasting finish. It is time-consuming and expensive so most manufacturers abandoned using it after the 1930s. Today lacquer and varnish give a more durable finish, which is less susceptible to damage from heat and water. French polishing is a highly skilled process and valuable pieces that require repair or restoration should always be professionally refinished.

You can test whether a surface has been French polished by gently wiping a hidden area with a soft cloth moistened with methylated spirits. If the surface softens and there is a deposit left on the cloth, it's French polished, otherwise it's probably polyurethane varnish.

French polish can still be bought ready-mixed from hardware stores, although you'll find it's called garnet polish, white polish or button polish. They're all based on shellac and vary in shade. The secret of the technique is the method of applying the polish. If you fancy trying this – preferably on a scrap piece of wood – take a wad of cotton wool and pour a little polish into it, then wrap it in a fluff-free cloth such as a handkerchief, ensuring there are no creases. Squeeze the pad so a little polish oozes through and then rub the wood in a figure of eight motion. Allow a few minutes for the surface to dry before building up further coats.

After about eight hours when it has dried, the polish must be 'spirited off' using the same motion, but with a clean pad and the tiniest amount of methylated spirits (otherwise the polish would be removed). This process removes any marks left by the rubber, with the pressure increased as the pad gradually dries out. Replace the cloth from time to time and then eventually work in the direction of the grain. The polish dries fairly quickly, but will take several days to harden before it can withstand use.

Scuff marks can be removed with a solution of five parts methylated spirits, two parts raw linseed oil and one part pure turpentine. Use the above technique to rub the surface. If there are deep scratches, apply neat methylated spirits to further soften up the surface and blend together the finish.

Oiling tropical hardwoods

Some timber (mainly hardwoods, including polished and unfinished teak) are oiled rather than waxed. Raw linseed or teak oil should be applied with a soft fluff-free cloth or paintbrush and then left to soak in. After a few minutes, redistribute the excess oil to the drier areas and then wipe away any residue.

Untreated teak doesn't have to be oiled. Left outside it will weather to a silver grey finish, which many people find attractive. If you apply oil it will preserve the natural colour of the wood because it stops water penetrating the surface. You can tell when oiled wood left outside requires re-oiling to maintain protection because raindrops will stop 'beading' on the surface.

Beech is another timber that can be oiled. It's hard wearing and so a popular timber for butcher's blocks, kitchen tables and work surfaces. The surface is protected from water and food stains with Danish oil applied in the direction of the grain with a soft fluff-free cloth. If you want a high gloss finish, sand the surface with a fine-grade glass paper between coats. Remove the dust with a cloth dampened with a little white spirit. Fewer coats of oil will produce a more matt sheen.

Woodworm

Wax won't prevent woodworm from entering furniture; in any case, polish isn't applied to the undersides. Signs of an active infestation are small 1.5–2.0 mm ($^1/_{16}$–$^1/_{10}$ inch) bored holes, but these aren't the only evidence. Small amounts of frass or sawdust usually indicate active woodworm. If you're unsure if woodworm is present, tap the item sharply and see if more dust falls out. If so, treat as soon as possible with a branded treatment (available from hardware and DIY stores).

When buying second-hand and antique furniture, always examine it carefully from top to bottom for signs of infestation. Undetected woodworm will eventually spread to other furniture and timber in your home. Serious infestations of house timbers can damage the structure. Professional treatment is necessary, which is expensive and disruptive because it involves spraying surfaces with insecticide.

Removing marks from wooden furniture

Preventing damage is always easier than trying to repair or disguise it. Valuable pieces should be taken to a restorer because amateur attempts at repair may seriously reduce their value.

Traditional fixes for damage to wooden furniture

Damage	Treatment
Alcohol spots	Remove the marks by rubbing with a cream metal polish and then reapplying wax. The marks are caused by alcohol reacting with the wax.
Greasy fingermarks	Wipe with a barely damp soft cloth wrung out with a solution of soap flakes or washing-up liquid.
Grease marks on unsealed wood	Sprinkle the surface with talcum powder. Lay some kitchen paper on top and press with a warm iron to absorb the grease.
Scratches	Cover up scratches with a matching coloured wax crayon, artist paint or shoe polish. Once absorbed, polish with wax to help fill any indentation.
Watermarks	Rub with a cream metal polish to lightly smooth the surface, then rub a little ash or shoe polish into the grain to cover up any colour loss. Watermarks happen because the water swells the wood, causing unevenness and colour loss.
White heat marks	Rub with a cream metal polish, covering small areas with repeated applications. The polish is mildly abrasive and will physically remove the damage.

Upholstered furniture

Sofas, chairs, chaises and ottomans, among others, are all made more comfortable, decorative and luxurious by padded fabric or leather coverings. Upholstered furniture is manufactured with a variety of methods and fillings, from the cheapest foam-filled stretch cover right up to sprung interiors topped off with luxurious down-stuffed cushions.

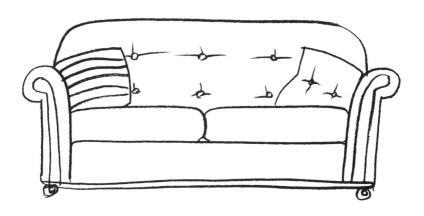

Fixed and loose fabric covers

All upholstery, no matter how hard wearing or expensive, gets dirty. Fabric will eventually wear out, but with regular vacuuming, spot removal and by exercising some care, you can keep covers looking good for many years.

Ten tips to make upholstery last longer

- Dirt, grit and crumbs dull colour and rub the surface, which cuts the fibres. Avoid dirt by eating snacks from plates and vacuuming thoroughly every week.
- Spot remove stains as soon as possible before they set.
- Don't lay newspapers on fabric; the print transfers easily.
- Beware of sharp objects such as jewellery, buckles and toys, which can tear.
- Don't sit on the edges of cushions or padded arms. It causes permanent distortion to the shape and fillings.
- Plump up all the cushions regularly to prevent creases setting, which accelerate wear and trap dirt.
- Rotate all seat and back cushions regularly to ensure even wear and uniform fading.
- Direct exposure to heat and light causes fabrics to fade. Place furniture away from windows, radiators and open fires.
- Keep pets off all upholstered surfaces.
- Cover upholstered sofas and chairs with throws to protect fabric from soiling by pets and young children.

Cleaning fabric upholstery

Some sofa and chair covers are removable and fully washable. It's worth ordering an extra set of covers at the time of purchase because you can be sure that by the time the original covers are worn out, the ready-made replacements will no longer be available. If covers are washable, follow the manufacturer's care instructions. These usually recommend a cool wash using detergent without bleach or optical brighteners. Wash the covers inside out to prevent the fabric fading. Allow the covers to dry naturally and refit them while they're slightly damp because they'll be easier to stretch. Wash all matching covers in consecutive loads with the same brand of detergent to ensure any colour variation is uniform.

Some removable covers and cushion pad covers can only be professionally dry-cleaned. If this is recommended, clean all the removable covers at the same time in case there is any variation in colour during cleaning.

Fixed covers have to be cleaned *in situ*. The best results are usually achieved with professional steam cleaning. Some fabrics have stain protection applied, which prevents spills and dirt penetrating the surface. Always follow the manufacturer's instructions for cleaning these treatments otherwise you'll invalidate the warranty. Stain protection treatments usually have to be reapplied after cleaning.

If you decide to attempt to shampoo fixed covers yourself, remember that it is the foam that lifts the dirt, not the water, so avoid overwetting the fabric. Professional steam cleaners blast the surface with foam under pressure and then immediately suck out the dirt and moisture. Follow the instructions on the shampoo and avoid leaving any residue because otherwise new dirt will quickly stick to it.

To remove pet hairs from upholstery, gently rub a barely damp rolled chamois leather over the surface, gathering the hairs together. Gently brush your hand over the fabric while wearing a rubber glove to collect hair.

Leather

Leather is more durable and easily cleaned than fabric, although it's often more expensive. It's a practical covering for dining chair pads and backs because unlike with fabric, spills can be wiped away quickly. However, that doesn't mean leather isn't delicate and won't be damaged by careless treatment, so don't expose it to bright sunlight or heat from radiators. Always refer to the manufacturer's care advice before attempting to remove any stains and always experiment first on an area hidden from view.

Wipe leather upholstery with a barely damp soft cloth to remove dirt and dust. Remove greasy marks by wringing out a soft cloth in a mild solution of soap flakes and gently wiping the surface, then buff dry. Don't use detergents because they can harden the surface. To more thoroughly remove ingrained dirt from most leather seating use saddle soap (available from hardware and riding tack shops), though this isn't suitable for soft aniline leather. Saddle soap nourishes the leather and removes dirt. It resembles a waxy polish and is rubbed into the surface with a soft barely damp cloth or sponge. When you apply it, avoid overwetting the surface – especially the seams – because water may stain the surface or lead to mildew. It's worth using hide polish to nourish leather and prevent it from drying out.

Look after your leather upholstery by taking the same care as you would with fabric. Don't sit on the arms and take care with food, drink and sharp objects. Leather won't tear as easily as fabric, but it will show scratches.

Removing stains from leather upholstery

Even leather can stain permanently unless spills and marks are treated quickly. Dab or scrape off excess liquid or spills immediately using white cloth or absorbent kitchen paper. Always try and remove stains with clean water before attempting anything else. Always refer to the manufacturer's instructions if you have them. Don't try using dry-cleaning solvents on leather because they won't remove grease or any other stain.

REMOVING STAINS FROM LEATHER UPHOLSTERY

Grease and stains First try wiping with a solution of soap flakes or saddle soap. Try absorbing grease with a sprinkling of talcum powder. If this doesn't work, test colour fastness in a hidden area, then gently rub the mark with a pencil eraser. Alternatively, cover the stain with a rubber solution – the type of glue included in bicycle puncture repair kits. Smooth a little over the surface and allow to dry. Leave for 24 hours and rub away.

Ballpoint pen Dab the marks with a pad of white cotton wool dipped in milk. Then wipe with a solution of soap flakes and dry. If this doesn't work, try spraying with a little hairspray and rubbing gently with a soft cloth.

Scuff marks Scuffing can be disguised by applying hide polish or a small amount of matching leather dye.

Plastic and vinyl

Plastic and vinyl can be wiped with a soapy cloth. A little bicarbonate of soda may help rub away any scuffs or marks, but don't do this on high gloss finishes or you'll dull them. Otherwise, try a branded cleaner designed for car upholstery. Don't use detergents or solvent cleaners as these may remove the colour and make the material hard. Try rubbing off ballpoint pen marks with a pencil eraser if washing doesn't work.

Cane, rattan and wicker furniture

It's worth vacuuming cane furniture to prevent dust from clogging up the weave. If dirt is ingrained, free it with a stiff brush. Wash very dirty canework with warm soapy water, rinse with a soft cloth and leave to dry in the sun. There are some oil-based aerosol sprays available (from hardware stores) that will help prevent cane from drying out and breaking, but pat off all the excess oil before reuse otherwise it transfers to and spoils clothing. Never stand on cane furniture because the excess weight can crush and snap the weave.

Lloyd Loom furniture

Lloyd Loom furniture isn't made from natural cane at all. It's still manufactured today using the same method invented in 1908 by the American, Marshall Burns Lloyd. Kraft paper is spun on to steel wire and machine woven and a chair can be produced in a quarter of the time it takes to weave by hand. Brush regularly to keep the weave free of dust and wipe clean with a barely damp soft cloth, but be wary of overwetting the kraft paper because the wire inside can rust.

Metal furniture

Wipe metal furniture over with a damp cloth and dry thoroughly to prevent rusting. Marks can be removed from chrome by wiping over with a little bicarbonate of soda. Rust marks can be rubbed away with wire wool, but exposed bare metal on painted metal should be treated with rust inhibitor paint.

Plastic and acrylic furniture

Wipe over with a cloth wrung out with a mild solution of washing-up liquid. Treat marks and scratches by rubbing gently with a little cream metal polish, which is very mildly abrasive. Don't use harsh cream cleaners because they will leave fine scratches, which show up like skate marks on an ice rink. Stubborn stains on less precious surfaces can be rubbed with a paste of bicarbonate of soda and water, or cream cleaner.

The outside

The walk up to your front door says a lot about what lies in store for your visitors. If the gate is hanging off its hinges, the path weed infested and the windows dirty, your home won't look very promising, however much care you've lavished on the inside. You don't have to be green-fingered to keep the outside of your property looking good.

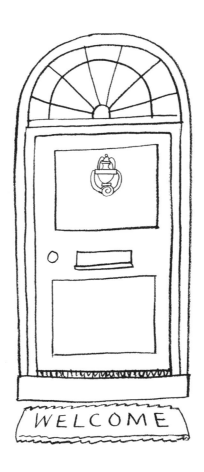

Kim When I was growing up in one of the little terraced houses in Portsmouth, none of us had a penny, but everything was kept spotlessly clean. By 9.30 am at the latest, you would take a broom and brush the front step. Then you'd take a bucket and wash the step, the path, and swill the water out across the front pavement. If you weren't out by 10.00 am, well, heaven help you. All the other women would gossip, 'Ooh, look at that, she hasn't done her step! The dirty madam!' You were letting the side down if all the slops weren't joined up across the pavement.

When I was young the front steps were all painted grey, but then there was a fashion for the red Cardinal polish. Well it didn't look very good at first, with bits of the old grey showing through, but after a few weeks the polish started to impregnate the stone and the red really started to shine. Soon everyone did it; it was quite a craze. It was a massive pride thing; everyone had to have a matching step and a shiny letter box. That pride has gone today.

People worry a lot less about the outside these days. But whatever you do, make sure your gutters are covered with wire mesh to keep them clear of leaves and the drains are covered over to stop the leaves blowing in and blocking them up or you'll be in terrible trouble come the winter. I like to run a household where you're thinking ahead to prevent problems, that way you can save a lot of time and enjoy your home.

Aggie My husband Matthew does all the outside stuff like clearing the drains, which are all covered over; it's chaos with the leaves otherwise. We paved our front garden over to keep it tidy. Before there was a planted area but it just attracted all the neighbourhood cats. Now there are simple window boxes, which

I love. Our front garden also holds all the rubbish and recycling bins. We have three aluminium dustbins – why three? Two just aren't enough! Then there's the composting bin, which the council supplies, and the green boxes for glass, tins and newspapers.

Round the back we've got another composting bin for the vegetable waste, which Matthew uses on the allotment. Eating outside is what summer's for. We have a barbecue, a charcoal one with enough room for a whole chicken or a joint of beef, and a large wooden table with foldaway chairs. I leave the table outside all year long because I like the weathered look, and anyway if it was covered it would go mouldy. We do have a patio heater, but it's only been on once. I don't feel good about having one, they're very wasteful.

Inspect the outside of your home twice a year

The outside of your property has to withstand the full force of the elements. Any damage done here, missing roof tiles or peeling window frames, can quickly deteriorate and lead to expensive repairs. It's worth carefully inspecting the outside of the building every spring to see what damage the winter has done, and make another tour at the end of the summer to make sure everything is in good repair before harsh weather returns.

Prevent water damage and damp

Water is one of the greatest potential dangers to your home. You should inspect guttering, damp-proof courses and drains to ensure that rain water is running away from the building freely and quickly.

Maintaining pipes and gutters

Gutters should be kept clear of leaves so that rainwater runs off the roof and through the downpipes. If rainwater cascades over the edge of the guttering, it's a sure sign that the gutter or downpipe is blocked. Clear obstructions as soon as possible otherwise the exterior walls of the property will become saturated and damp will transfer indoors. Any leaks or drips from guttering should be repaired or patched.

The exposed drains where waste pipes and gutter downpipes discharge should be covered to prevent them from blocking up with leaves. If the drains smell or there is an unpleasant odour from basin and sink plugholes inside, flush the outside drain with a strong solution of hot water and washing soda crystals, which will break up greasy deposits, or disinfectant.

If you're unable to clear internal sink blockages (*see* The kitchen, p. 148), then check the outside drain is clear. If it is, but the water still isn't flowing away, the underground pipe leading to the sewer may be blocked. Lift the exterior drain inspection covers, which are usually metal and oblong-shaped, and check that the open section of drain below is clear. If the chamber is full of water, it is obstructed. Lift the covers back until the next empty chamber to pinpoint the blockage. Either call in a specialist blocked drains service (but try and do it during regular hours as emergency call outs are more expensive) or hire flexible drain rods to push out the obstruction in the direction of the empty chamber. To unblock a frozen exterior water or waste pipe, wrap it with old towels soaked in hot water. Don't pour hot water directly on to frozen exterior pipes or use a hairdryer because the pipes may crack.

Maintaining the roof and walls

Early autumn is also a good time to check the roof is in good repair before the wind and rain come back in earnest. The roof isn't the easiest thing to get a good look at. Are there any signs of water damage inside the house on decorated ceilings? Lift the loft flap and check that everything is dry inside the roof space, and open skylight windows and look around the roof covering. From outside in the street look up at the tiles, slates or felt; borrow a pair of binoculars; or look through the high-powered zoom lens of a camera. Any missing or leaking roofing materials must be replaced or repaired as soon as possible because rainwater can cause a lot of damage.

Have a look at the exterior walls of the building too. Check that nothing is breaching the damp-proof course (the thin black layer a few brick courses from the ground), for example soil in flowerbeds or bags of compost or masonry. A breached damp-proof course can lead to rising damp inside. Check that low level airbricks are free from obstructions and properly ventilating the building – take a thin stick and poke it carefully into the vents. Also check that the pointing – the mortar joints linking the bricks – is in good condition because this is also a barrier against water penetrating inside.

While you're inspecting the condition of the building, take a close look at any woodwork. Bare softwood decays rapidly, so it's better to touch up damaged paintwork as a temporary measure than wait until the entire exterior is repainted. Touching up needn't involve extensive stripping back, but separate coats of primer, undercoat and gloss will give longer lasting protection. Check that the gaps where windows meet the brickwork are sealed with flexible silicone sealant to prevent water and draughts penetrating inside.

Avoiding storm damage

Large trees should be regularly maintained. Have a tree surgeon trim the branches every few years to lessen the risk of the tree toppling during storms. Tell your buildings insurer if you have a large tree within ten metres (thirty feet) of your property in case you ever have to make a claim for storm damage or subsidence.

During the summer, take time to walk alongside the fence, gently shaking each of the posts to check they are secure. It's much easier to reinforce a single post than to replace a whole length of fence that is blown over and smashed by a gale-force wind.

CHECKLIST: TWICE YEARLY EXTERIOR INSPECTION

- Check gutters are free from obstruction and that rainwater can freely run into downpipes.
- Check drains are clear and covers are fitted to prevent leaves causing blockages.
- Flush drains with a strong solution of hot water and washing soda to remove grease and prevent smells.
- Ensure damp-proof courses are not breached by soil or masonry piled against walls.
- Check air bricks are not blocked or obstructed.
- Check pointing in brickwork is in good condition.
- Inspect paint on woodwork. Prime and paint exposed surfaces.
- Inspect the roof inside and out for leaks and missing or damaged covering materials.
- Have tall trees regularly maintained.
- Inspect and repair boundary fencing and posts.
- Check outside security features are working.

Security

Fitting exterior security lights increases security and deters intruders. These are best when operated by dusk-to-dawn sensors, which won't disturb neighbours or distract passing traffic. Before the winter evenings set in, check these are working and replace any broken bulbs or sensors. Other worthwhile security precautions are a light outside the front door and a spyhole or intercom so that you can see who is calling. Only open the door to uninvited callers with a door chain in place if you are unsure about their identity. All officials carry identity cards, so ask to see them. Don't invite strangers in if you are alone; ask them to return by appointment when you have company.

○ If you are going away in the summer for several weeks, arrange to have your front lawn mown so that you don't advertise your absence.
○ Don't let hedges and bushes become so overgrown that burglars can break in unseen or gain cover behind them.
○ If you're concerned about security, ask at your local police station if the local crime prevention officer can visit you. There's more official police information and crime prevention advice at www.securedbydesign.com.
○ The Home Office produces several comprehensive leaflets containing useful advice on home security, including recommendations about alarms and locks. These are available at libraries, police stations and at www.crimereduction.gov.uk.

349

Garages, sheds and outbuildings

When you think about it, we store quite a lot of valuable items outside our homes. Cars, garden tools, equipment and toys all need protection from thieves as well as the weather. Garages and sheds provide plenty of storage, but they can quickly become filled with junk too. As much as three-quarters of all motorists can't park their cars in their garage because there is so much junk in there. Park your car in your garage – it reduces the risk of theft and saves on insurance premiums.

The garage can provide useful storage for toxic materials such as paint and weedkiller, but ensure chemicals are locked away from children and pets.

Sheds are very useful for storing garden tools and furniture, but burglars know this too – most people don't lock their sheds. Burglars won't only steal your expensive garden equipment; they'll also climb on your garden furniture or use your tools to break into your home.

To clean outside windows

If you don't employ a window cleaner, there are loads of gadgets to help you. The latest design of tilt and clean windows revolve completely on their hinges so that the outside glass can be cleaned from inside. If your windows don't do this, there are combinations of sponges and squeegees on extending poles, which will reach first- and ground-floor glazing. If you want to wash the window frames too, do these before you clean the glass.

There are commercially available products to clean UPVC window frames, but a strong solution of warm water and washing soda is also effective. Apply with a sponge or soft cloth to avoid scratching the surface.

Take extra care when cleaning glass roofs, such as conservatories. It's very dangerous to stretch across or put any weight on glass. Always use a pole to extend your reach.

Cleaning windows

- A drop of washing-up liquid in a bucket of warm water is ideal for cleaning exterior windows.
- Apply the foamy water with a sponge – working from top to bottom. There's no need to rinse.
- Place a squeegee (rubber-edged window cleaner) in the top corner of the glass with the blade pressed up against the vertical frame.
- Use a single sweeping horizontal 'S' shape down the entire width and length of the glass to produce a smear-free finish.
- Give the glass a final polish with a dry chamois leather.
- Methylated spirits will remove stubborn marks from glass. You can also use a half/half solution of clear vinegar and water from a spray bottle. Spray liberally on the glass and rub off with scrunched-up newspaper.

If you wash inside as well, use a vertical 'S' movement from top to bottom so you'll know which side of the glass any remaining smears are on.

Cleaning and caring for garden furniture

New garden furniture can represent a considerable investment so you'll want it to last several summers. Most materials are hard wearing and will weather well, but protecting with covers or moving inside during the winter months will preserve the life and appearance of outdoor furniture. In addition to the specific advice, you may want to use the hose or pressure washer to clean grime from your garden furniture.

Choosing garden furniture

Hardwood and teak
Hardwood furniture, including teak, will last unprotected for many years. Light sanding followed by painting or wiping over with teak oil preserves the natural colour of the wood and helps prevent splitting. The wood can also be left to 'weather'. Teak turns an attractive silvery grey, while some other woods turn black. Sand lightly weathered surfaces and protect with oil to prevent further weathering. Remove dirt and algae with a scrubbing brush and warm soapy water. Hardwood furniture will last longer if stored under cover during the winter.

Soft wood
This is only used for inexpensive outdoor furniture and is not enduring. It must be painted or varnished to seal the surface; without this protection it will quickly rot. Once painted or varnished, it can be washed with warm soapy water.

Cast iron

It's usually painted, which prevents rusting. It is durable and long lasting, but heavy to carry. Paint is easily wiped or scrubbed clean with warm soapy water. If the finish becomes chipped or scratched, rub off any rust with a wire brush and touch up with a rust inhibitor paint.

Stainless steel

This is increasingly popular as a finish because of its contemporary look. It's durable but quickly becomes dulled with a whitish bloom and scratches easily. Don't clean with anything abrasive – warm soapy water will remove grime. Wipe over with clear vinegar to cut through dullness and rinse with water or use metal polish to restore the shine.

Aluminium

This is lightweight and doesn't rust, but it does bend easily. Wash with warm soapy water or wipe with methylated spirits to clean.

Plastic or UPVC

Hardwearing, lightweight and reasonably inexpensive, but it does show dirt. Hot soapy water and a soft cloth or sponge will remove grime, but avoid anything abrasive – even cream cleaners – which will scratch the surface.

Rattan

A natural material, which is reasonably weatherproof. Scrub clean with a stiff brush and warm soapy water.

Cleaning the barbecue

You need to keep your barbecue as clean as your cooker for obvious hygiene reasons (*see* The kitchen, p. 148). If you can smell food odours from your barbecue before you start cooking, then it isn't clean enough.

There are many different styles of barbecue, but they all suffer from grease, soot and burnt-on food. Clean the surfaces as you would with any cooker, though you may be less concerned about preserving the finish of something stored outside and decide to use more abrasive cleaners. Scrub metal barbecue racks with scrunched-up aluminium foil, a wire wool brush or pumice stone to get them looking like new.

Cleaning paths, patios and driveways

Driveways, paths and patios are regularly wet during the winter months and the damp leads to moss and algae. Joints between the slabs and surfaces fill with soil and weeds quickly take hold. You can use chemical treatments to kill moss and weeds, but it isn't necessary and you'll still have to pull them up or sweep them away once they're dead. Warm soapy water and vigorous sweeping with a stiff yard brush will remove most moss and dirt from outside paths. Vinegar will kill many weeds that grow in paths.

One of the most effective ways of cleaning outside paths and patios is with a pressure washer, which is relatively inexpensive to buy now. You'll need access to an outside tap and electricity. You can use a pressure washer with detergent or chemicals, but the high-pressure action of the water is sufficient to dislodge most dirt and even moss. This is a tiring, dirty and very noisy job so large areas are best tackled in several stages for your own and your neighbours' sake.

Outside safety

✚ Ensure ponds and water features are covered or supervised when young children are present.

✚ Keep pesticides and garden chemicals safely locked away in clearly labelled containers.

✚ Secure powered garden tools such as hedge trimmers, strimmers or pressure washers away from children and thieves.

✚ Clean up any animal droppings from dogs, cats and birds, which could be harmful to children.

✚ Lay ladders horizontally and lock to a secure fitting.

Kim's housekeeping tales: Eaton Square, London

When Pete and I arrived back in England in 1995 we finally managed
to get our first live-in, part-time residence. Not only that, but at one
of the top addresses in London: Eaton Square. These grand houses
were built in 1826 and most of them had been divided into apartments,
but not this one. It was owned by a German industrialist and his wife,
but they only stayed there for a four-day weekend every six weeks.
Let me tell you, these are the really lovely jobs. It's called a part-time
residency in housekeeping circles. That's not because you're part
time, no you're full time, it's the owner who's there part time.

These placements are like gold dust and you have to earn your
stripes before the agencies will even consider you. You must have
at least three years' live-in experience and excellent references.
Well I'd just come back from working in the States with eleven years'
service and my last employer, she was pleased to vouch for me and
my previous employers furnished me with very good references, so
I went along to the interview. The owners were very unhappy with
the standard of work they were receiving. 'Well ma'am I can
see that,' I said, 'there's dust in that corner and a cobweb hanging
from the ceiling.' I think it's only right to show respect, so I always
called my prospective employers 'sir' and 'ma'am'. You can always
tell right away whether they like you.

The lady also wanted to know if I could arrange floral displays.
They were employing a company to do them and it was costing
£1200 a month. Well I've never had any formal training, but I'm
interested in flowers and I like to make things, so I showed her how
I would do it and she liked the result very much. Pete and I were
offered the job to live-in and with Pete being an ex-policeman,
they were pleased to have the extra security too.

The whole house had been remodelled in a modern style with oak
stripped floors and white sofas. The upstairs had been converted into

a penthouse apartment for his son, but his son didn't want to live there so that's what we were offered. Originally there had been a servants' hatch and pulley system for lifting the furniture and the huge gowns up through the house. This had been converted into a small lift, which opened right into our kitchen. We even had our own balcony – ooh we were living in luxury! We earned about £600 a week between us after deductions, which isn't bad because of course all your living expenses are paid for, so you only need to buy your food.

As I said, the house had been completely renovated. Up the middle of the house was the huge original sweeping stone staircase. It was a beautiful thing and they didn't want it carpeted, so they'd decided to have it stripped right back to the bare stone and polished. When it was done, you could see every other step was worn at the front. The specialist told me that was because when the maids used to be run ragged from morn to night, they would skip every other stair because they were dashing about for their lady so much.

These kinds of homes are nearly always filled with expensive art, so they have to be occupied for the insurance. If the house was empty half the time, the insurance would be double. If your art is worth millions you want to employ the best housekeeper you can find. The owner had a collection of African masks on plinths. They were very rough wood, so you wouldn't dare dust them because the cloth would snag. Instead I blew the dust off each and every one.

This house also had some seventeenth-century Ming dynasty furniture. I thought it was Ming when I saw it. I don't know a lot about antiques, but you pick it up as you go and I always watch the *Antiques Roadshow*, which has taught me a lot. This dark, wooden Ming dynasty furniture had an amazing sheen and was lacquered, like so much Chinese furniture. It's very important to keep wooden furniture away from bright sunlight or direct heat, so the chairs were stood in the middle of the room – the designers saw to that. Of course if you're looking after antiques, you have to treat them in the right way, so I phoned up Sotheby's and spoke to the expert. They advised me to keep the sheen by applying just a tiny bit of beeswax every six months. For regular dusting, you just wipe it over with a barely damp soft cloth and then buff with a dry cloth. If you look after your own furniture like this, you can be sure you'll be giving it the very best treatment.

As so many owners of these grand homes are, these people were very particular. They took all their clothes back to Germany for the regular staff to launder – even the shoes went back to Germany for resoling. They wouldn't let them near a cobbler here and, of course, you have to go along with their habits. I would always launder the fluffy dressing gowns and take them out of the closet when they were expected. I'd also brush down Sir's suit and coat in the hall before he stepped out for an engagement, which he was always very grateful for. We would have happily stayed in that house. It was wonderful living in a penthouse in Eaton Square, but unfortunately Sir started coming over less and less and eventually he decided to sell it. By June 2000 it was time to move on again, but I've never been short of a good job because I've got good references – you see, I love cleaning.

Household management

Hosting a dinner party

Some people don't need any excuse to throw a dinner party; they enjoy it so much they even plan the next one while they're clearing up. The rest of us only entertain a couple of times a year; usually to celebrate special occasions. When it comes to dinner parties, we're certainly chalk and cheese.

Aggie Friday is a great night to have people round for supper; it gets the weekend off to a really sociable start. Your guests are forgiving because they can't believe you've managed to work all week and cook a big meal, and then you have the whole weekend to yourself without all the worry of shopping and cooking.

I love planning what I'm going to cook, and everything – even the rolls – is made from scratch. I think six people is about the optimum number – couples or singles, it doesn't matter.

Once I've decided what to make, I do most of the shopping in advance and last-minute bits on the day. I like to spend the whole day cooking, so I ask people to come at 8.00 for 8.30. I like everything to be done by 7.40 and if it's all gone according to plan, I'll have a nice relaxing gin and tonic before the first guest arrives.

When the guests arrive, I like to serve some fizz because that always gets the evening off to a good start. Dinner is usually three or four courses, followed by coffee and posh chocolates or homemade truffles. I do like my guests to go home before 1.00 am, but it's amazing how quickly the time passes when you're having fun. If anyone gets stranded, I'm happy for them to stay the night – in fact I immediately start planning what I'm going to cook for breakfast.

Kim I prefer to cook very plain food: soup, salad, chicken, steak, and trifle for dessert, so that's what I serve for my guests. Only my close friends get asked over anyway; so they know what I'm like.

For drinks we'll have some fizz; one of my favourite drinks is a mimosa – champagne and orange juice. It's an American drink 'mimosa'; here we call them plain old buck's fizz, which doesn't have quite the same sparkle does it?

I'm not one for tablecloths; I think they're rather old fashioned, except for Christmas. Dinner is three courses with red and white wine. I prefer to put water in jugs because I don't like bottles on the table. At the end of the meal I always have a cheese board because it's lovely with a last drink, and then coffee and chocolates to finish.

The one thing I absolutely won't allow is anyone to smoke in my home. I never put out ashtrays, but if they want to take themselves off outside, well, that's up to them. On the other hand, I'm very relaxed about when people go home because the last thing you should ever do is throw a dinner party when you have to work the next day. Of course I wouldn't want my guests still around at 7.00 am – who would? If they seem a bit slow to leave, come 2.00 or 3.00 am I start making a joke like, 'It's OK for you, some of us have got to be up in the morning,' even though I'm fibbing of course.

The secret is good preparation

Deciding to throw a dinner party starts with a feeling of excitement and anticipation, but as the date approaches you may be overtaken by nervousness. When the day finally arrives, you may even need to suppress an overwhelming urge to suggest going out to eat instead. As with most events, good preparation is the secret to a successful dinner party, and with a little forward planning you might even be able to relax and enjoy yourself. If you leave everything until the last minute, you may feel inclined to panic, which usually leads to disaster.

Invitations

These days there's no need to send out formal invitations to guests, except for weddings or a special party. It's perfectly usual to invite your guests by phone and then follow up with an email or text message to confirm the time and date. A follow-up is always a good precaution to prevent mix-ups. It's amazing how people can confuse instructions like 'the weekend after next' and you discover hungry friends on your doorstep a week too early.

Dinner parties are more interesting if you don't invite the same crowd every time. Introducing colleagues to friends can be fun, and your friends will stop the whole thing turning into a moan about work. Mixing friends and family can also be fun. Around six to eight people is an ideal number, but your decision will probably rest on how many of your guests are couples and how many you can seat and feed comfortably.

Don't forget to be clear about what time your guests should arrive, which will help them and you. A half hour window is a good idea; say 7.30 for 8.00. On weekdays, if your guests will arrive straight from work then an earlier start may be better, perhaps 7.00 for 7.30. At the weekends, you can slip back to 8.00 for 8.30, but don't serve heavy main courses too much after 9.00 – your guests won't appreciate it. If you're hosting the party on your own, you might want to invite a friend to come early and keep you company.

What to serve

When you invite your guests, ask them if there's anything they don't eat. Most of us find it awkward when we're accepting an invite to launch into a list of things we don't or can't eat. What's likely to happen, if you don't ask, is that one of your guests will eventually decide they should warn you that they're a vegetarian a few hours beforehand, just as you get back from the butcher. If you have lots of friends with demanding diets, invite them to the same party to make cooking easier.

Do I need to bring anything?

Your guests may ask whether they need to bring anything. The answer is probably 'no', although the truth is you'd love them to bring wine, chocolates or flowers – or all three! This is a good chance to ask someone to bring spare glasses or anything else you need. If your party has a theme – and especially if it's someone's birthday – be sure to mention it.

Lots of people decide to share the cost and effort of hosting a party by each making a course. If it's your turn to coordinate, then make sure everything comes together by remembering the things that may get forgotten, like music, flowers, napkins and chocolates.

No time to experiment

Dinner parties are no time to experiment; even the most talented cooks should have a dry run if they plan to serve a new recipe. No top chef would dream of putting a dish on the menu until they had perfected it. Stick to your tried and trusted successes when you're entertaining. Playing it safe is the motto – it ensures you'll know exactly in which order to do things and how to rectify mistakes.

Do as much shopping in advance as possible. Some good advice from the professionals is to buy the best ingredients you can afford. Leave all the fresh produce until on the day if you can. If you decide to have everything delivered, give yourself time to rectify any mistakes or no-shows. Estimate on the generous side when it comes to buying supplies – no one wants to waste food, but it's better than hungry guests. Note how many people recipes say they serve and try them out first. Ask advice from the fishmonger or butcher about weights – joints of meat from the supermarket also often indicate how many people they serve.

Devise a menu that allows you to do as much of the preparation in advance as possible. You don't want to be stuck in the kitchen while your guests are having fun. Choose chilled starters or dishes that can be quickly heated. Make sure your main course is easy to serve and the dessert is prepared in advance and chilled or ready to bake as necessary.

Kim & Aggie The Cleaning Bible

Wine and cocktails

When you've planned your menu, decide which drinks to serve. If you're throwing a themed party, your drinks will help with the theme. You can serve cocktails or more traditional apéritifs like gin and tonic. Champagne, or a less expensive sparkling wine such as Spanish cava, will get any party going.

If you don't know much about wine or don't drink it, ask a friend or off-licence to help. Don't choose anything too dry or too sweet. A chardonnay or a sauvignon blanc is a safe bet for white, and a cabernet sauvignon for red. Allow three glasses for each guest, which is half a bottle each. If you don't know whether your guests will drink red or white wine, buy equal supplies of both. Your main course may suggest a choice – lighter dishes go with white and heavier meat and pasta dishes red, but nowadays people drink whatever they like, despite what's on the menu.

Serve white wine chilled. If space in the fridge is at a premium, buy some bags of ice cubes and chill the bottles in a plastic bucket. Red wine is served at, or just below, room temperature. Some red wines benefit from being opened to 'breathe' in advance, but this is probably unnecessary. Don't economize by buying cheap wine or serve anything you've never tried before. Remember the rule – don't experiment!

Don't use your best wine glasses if you can't bear the risk that one might get broken. Either buy some inexpensive glasses for entertaining or hire some from the off-licence – many offer free glass hire if you buy your wine from them. Red wine glasses are larger than white, but never fill a wine glass to the rim – half to two-thirds full is the correct measure.

If you're serving pre-dinner drinks and you have delicate furnishings, leave out plenty of coasters. If you're worried your guests won't see them, hand out coasters with the drinks. You'll probably also want to serve some appetizers or dips, but never let chilled foods sit for more than two hours (*see* The kitchen, p. 148).

Your guests may bring a bottle of wine with them. It's perfectly acceptable to open these, and hard not to if they ask you to try something they've brought. If one of your guests brings chilled champagne, you might want to open that too – a single bottle contains six good measures. Not many hosts offer liqueurs after dinner, so if you don't usually have them, there's no need to get them in especially. Port and brandy are safe choices if you do feel the need.

Don't forget some people may choose not to drink alcohol. Serving exotic fruit juices, herbal teas and posh carbonated mineral water will show you've thought about them too.

How to lay the dinner table

The table is the focus for your feast, so you'll want it to help create
the atmosphere. If you only own a small table, you can hire a larger
one, and extra chairs, from many catering companies – they'll even
deliver and collect. You'll probably want to dress the table up and lay
formal place settings (*see* The dining room, p. 196). You don't have
to use a tablecloth, but napkins are essential. Create a centrepiece
such as flowers, fruit or candles to show the table off.

When guests arrive

Before your guests arrive, choose some music to create an atmosphere, don't just stick on the first thing that comes to hand. Light some candles and check there are clean towels, fresh soap and adequate toilet roll in the loo.

Hopefully your guests will start to arrive shortly after you asked. You shouldn't aim to serve dinner until at least half an hour after your last guest arrives. Greet everyone personally and take their coats and bags. If you're going to ask your guests to remove their shoes, when they arrive is the time to do it – although if they already know you well, you probably won't have to ask. Introduce your guests to each other and start a conversation with them so that they can continue chatting when you leave to greet your next guest.

If you're happy for your guests to smoke, then leave out ashtrays. Put matches in them and smokers will know they're not ornaments, but these days it's unlikely any smoker will light up in your home without asking first. If you prefer people not to smoke, ask them to go outside. Discourage smoking at the table until dinner is over. Your non-smoking guests will much prefer it, whatever they might say.

The dinner

When you seat guests at the table, think about who they'll be sitting opposite, as well as next to. If a seating plan is important to you, work one out in advance. For more formal dinners, the host should sit at the head of the table unless you have a special guest, and then you should sit next to them, although as the host you may prefer to take the seat closest to the kitchen. Some hosts like to suggest their guests change seats between courses so that everyone gets to talk to each other.

More and more of us entertain in open-plan kitchens. If this is your layout, you'll need to maintain an air of calm in the cooking area. If disaster does strike – the meat is burnt to a crisp or the soufflé doesn't rise – own up rather than make up some elaborate lie. If it really is a disaster, dial for a takeaway and laugh it off – if they really are your friends, they'll forgive you.

Decide when you plan your menu whether you're going to serve the main course or ask your guests to help themselves from serving dishes. You might do half and half and serve the meat or fish and let your guests help themselves to the vegetables. When each course is over, collect the plates but don't scrape or stack them at the table. Once the main course is finished, remove all the condiments from the table, wipe it clean and reset for dessert. If you can, avoid washing up between courses because it will delay things and make your guests feel like they are putting you to a lot of trouble.

If you need your supper to end earlier than 11.00, invite your guests for an 'early supper' so they won't wonder what went wrong. If you have difficulty getting your guests to leave, try the subtle approach and mention you have a busy day ahead or ask whether anyone needs a taxi booked.

Putting off all the clearing up until the following morning may seem like a good idea at the time, but it will take the edge off most dinner parties and makes the dirt on the dishes even more stubborn.

Entertaining house guests

Some people don't like the disruption of having people to stay, while others love to play the host. When it comes to welcoming visitors, we're at opposite ends of the scale!

Aggie I love having people to stay, it's such a pleasure. We probably have house guests at least once a month, and I especially enjoy planning what I'm going to cook for them. If they have children, that's great too, because it eases my guilt about spending less time with the boys.

Kim I have to admit, I'm afraid I don't like having anyone come to stay at all. My friends know how fastidious I am, so they understand. I don't like having my routine interrupted. The agreement is this: I book them into a hotel and I pay. I wouldn't go and stay with people either. When I go visiting, I much prefer to stay in a hotel.

Aggie I like to do some advance preparation to make sure the guest room is neat and tidy, with fresh towels laid out on the bed and an extra blanket – and in winter I always offer a hot water bottle at bedtime. I think a bed looks naked without four pillows, and I leave out a spare dressing gown. I'll always make some hanging space in the wardrobe and finish the room off with some fresh flowers.

Kim When I kept house for the Sheik, I prepared the bedrooms as if there were guests coming – even though they owned the place! A fresh bathrobe is very welcoming. One tip would be line your guests' waste bins with a plastic bag, then you can just simply scoop the whole lot out and you won't be trying to fish someone's cotton wool pad out of the darkest recess. Keep some spare bags folded at the bottom of the bin, so you can stretch another one straight into place.

Aggie When it comes to breakages, I try not to be too precious – they're only things. I do have some handmade Austrian wine glasses and I always insist on washing them myself because then if they get broken it's my deal.

Kim When it comes to any accidental breakages, handle them with grace. I break things, we all break things, none of us means to. If something out on a shelf is terribly precious, then put it away; don't make people feel awkward.

Sharing your home

Having guests to stay can be fun and disruptive in equal measure, but whether they're friends or family, you'll want to make them feel at home. With some advance planning, they'll feel more welcome and your routine will be less disrupted. Even if someone arrives unexpectedly, don't panic, there are plenty of things you can prepare, even with just an hour's notice.

Preparing the guest room

If you're lucky, you'll have a spare guest room, if you're unlucky, you'll be giving up your own bedroom and sleeping on the sofa. If you don't have a sofa bed, it may be worth buying an inflatable mattress – they're often advertised in newspaper classifieds or sold in outdoor activity shops. The deluxe versions are flock-lined and can be inflated with a hairdryer. It's bad etiquette to expect your guests to sleep on the floor – even if they offer.

To prepare the guest room start by opening the windows to let the fresh air in. Whichever room your guests will be sleeping in should be clutterfree. You can't expect guests to sleep surrounded by heaps of your dirty laundry, piles of toys or abandoned bits of furniture. Ideally, don't leave guest beds made up with sheets when they're not in use – just cover the mattress.

You'll need fresh bed linen. If the sheets were clean, but the bed has been made up for some time, it may be worth remaking it. If the sheets are soiled and you only have an hour's notice, strip the bed and get them straight into the washing machine for a quick wash and tumble dry (which should take just under two hours). If you're desperate, larger supermarkets stock bedding and some stay open twenty-four hours. Everyone needs at least one pillow and, if possible, leave out a spare (all the best hotels leave a spare pillow in the wardrobe). While you're leaving out spares, fold an extra blanket along the end of the bed. It makes the bed look inviting and is very welcome if your guests are cold during the night because we all tend to heat our homes to different temperatures.

Once you've made up the bed, dust and vacuum the bedroom. Clear some space in the wardrobe and leave out some hangers so your guests will know you've left space inside on the rail. If possible, empty a drawer and leave it slightly open. If you don't leave some storage space, your guests will be forced to drape their clothes all over your furniture, and they won't feel at home.

Organize a bedside table – even if there isn't usually one – with a lamp and a coaster for a glass of water, and line the wastepaper basket with a plastic bag. Leave some guest towels folded on the bed – a hand and bath towel size.

Finishing touches

Your guests may also appreciate a small supply of toiletries: some fresh soap and perhaps even some shampoo and body lotion – just as all the best hotels do. In fact, why not bring some spares home next time you're travelling? Lots of pharmacies stock special miniature, travel-size toiletries. To make the ensemble especially tempting, line a basket with a fresh face cloth and place it on top of the towels. Your guests may also appreciate a hairdryer and a dressing gown if you have a spare one freshly laundered, and a vase of flowers is always very welcoming.

If you're sharing the bathroom and you need to get up and out early, it's a good idea to tell your guests, so they don't delay you. It's also worth warning your guests about any peculiarities or eccentricities associated with your plumbing so that they don't end up with a cold bath, scalding shower or blocked toilet.

If your guests are staying with you for a few days or over the weekend, you might want to get out a map and a guidebook with some tips on where to park or how to use the public transport. If you don't plan on spending the whole time together, some suggestions for places to eat will also be appreciated.

CHECKLIST: PREPARING THE GUEST ROOM
- Open the window to air the room.
- Make up the bed with fresh bed linen.
- Dust and vacuum the room.
- Leave out a spare pillow and blanket.
- Leave a fresh hand and bath towel folded on the bed.
- Clear some hanging space and provide a few hangers.
- Empty a spare clothes drawer.
- Provide a bedside lamp and a waste basket.

Finishing touches
- Leave a selection of miniature toiletries and a hairdryer.
- For longer visits – a map, guidebook and local transport information.
- A vase of fresh flowers.

Preparing the rest of the home for visitors

Now you can turn your attention to the rest of the home. If you're normally fastidious – and let's hope you are! – you won't need to do much except run the vacuum round, plump the cushions, gather up the newspapers, turn the TV and computer off and put the kettle on.

The untidy home

If your home is normally in a state of chaos, don't panic – there's still plenty you can do to make your guests feel welcome. Obviously this isn't the time for spring cleaning, but you can smarten up the rooms your visitors will notice first. If possible, mobilize everyone in your household to help and each take one room. Allocate the most challenging room to the most capable person, put on lively music and set a deadline to finish.

Open up some windows to change the air; gather up all the clutter into bags or boxes; and pick one room or cupboard to hide them all in. Empty all the waste bins and put the newspapers into the recycling. Collect all the crockery and glasses into the sink or dishwasher. Rinse the bathroom hand basin, wipe over the toilet seat and rim, freshen the pan with cleaner and flush. Polish the mirrors and dust all the surfaces with a damp cloth. Finally, mop and vacuum all the floors and pull the doors closed on any rooms you didn't get round to. Finally, put the kettle on – you've earned it.

The tidy home

- Plump up the cushions.
- Vacuum the carpets.
- Turn the TV and computer off.
- Put the kettle on.

The untidy home

- Mobilize some help and take one room each.
- Open all the windows and let the fresh air in.
- Gather all clutter into boxes and bags and hide in one room or cupboard.
- Empty all the bins and put the newspapers into the recycling.
- Collect all the dirty crockery and glasses into the sink or dishwasher.
- Clean the bathroom basin and toilet.
- Polish the mirrors.
- Dust surfaces with a damp cloth.
- Mop and vacuum all the floors.
- Close the door on any rooms you didn't have time to attend to.

How to greet your guests

However fraught your preparations have been, remember to smile when you greet your guests. Let them know you're eagerly expecting them by turning off the television or computer and putting away whatever you've been doing. You don't want them to feel as if they're intruding.

As you'll know by now, we don't think you should wear your outdoor shoes inside your home, and we don't think your guests should either. In some countries, such as Japan, you wouldn't even have to mention it, and of course if your guests know you well, they won't mind. If you're welcoming guests for the first time, ask them if they mind taking off their shoes. You could even provide some inexpensive slippers for them.

Catering for your guests

You'll want your guests to feel at home, especially if they're staying for a while. Invite them to help themselves to anything they'll need and show them where things are, although you'll still need to offer drinks and snacks because most of us are shy about helping ourselves. Guests staying for a few days may offer to cook a meal. Your first instinct will probably be to decline their offer, but why not let them repay your hospitality? If you don't like the idea, suggest going out to a restaurant instead.

Sharing your home with guests

Children's activities
When you have children come and stay there are a few extra
considerations. Firstly, if you don't have any of your own, is your home
safe, are there fragile things on show, where are hazardous things
stored? If you do have children, decide if any toys, computers or video
games are off limits. You may also want to agree with your guests
when kids' bedtime is.

Cleaning routines
It's important that your guests don't feel as if they are intruding into
your usual routine, but at the same time you'll want to keep on top
of things as usual. You should certainly clean the bathroom and toilet
every day and change the towels every couple of days. You'll want to
vacuum the main areas most days, and stay on top of any extra clutter
that builds up – newspapers, crockery, toys and books. You won't
need to change your guests' bed linen unless they're staying for more
than a week. If you're sleeping on the sofa, or an inflatable mattress,
you'll need to pack them away every day so that your guests aren't
constantly reminded that they're disrupting you.

Accidents and breakages
One other eventuality is how to respond when your guests damage
or break something. If the breakage is unimportant you won't mind
much – so say so. If you have valuable or delicate possessions, it may
be more considerate to put them safely away before welcoming
guests – especially if they include young children.

Renting and letting your home

Some people choose to rent their home, for others it's a necessity. You may decide to rent because you can't afford to buy, or while you're working away from home. There may also be a time in your life when you have to rent out your own home because you decide to go travelling, move away for work, or move in with a partner. Both renting and letting require careful consideration to ensure you end up making the best arrangements.

Renting your home

Advantages

There are some benefits to renting your home. You don't have to save up a large deposit or take out a long-term loan. Renting in a new area gives you the opportunity to discover whether it's somewhere you'd like to live permanently first – and saves making a costly mistake because buying and selling property incurs considerable fees and costs. Renting will save you from other expenses too because as a tenant you're not usually responsible for regular repairs and maintenance.

Disadvantages

The disadvantages of renting are that you usually have to accept the décor and furnishings that are offered, although the higher the rent, the better quality these usually are. The money you pay out in rent doesn't give you any investment return, so if property prices rise it can be more difficult to afford to buy your own home later. However, if property prices fall, you won't be left with a home worth less than you paid for it.

Finding a property to rent

There are plenty of ways to find a property to rent. You can ask friends and colleagues, search the small-ads, sign on with an agency, or if your employer is relocating you, ask them to pay for a relocation agent.

Most agencies charge the landlord commission, so as a tenant the service should be free, although you may have to pay some legal and inventory charges. Viewing properties is time consuming and can be frustrating, so work out your budget and exactly what kind of accommodation you're looking for – furnished or unfurnished. Besides the rent you'll normally have to pay council tax, utility bills and a deposit against any damage.

The best way to find a property is to build a relationship with the local agents and prove you're seriously looking for somewhere to rent by phoning them to see what's new, and viewing suitable properties quickly. Many agents will start by showing you properties that are already on their books. These may have already been rejected by lots of other people, so try and find out why a property hasn't been let before you waste time viewing.

Tenancy agreement

Once you've found a property to rent, you'll have to sign a tenancy agreement with the landlord. This contract lays out all the conditions you must abide by, the length of the tenancy and the rent you have agreed to pay. It also gives the landlord an absolute right to possession of the property at the end of the tenancy once notice has been served. If you leave before the end of the agreement, you'll still be liable for all the rent payable. If you become a joint tenant with another person, or group of people, the terms of the agreement will apply to all of you. The landlord can claim the full rent from any of the tenants, which is worth remembering if one of you leaves the property – the remaining tenants will have to cover the rent.

You'll be asked to provide references from an employer or previous landlord, and you may have to agree to a credit check. You'll also be required to pay a deposit equal to between four and six weeks' rent. If you're using an agent, ask for the deposit to be lodged in trust in case the agent ceases trading before your tenancy ends, otherwise you may not get your money back.

Tenancy agreements restrict what you can do to the property – after all you don't own it. You won't be able to decorate or make any alterations without prior permission – you may not even be able to put up any pictures in case you damage the decoration. You'll have to leave the property and carpets clean and perhaps even the garden in the condition you found it.

The landlord or managing agent is entitled to make an appointment to inspect the condition of the property at any time, but they can't enter without your permission. They would normally ask to do this only towards the end of the tenancy or if you report damage or a problem, but they may also inspect if they receive any complaints from your neighbours. If a visit is requested, ask what the purpose of it is and arrange to be present.

Inventory

An inventory will be made of all the fixtures, fittings and furnishings along with a description of their condition. Check that you agree with this list and record any existing damage, otherwise part of your deposit may be withheld at the end of your tenancy.

Take digital photographs of the general condition of carpets and decoration in case the deposit is later withheld to cover damage that was already done. Email the photographs to the agent as proof of the date. Disagreements over the repayment of deposits are the most common disputes.

Establish who will be managing the property – will it be the agent or the landlord? If the washing machine breaks down or the roof leaks, this is the person who'll be responsible for arranging and paying for repairs, so you'll want to be confident they are readily accessible, which they may not be if, say, your landlord is working abroad. When you first viewed the property it was probably occupied by the former tenants or even the owner. Ask what arrangements have been made to clean and prepare the property before you move in. You'll be required to leave the property in a clean and well-maintained condition.

When you're preparing to vacate the property at the end of the tenancy, remind yourself what is required under the terms of the agreement. You may have to arrange to have the garden tidied up or the carpets professionally cleaned in order to get back your full deposit. If you default on these obligations, the landlord will be within their rights to hold back their costs. If you are short of time, it may be worth paying to have the cleaning done by a contractor, but get two quotes because it can prove expensive.

Disputes

As a tenant you have legal rights. If a dispute arises because your landlord refuses to carry out repairs, wants to increase the rent, or threatens to evict you, you should seek help. The local Citizens Advice Bureau can give you help and advice (www.adviceguide.org.uk) and the charity Shelter (www.shelter.org.uk) has further information about your rights.

CHECKLIST: BECOMING A TENANT

- Decide on a location, budget and property type – furnished or unfurnished.
- To find a property, ask friends, colleagues or sign up with agents.
- Build a relationship with agents to hear about the best properties before anyone else.
- You will have to pay council tax, utility bills and find a deposit.
- You'll have to sign a tenancy agreement.
- Joint tenants are all equally responsible for the rent if someone leaves early or can't pay their share.
- You'll have to pay a deposit against breakages and damage.
- If you use an agent, check your deposit is held in trust in case they go out of business.
- Check that the inventory is correct.
- Take photographs to prove the condition of decoration and carpets when you moved in to help get your deposit back.
- When it's time to move out, check what you must do to get your full deposit back.

Becoming a landlord

There are two main reasons why you may become a landlord.
Firstly, you have to let out your own home while you're travelling,
living or working somewhere else or living in long-term residential
care. Secondly, you may have a second investment property
for rental income and the potential for capital appreciation.

Advantages
Letting your own home allows for a temporary or long-term change
in your living arrangements, without incurring all the costs of selling.
Letting a property that would otherwise stand empty provides a rental
income and can help maintain and protect the building by keeping
it occupied.

Disadvantages
Becoming a landlord is not risk-free. If you're unable to find a tenant;
they leave owing you money; or cause damage to your property; you
may struggle to cover your costs or recover your loss.

Managing a rental property yourself is a serious commitment.
Appointing a professional agent will reduce your responsibilities, but
increase your costs significantly. You'll also need to keep accounts
and file a tax return showing the rental income and your expenses.

Preparing your property for market

Prospective tenants have a wide choice of properties so you must make yours as attractive as possible. You'll have to decide how long the let will be for (six or twelve months is the usual length of each agreement) and whether to let furnished or unfurnished. Any furnishings you include in the property must comply with current fire safety legislation.

If you do provide furnishings, the quality should be reflected in the amount of rent you demand – poor quality furniture won't help sell a penthouse. The fixtures and fittings need to be robust to withstand use by tenants who may take less care than you would. You're also responsible for the safety of all gas and electricity appliances, and you'll need to obtain landlord's safety inspection certificates every year.

If your property has a mortgage or loan secured on it, you'll need to notify your lender that you're planning to let the property. They may make an administration charge and increase the rate of interest they charge to cover their increased risk. You should also notify your buildings and contents insurer, but it can be very difficult to insure any furnishings if they're not in your care.

You need to decide whether to market and manage the property yourself or appoint an agent. An agent will find and vet a tenant and draw up a tenancy agreement, usually for a fee of around 10 percent (+ VAT) of the total rent payable for each of the periods their tenant stays. If you also want the agent to manage the property, collect the rent and appoint contractors for repairs, they typically charge 15 percent (+ VAT) of the rent for this service.

Talk to several agents, as they'll help you decide the state of the market and how much rent you can ask. It's also worth negotiating agents' fees if you can. Ask the agent to reduce their fees in subsequent years if your first tenant decides to stay longer and they don't have to find you another one.

You don't have to use an agent; you can advertise locally and put up notices at work and any clubs you belong to, but even if you rent to a friend, you must use a professionally prepared shorthold tenancy agreement. This will be your protection if anything goes wrong. It will also give you the absolute right to reclaim your property at the end of the agreement, and give you legal protection if the rent isn't paid or your possessions are stolen or damaged. Be wary of using a standard agreement downloaded for free from the internet. This is one area where legal fees are money well spent.

Ask prospective tenants to provide references from their employer and, if possible, their current landlord. You can also obtain a credit check from an agency if you have the prospective tenant's consent. For your own protection, before you hand over any keys you must have a signed tenancy agreement; a month's advance rent; and a deposit equal to at least four to six weeks' rent.

Disputes

Although you own the property, your tenant has legal rights and protection. Even if they default on the rent, you can't forcibly or physically evict them – you must obtain a court order first. As the landlord, you're also legally required to carry out essential repairs swiftly, and action can be taken against you if you don't fulfil these obligations.

The best precaution against legal difficulties is to vet tenants carefully. If you have any doubts about their suitability, wait for another tenant rather than take a risk. Applying to the court to evict a tenant is expensive and time consuming, and you may not even get your rent.

○ Decide whether to let furnished or unfurnished.

○ You must notify your mortgage lender and buildings insurer if you decide to rent out your home. They may charge you a fee and increase their charges to cover the extra risk and administration costs.

○ Ask agents to view the property and advise a realistic rent.

○ Agents' fees are negotiable, but they usually charge a percentage of the rent to find a tenant (typically 10 percent + VAT). Agents charge more if they collect the rent and manage the property (typically 15 percent + VAT).

○ Appoint an agent or advertise in local press or shops or on notice boards at clubs and work.

○ Always use a tenancy agreement, even with people you know. This will help provide legal protection if anything goes wrong.

○ Hold a deposit equal to at least four to six weeks' rent against damage or unpaid rent.

○ Draw up an inventory that lists fixtures, fittings, furnishings and their condition.

○ Furnishings must meet current fire safety regulations.

○ Landlords are legally required to have gas and electrical installations certified safe every year.

Hiring domestic help

However essential it may feel, hiring a cleaner is a luxury because, let's face it, most of us can clean for ourselves. It's surprising how superhuman we think other people are when they're doing work we don't want to do ourselves. We're fooling ourselves if we think a professional can clean a whole house in three hours a week. Come on, let's play fair with our unsung cleaning heroes!

Aggie People expect too much from their cleaners, they really do. I think they get a raw deal. You're more likely to notice what hasn't been done, not what has – you won't get perfection every time. Before hiring a cleaner, you need to do a test run yourself to find out how long it takes you to clean your home to the standard you expect, and then be prepared to pay for it.

Kim A lot of cleaners, in our day and age, live in their own homes and they want the work to fit around their own lives – perhaps because they've got children at school – but I don't think that's a good reason to clean. Very few people know how to clean properly. When you hear someone say, 'I went through twenty cleaners and I've had this one two years,' well, for heaven's sake don't lose them, give them a raise – they're worth it.

It's very difficult to find a good cleaner; you really need to see them in action. Of course you must take their references, but take a good look at their appearance too. If they've got scruffy shoes and are poorly turned out, they're not going to do a good job on your home either. When they start work, for goodness' sake, be there too. The number of times people have said to me that they have a new cleaner starting on Thursday, and they're not even going to be in! I say, see what she's cleaning, and more importantly what she's leaving behind.

Aggie We first had a cleaner when I went back to work after my first son was born. Now the boys are older we have a live-in au pair, who looks after the day-to-day vacuuming, dusting and keeping the bathrooms in order. Before Pawel came to us, I preferred the cleaner to come once a fortnight for a whole day, and do a really thorough clean. That felt better to me than getting the place skimmed over for a couple of hours once a week. You definitely need to make a list of jobs. Discuss them with any prospective cleaner before they come to work for you, and check they're happy to do all of these jobs. You may need to get in the supplies they ask for, but do tell them if there are things you would rather they didn't do. I once had a cleaner who sloshed bleach everywhere, which wasn't what I wanted at all. You'll also need a decent vacuum cleaner. No one can clean if you don't provide the proper tools for the job.

Kim If I was ever going to need a cleaner, I think I'd ask for one whole day every week. I'd get them to vacuum the whole house, dust it, and clean the loos. If she was any good, I'd pay her good money. Invariably a cleaner pays her own taxes, and she should sign to say she does, so I'd pay £10 an hour to give her some inspiration and, if she was good, I'd put it up to £12 because if you're stingy, they'll go elsewhere. I'd also say, 'Once you've done a year, I'll pay for your holiday time.'

Aggie I'm not sure about paying a visiting cleaner for holidays, it's difficult isn't it? When you're away it's an added expense you don't need, but cleaners can't afford to take a holiday just because you do. What I would do is set some extra jobs there wouldn't normally be time for, such as washing down paintwork. As for paying while your cleaner is on holiday, well, I think that's something you'll only want to do once you've developed a good working relationship.

Kim Absolutely you give them a Christmas bonus. I've been a cleaner and let me tell you, you look forward to your bonus. This is the most important person in your life after your family. If you can afford a cleaner, you can afford to reward them. My biggest bonus was £500.

Aggie I would definitely tidy up before my cleaner came to work – how can anyone clean a surface if it's covered in clutter? As for people who leave the previous evening's washing-up for their cleaner ... I think that's unforgivable.

Kim Frankly I dread the day when I have to hire a cleaner; they can make or break your house. I'd hate someone bumping the vacuum into my sofa and skirting boards. I don't think I'm fastidious, I just want a good cleaner – that's why I do it myself.

Hiring extra help

If you don't want to, or are unable to, keep your home clean yourself, there's no shortage of people ready to help you. Hourly rates of pay have reached realistic levels, so expect to pay between £5 and £10 an hour. You'll probably have to make a minimum booking of two or three hours every week so expect to pay as much as £20, but a good and reliable cleaner is worth their weight in gold.

There are also agencies and firms who will quote to do extra one-off cleaning, for example when you're moving into a new home, after building work, or while you're busy caring for someone else. This usually involves several cleaners working at once for a half or a whole day and can be expensive. Expect to pay £200 to £300 for a big job, depending on where you live. Contractors usually bring all their own equipment and materials.

It's a good idea to decide, before you hire a cleaner, exactly what it is you want them to do, when you would like them to come, and for how long. Some cleaners may not want to do certain tasks – for example, ironing, cleaning windows or polishing silver. If having your ironing done is a high priority, you'll either need to look for another cleaner or find a laundry that offers an ironing service.

While there's plenty of choice available, choosing the right cleaner isn't always easy. When you're hiring help, ask your friends and family first because they'll always have the most reliable recommendations, although you may discover some people jealously guard their cleaners' names and telephone numbers! Be wary of people who push handwritten cards through your letter box and before you hire any cleaner, always take up references from their current clients.

Most cleaners will want to come at the same time every week to fit your job into their existing commitments. They may not offer much flexibility unless a current client is happy to change time or day.

Because professionals clean for a living, they tend to have established ways of tackling tasks, so if you have very fixed views about how things are done, you may need to be a little flexible. If you have something precious, suggest how to clean it or ask them to leave it. Most professional cleaners prefer to use certain cleaning materials, which they will bring or ask you to buy. If you have strong views about which products are used in your home, for environmental or health reasons, remember to say so.

We've all heard about the people who feel compelled to clean or tidy up before their cleaner arrives. This really isn't as silly as it sounds. Your cleaner can't reasonably be expected to tidy things away for you and you shouldn't expect anyone to pick up your dirty underwear. Tidying is a waste of your cleaner's precious time – time which they could better use to clean. If you clear all the floors and surfaces before your cleaner arrives, they will be able to get straight to work with the mop, duster and vacuum cleaner.

Agony and household etiquette columns are filled with queries from householders who don't know how to communicate with their cleaners. They moan that their domestic help gossips too much, smokes too much, damages too much, is always off sick, refuses to go sick, expects holiday pay, more pay and so on.

You have to be responsible for managing your relationship with your cleaner, just as you do with everyone else in life. Once you develop mutual respect, the relationship will be at its most productive. Agree some ground rules between you at the outset about how you'll deal with holidays, sickness and breakages (some cleaning agencies carry liability insurance) and ask that the goings-on in your house remain confidential – so, if you hear any gossip back from your neighbours, you'll know where you stand.

Finally, do thank your cleaner. Comment on the things they do that you like, we all like our work to be noticed and appreciated, and feel free to reward your cleaner with bonuses and gifts.

- 🌿 Decide what you want help with, for how long and how often.
- 🌿 Some firms provide one-off cleaning when you're moving in or after building work.
- 🌿 Always ask friends and neighbours for recommendations.
- 🌿 Check references with current clients.
- 🌿 Discuss your requirements at the outset.
- 🌿 Agree your requirements during holiday time.
- 🌿 Build a good working relationship with your cleaner.
- 🌿 Remember to tell your cleaner that you appreciate their help and remark on any nice touches that please you.
- 🌿 Do reward your cleaner with cards and gifts – we all like our work to be noticed and appreciated.

Hiring builders, renovating and decorating

Most of us have grand plans when it comes to decorating and designing our homes, but we have to reconcile our dreams with our budget. There's no doubt that freshening up the decoration makes cleaning easier and more pleasurable, but carrying out renovations can be very disruptive.

Aggie We moved into our current house eight years ago and since then we've completely renovated it. We started with the big jobs: the roof, the wiring, a new bathroom, and finished up with a new kitchen, which was a major job. In the past I've wallpapered, painted, cut tiles and laid floors, but nowadays I would rather spend time with the family and pay someone else to do it.

Kim We've only recently moved into our new house. It was the showhome actually, so everything is brand new, and we like the colours very much. Normally we wouldn't choose a new house, but we didn't have much time to look around, so this was ideal. We used to do our own decorating, but now I say, 'Come on Pete, we've got the money, let's give someone else a chance!'

Aggie When we had the building work done we did get three quotes with all the different jobs costed out. That's the only way you can see where all the money is going. I wouldn't choose a builder purely on cost because reputation is very important too. We're lucky, though: because Matthew is an architect, he knows the best builders.

Kim I'm not one for picking trade people out at random, in my opinion you'll never beat a recommendation. I'm very mistrustful of decorators I don't know. Don't go for the cheapest quote, that's foolish, you have to pay to get a job done well; it saves a lot of heartache.

Aggie I think the lesson with builders is that if there's any room for ambiguity whatsoever, they will do it differently from how you'd imagined. If you're picky, you must explain every aspect of the job clearly; that way you'll have more chance of getting the end result you want. Do keep a diary of the work done, record all the payments you make, and agree in advance about any penalties if the work goes on longer than promised.

I think it's very difficult to stay sane, or clean, when you have the builders in. I remember going to clean my teeth and finding there was brick dust on my toothbrush. At moments like that you just think, 'What's the point?' I do love it when builders clean up properly. It's a very stressful time having work done on your house.

Kim One other thing about decorating your home – I think it's a smashing idea to keep a home journal. I do, and I wait until sale time for the big purchases – you can get some bargains, especially on fitted kitchens. My other tip is to always keep some spare matching paint or paper at the end of the job, especially if you've used a lot of a particular colour throughout the house. It's a devil to get an exact match afterwards, and you'll have to start again, when you could have simply done some touching up. I'll always spend the extra money on special washable paint for kitchens and bathrooms. Even some matt emulsion is wipeable now, aren't we lucky?

Create a home journal

It's a good idea to create a home journal so that you'll always have a record of your room and window measurements, paint and paper finishes, fabric colours and dimensions for any furniture you need, such as shelves.

An A5 (half the size of A4) notebook or folder is a convenient size journal. Create a double page spread for every room in the home, marking the dimensions of the layout, the window sizes and the widths of the doors (so that you'll be sure you can accommodate larger items of furniture). Take photographs of your rooms to help you visualize how new furniture will fit in. Attach paint, paper, carpet and fabric samples so that you can match up the colour schemes (if you don't have a fabric sample for upholstery or curtain material, buy a reel of matching cotton thread). Finally make a shopping list of the things you're looking for, from carpet to cushions.

Take your home journal with you on shopping trips and take your own tape measure along too so that you can measure up furniture without waiting for the assistant. Stores often won't reserve or make refunds on sale clearance items because the discounts can be so exceptional; ex-display curtains and furniture can be reduced by as much as 70 percent. You'll also find cancelled customer orders and ends of ranges can be heavily discounted. Nonetheless, it's always worth being cheeky and asking for an extra discount on top because shops are usually keen to shift display goods and ends of ranges to make space for new stock.

Test your negotiation skills by asking for a further 10 or 20 percent; especially if you're planning to buy more than one item or you can take it away there and then. If there's any damage, point that out too as a way of securing a further knockdown. You'll only want to impulse buy at sale time if you're sure that 'bargain' is the right colour and size, so make sure you always have your home journal with you. The time you've invested keeping it up to date can quickly be rewarded.

Finally, keep all the receipts, instruction manuals and guarantees for all your household purchases (*see* The home office, p. 38). Most household goods, from kettles to televisions, are guaranteed for twelve months and even fabric protection finishes and flooring materials come with guarantees of durability. Store them all in one place so you'll always be able to refer to them quickly when things go wrong. Manuals are full of invaluable information including cleaning tips, troubleshooting guides and contact details for service agents for when things go wrong. It's a good tip always to check the troubleshooting section of the instruction manual before taking goods back or calling for an engineer.

CHECKLIST: CREATING A HOME JOURNAL

- Use a portable-sized notebook – no larger than A5.
- Take your home journal out shopping with you – especially at sale time.
- Record the room dimensions on a floor plan so you'll know sizes for carpet remnants and furniture. Mark the locations of doors, windows and radiators.
- Record the width and height of door and window openings to be sure new furniture will move in painlessly.
- Record window dimensions and drops from ceiling to floor for curtain and window dressings.
- Attach paint charts, wallpaper, fabric and carpet swatches to help match colours.
- Create a shopping wish list for each room, covering everything from shelves for a tricky alcove to rugs and lampshades.

Decorating

Unfortunately, keeping your home looking good, year after year, requires a little more effort than just regular cleaning and maintenance. However spotless you keep the décor, paper and paint will become dirty and faded over time, carpets begin to show signs of wear, and furnishing fabrics fade.

A good tip is to freshen up, or redecorate, one room in the spring and another in the autumn. If you do this, a four-bedroom home will be redecorated every four years (if you count in kitchen, bathroom, living and dining rooms). If you only have a couple of bedrooms, you can relax and decorate one room a year. There's no need to spend a fortune on a new look; complete redecoration isn't always necessary. Sometimes the simple addition of new cushions, throws, bedcovers and lampshades can work miracles in refreshing the appearance of a room.

Soft furnishings are always included in summer and winter sales to make way for new season collections. Furnishing fashions don't change as often as stores would like us to believe so, if you avoid garish designs, your bargains won't look dated. It's worth buying lampshades, cushions and throws all from one designer's collection if you don't feel confident enough to create a coordinated look yourself. If you do decide to redecorate a room from top to bottom, plan the look you're going for first – you'll get a much quicker and more successful result. Clip photographs from magazines and home furnishing catalogues.

Plan ahead when decorating

- Snap up bargains. Summer and winter sales offer reductions on furniture, furnishings, paper and paint.
- Decorate one room in the spring and another in the autumn and the house will always look good.
- Decide whether you will do the decorating yourself or hire help.
- Professionals can be in short supply and the good ones are usually booked up in advance.

Hiring a professional decorator

If you don't fancy or are unable to do the job yourself, look for
a professional decorator. Ask friends and neighbours for their
recommendations because it's always the most reliable method of
hiring help. If this doesn't produce a result, look up registers of trade
associations and qualified professionals, which you can access on
the internet. Some paint manufacturers list approved contractors
whose materials and work they vouch for. It's always worth getting
three quotes, but the most competitive price shouldn't be your only
consideration when making the final decision about who to hire.

Always use your common sense when you invite people to come
and work in your home. Make sure you have their address on a written
quotation – not just a mobile telephone number. Make a judgement
about their appearance and mode of transport, which may reveal a
lot about their likely standard of work. If possible, view their previous
jobs and ask their recent clients if they were happy. A decorator will
always be able to provide a reference if he has happy customers. If a
contractor doesn't turn up as agreed to give an estimate, it's unlikely
they'll be reliable when it comes to doing the job either. These are just
some of the things you should bear in mind when you decide which
quote to accept – reliability may be worth paying a bit extra for.

When you're getting quotes, don't feel intimidated about asking
questions. If you agree what you want done at this stage, it will avoid
unwelcome surprises later and help the project run more smoothly.

- ○ Always ask friends and neighbours for recommendations.
- ○ Get written quotations and inspect previous work.
- ○ You may have to pay for materials in advance, but never pay for labour upfront.
- ○ Be wary of 'trade discounts', which may not always be a better deal than you can obtain.
- ○ Remember to check if the price includes VAT.
- ○ Agree a start date and how many days the job will take.
- ○ Ask who is responsible for moving and protecting flooring and furniture.
- ○ Don't make the final payment until you're satisfied with the work.
- ○ If you're pleased with the work, make an advance booking for next time and tell your friends. Everyone should benefit from good service.

Do-it-yourself decorating

Modern decorating products are all designed with the home user in mind, so you can achieve a good quality, professional looking finish. Good preparation goes a long way towards getting the best results and causes the minimum disruption to home life.

Decide sensibly how long the job is likely to take – can it all be done in a weekend, or will you need to allow some extra days? Will you be able to work during the evenings, or would a day or two off work get things finished and back to normal more quickly? The answers to these questions will depend on which rooms you are tackling – essential spaces such as kitchens, bathrooms and bedrooms should be decorated or renovated as quickly as possible with minimum disruption.

Before you start work, shop for all the materials you are likely to need. Most stores will make refunds on surplus supplies (except special orders or custom-mixed paint). At all costs, avoid having to down tools on the job to go shopping because it wastes valuable time.

Completely remove all the furnishings from a room if possible – it's much quicker in the long run because you won't be constantly shifting things, and more importantly nothing will get damaged by paint or dust. Try and clear the space the evening before you plan to start work so that valuable daylight is saved for decorating. If you're unable to remove heavy furniture, move it to the centre of the room and cover it in heavy-duty plastic sheeting. If the carpet has plenty of wear left, protect it with plastic and dust sheets. Always decorate before, not after, laying a new carpet.

As a general rule, the time spent preparing surfaces determines the quality of the finish and how long it will last. You should spend the same amount of time washing, filling and sanding surfaces as you do applying paper and paint.

- Plan the job before you start.
- Buy all the materials in advance. Most shops will make refunds for unused supplies (except for specially mixed paint).
- Buy the best quality materials you can afford. The job will be easier and quicker with quality paint and paper.
- Clear the room completely, or move heavy furniture to the centre and cover in clean plastic sheeting.
- Cover the floor with plastic and dust sheets.
- The secret of a good finish lies in good preparation. Time spent preparing surfaces should be equal to time spent painting and papering them.
- Open the windows to reduce harmful odours.
- Apply paint in natural daylight whenever possible.
- Paint the ceiling first, followed by the walls and finally the woodwork.
- When hanging wallpaper, paint the ceiling, followed by the woodwork and hang the paper last.
- It's quicker to apply paint with a roller than a brush.
- Use water-resistant emulsion for kitchen and bathroom walls.

Renovations and hiring builders

Renovating and building work differs from redecoration because it involves structural, not simply cosmetic, alterations. Most of us want to improve our homes and some of the work required may be remedial – a new roof or damp-proof course – while new kitchens or bathrooms are improvements, not renovations.

Never accept offers from builders 'just passing by' who claim to have noticed repairs that require immediate attention. Always get a second opinion from a respected and recommended contractor because some people have been conned into paying huge sums for unnecessary and overpriced repairs.

The cost of home improvements can be considerable, and usually ends up exceeding the original budget once new problems are uncovered or extra improvements are added. It's wise to have a contingency fund of up to one-third of the value of the planned work. If you plan to spend a lot of money, check that your changes will increase the value of your property by asking an estate agent or surveyor how much your home is likely to be worth before and after the proposed work.

Before you turn your new home into a building site, it can be worth living in it for a few months first. You may find you use the space differently to how you'd imagined or discover the neighbours have a more ingenious improvement than you'd planned. If you have big ambitions, hiring an architect may prove a very wise move. Ask the local authority about any planning permission or Building Control Regulations that affect the proposed work.

413

Cleaning up during building work

Improvements can provide the opportunity to have the kitchen layout you've always dreamt of, the en suite you're hankering for, or a conservatory built, but large-scale work can also involve tearing down walls or extending into lofts and basements. The cost can be considerable, to both finances and comfort. All building work is tremendously disruptive to home life; some rooms become inaccessible while others have to cope with the extra strain. Everywhere gets covered in dust and the constant dealings with builders can be very wearing. Regular cleaning may seem impossible or pointless when builders are working in your home creating chaos and dust, but there are some simple steps you can take to stay in control.

- Discuss with the builders which rooms they need access to and in which order. Keep them to this – otherwise they can tend to work in several rooms simultaneously.
- Wherever possible, seal off doors where very dusty work is taking place to prevent other rooms becoming contaminated.
- Cover up carpets and flooring with dust sheets, move furniture and take down curtains before builders arrive.
- Put away valuable breakables.
- Nominate one room (a bedroom or living room) as a safe haven. Keep this room as clean and clutterfree as possible.
- Clean the bathroom and toilet regularly so that you can freshen up in comfort.
- If you have separate toilet and hand washing facilities, ask the builders to use them.
- Ask builders to stow their tools and materials away at the end of the day and over weekends.
- If you're not hiring a skip, agree where the rubbish will be put – you may value your front garden much more than your builders do.

Choosing a builder

Don't pick a builder at random from the phone book; ask friends and neighbours for their recommendations. Ask your chosen builder for referees who will allow you to see some previous work. Get a written quotation, and insist on a contract for big expensive jobs (there are agreed standard contracts drawn up by recognized trade bodies). Agree a schedule for payment, and keep a diary of events in case there are problems. Don't try to avoid paying VAT; it's illegal, and will cause legal difficulties if disputes arise later. If your builder has a trade association logo on his letterhead, check that the membership is current, and ask to see a copy of the liability insurance, which will cover you if things go wrong.

Finally, let your neighbours know when work will start, how long it will go on for, and apologize in advance for any noise or extra traffic – a little consideration goes a long way.

Hiring builders

- Ask friends and family for recommendations.
- Always ask for references and visit previous work.
- Check current membership of recognized trade bodies.
- Insist on a written itemized quotation so that you can see the cost of each element.
- Don't try to avoid paying VAT by offering cash. It is illegal and proof of payment gives you legal rights if things go wrong. But do check for a VAT registration number before paying VAT.
- Ask for a guarantee and proof of current liability insurance.
- Agree a schedule of payments, but never pay all the money in advance.
- Check your insurance provides cover during building work and whether your mortgage lender has to be notified about improvements.
- Check with your local authority about planning permission and Building Control Regulations governing any work.
- Specify the design of any materials you have strong views about; builders may not share your good taste.
- Agree the cost of 'extra jobs' in advance.
- Be courteous – tell your neighbours when work will start and stop.

Renovating

- Live in a new space for a few months before making final decisions on renovations and alterations.
- Investigate your neighbours' solutions for updating and adapting similar spaces.
- Keep a scrapbook of ideas and design details.

Kim & Aggie   The Cleaning Bible

Kim's housekeeping tales: Westerham, Kent

I didn't know it at the time, but this would turn out to be my last live-in housekeeping job. We'd left Eaton Square and had a few months off in Pembrokeshire while we looked out for our next job. Through the agency we heard that a Saudi Arabian sheik was looking for a couple to look after his part-time country house. The sheik had an agent in London to look after his affairs, who we met, but of course we had to be vetted by the sheik himself when he flew in for his next business trip.

The sheik owned a London home, but we were hired to look after his country mansion in Kent, which he kept purely for the family summer holiday every August. The house had a grand frontage with fountains and five acres of gardens shielded by huge trees. There were dozens of rooms; I never even counted them. That was where we met the sheik, and we were served tea by the couple who were leaving. I remember thinking that we could do better – the tray they served from was dirty, the pot could have been shinier and the sandwiches weren't very neatly cut. The sheik didn't ask me much during the interview. He'd read my references and was impressed that Pete had been a policeman, and then he asked when we could start, which is unusual because usually it's the agent that offers you the job after the meeting.

The sheik and his family brought over all their regular staff when they came to stay, so our job was to tend the house the rest of the year. Even when a house is going to be used so little, you have to clean as you go to keep on top of everything, otherwise suddenly you're faced with five weeks of dust. If the sheik had turned up unexpectedly, which he never did, everything would have been beautiful.

When we took over, the house had been somewhat neglected. I discovered an infestation of carpet beetles which had completely eaten away one of the rugs around the planter that stood there.

Of course I had to call in the exterminator straightaway. In fact I arranged for a six month contract because there were mice in the attic too. All the carpets were sprayed and the doors shut for a couple of days and then when I opened up again, you could see all the dead beetles, which I vacuumed straight up and emptied the bag. Fortunately I think I spotted it in time, because the sheik had some beautiful rugs. There was a thick burgundy rug with a fleur-de-lys pattern laid in the main hall, which was so long you couldn't see the end of it as it stretched away towards the kitchen, dining and sitting rooms. With so much carpet, I did a lot of vacuuming.

The main cleaning challenge was the huge chandelier in the hall; honestly we would put Del Boy to shame. Pete would winch it down by a handle upstairs to my working height and then I would cup each of the individual crystals in my hand and wipe them over with a barely damp cloth tightly wrung out in some warm soapy water. The small chandeliers you could have done in twenty minutes, but this one took quite a lot longer to do every individual piece.

The art in these houses is always hung by the interior designers and they'll say, 'This is a wonderful picture, but it can't hang there because the light will damage it.' Some of these artworks can be priceless so you certainly can't go flicking them with a duster. In these houses there's always a maintenance contract with a specialist where any art is concerned, so if you notice a problem with any of the paintings, you just call them in.

The sheik's house didn't have any big collections because he wasn't there very much, but he did have some gorgeous tapestries hanging from the walls. With tapestries this rare and valuable you wouldn't dare vacuum them in case you pulled a thread, so instead I would brush them with a very soft broom. I would place a ladder against the wall and run the broom from top to bottom in long parallel sweeps. Of course from time to time they would need specialist cleaning. If you pointed out something to the sheik he would say 'get me a price' and we would always get three quotes before we had any work like that done.

It was while I was working with the sheik that I got the call to audition for the television show. Even when the show started filming I carried on working because the sheik didn't want me to leave. When it finally came on TV he asked to see the tapes and the whole family used to sit and laugh along, although eventually I did have to leave because I was too busy to clean for him too. Recently his granddaughter phoned me on her mobile from school because her teacher didn't believe she knew anyone famous, but of course when I started working for the family I was just the housekeeper, isn't that marvellous!

Appendix

Fabric stain removal

Stain removal isn't sorcery, it's chemistry. We remove stains every day, without even thinking about it, when we put detergent in the washing machine. It's only when we're faced with a more dramatic looking stain, often on a favourite item, that we panic. The secret to successful stain removal is working out which is going be the best agent or solvent to help unlock the stain. It may take several attempts, so it's best to work slowly and carefully.

Kim It's invariably the item you treasure that gets spoilt, but the quicker you can act the better. I always pretreat stains before they go into the washing machine. A little bit of liquid or hand soap will remove grime from cuffs and collars and most make-up comes off with soap too. Gently rub the fabric against fabric; a good old rub-a-dub-dub and it's gone.

Aggie The satisfaction in removing a stubborn stain is huge – just recently I managed to get a black grease mark out of a favourite striped T-shirt using hydrogen peroxide – very pleasing!

I don't keep a huge number of stain removal products in readiness, but I always have a packet of colour run remover in the cupboard. You can reverse some real disasters, for example when a stray red sock dyes all your whites pink. I find they work really well – just add the sachet and run the machine again.

Kim Of course you're not always near a washing machine when disaster strikes. I was on a plane when my white shirt got splashed with freckles of tomato soup. I used some white toothpaste and a cotton bud to dab the spots. You can get out most stains if you're quick.

Don't panic

Modern laundry detergents give the washing machine a tremendous amount of cleaning power. Detergent will remove lots of stains that traditionally were considered tough to shift, so most stains, including blood and grass, are easily removed with normal everyday washing. Some stains, however, especially those that are solvent and grease-based, for example ink, oil and fats, call for some extra action, otherwise you run the risk that a hot wash will set the stain for good.

Problems also arise when a fabric isn't washable either by hand or in the machine. If it can be dry-cleaned, take the garment to the cleaners as soon as possible. There are also some stain removal remedies you can attempt yourself, which are covered later.

The ten golden rules for successful stain removal

Rule number one for successfully tackling stains is 'act quickly'. For liquid spills, soak up as much as possible and with solids, scrape off as much as you can, before even thinking about the stain that may be left behind (*see* Treating carpet stains, p. 266).

Read the garment's care label and pay attention to all the instructions. Can the item be machine washed? What is the maximum temperature it can be washed at? Can bleach be used? If the care label advises 'dry-clean only', blot away the excess stain and take the item to the cleaners within twenty-four to forty-eight hours. Point out the stain and tell them what caused it so that they can use the most effective cleaning method.

When tackling a stain, always use the mildest remedy first. It's much more effective to work in several careful stages than launch one knockout assault, which may set the stain. Work from the outside of the stain towards the centre and from the reverse side of the fabric if you can. Before you use any solvents, check that the fabric dye is colourfast by testing inside a hem.

Never scrub stains. If you scrub you'll damage the fibres and leave a permanent marked area on the fabric even if you manage to get the dye or grease out. Instead, dab the stain with a white cotton cloth (so you don't transfer any dye) and if you can, lay the stain on another cloth so that it is absorbed from both sides.

Ten golden rules for stain removal
- Act quickly.
- Soak up excess liquid; scrape off excess solids.
- Dab, don't scrub.
- Use a white cotton cloth to dab with. Coloured fabric may leave dye behind.
- Lay the stain on a white cloth to help absorb the stain from both sides.
- Work from the underside of the fabric when possible to push the stain out.
- Work from the outside edge of the stain towards the centre.
- Always test the fabric in a hidden area for colourfastness before using any solvents.
- Use cool or warm water, never cold or hot, when soaking to avoid fixing the stain and making it permanent.
- Several repeated applications, starting with the mildest remedy, are safer than a single knockout assault.

The five types of stains

There are five main types of stains, which is why many branded stain removal products are sold as a range of products to target each of them separately. These can be washed out of fabrics that can be laundered.

Protein stains These include baby food, body soils (faeces, urine, vomit, blood), milk, egg, mud and grass. First scrape or blot away any excess and soak fresh protein stains in cold water. Rub fabric against fabric to help break up the stain. Soak dried-in stains in water with a little detergent for ten to fifteen minutes and then wash in warm water. Never soak protein stains in hot water because it may set or fix them.

Oil-based stains These include cooking fats, butter, mayonnaise, grease from bikes and cars, human grease soiling on collars and cuffs and make-up. Soap and detergent will remove oil-based stains, but they may need some concentrated pretreatment before going into the regular wash. Work some detergent into the stain and leave it to soak for ten to fifteen minutes, then wash in the hottest water the fabric care label allows.

Tannin stains These include tea, coffee, beer, soft drinks, fruit juice, perfume and wine. Never use bar soap on tannins because it makes them much more difficult to remove. First rinse with cold water and flush as much of the stain out as possible. Then wash with detergent in the hottest water the fabric care label allows.

Dye stains These include dye transfer from other fabrics, natural food colourings and dyes including cranberry, raspberry and mustard. First flush away as much of the colour as possible with cold water to avoid setting the dye. Presoak in detergent in cool water and then wash in the hottest water the care label allows. If you accidentally dye an entire load, use a colour run reversal product.

Combination stains (oil and dye) These include ballpoint ink, candle wax, crayon, lipstick, shoe polish and some foods, such as chocolate, gravy, ketchup and tomato-based sauces. These stains usually involve two components: oil or wax that is coloured with dye or pigment. You need to remove the oily part first and then tackle the dye. With waxy stains, scrape away as much as possible. You may also have to use a solvent such as dry-cleaning fluid, liquid lighter fuel or methylated spirits to dislodge oil and wax stains. Once the oily or waxy part is removed, soak the garment in cool water with detergent for ten to fifteen minutes to remove the dye. Finally, launder in the hottest water the care label allows.

Other cleaners that will remove stains from fabric

When you know from experience that a stain will be hard to shift with detergent alone, you may want to try one of the traditional stain removal agents, some of which will already be among your cleaning supplies (*see* Common laundry problems, pp. 290–291).

Stain removal agents

Acetate	This is very similar to nail varnish remover, but can also be used on acetate fabrics. It dissolves some paints and glues as well as nail varnish. Acetate is flammable and should be used with care.
Ammonia	A laundry bleaching agent usually sold in 10 percent strength and further diluted with water before use (usually 30 ml to 5 litres/1 fl oz to 8½ pints).
Bicarbonate of soda	A versatile stain remover. In paste form, mixed with a little water, it will shift greasy food marks such as butter, margarine, mayonnaise and cooking oil. Leave for 30 minutes and then soak in detergent. In solution, it can also be used to tackle perspiration stains.
Biological detergent	This washing detergent contains enzymes that are designed to digest protein-based stains such as egg, blood and milk. But don't wash wool and silk in biological detergent because the enzymes will weaken the fibres.
Borax	An alkali and therefore effective for neutralizing acid stains such as wine and fruit. Dissolve borax in water for soaking, but don't leave coloured garments to soak for more than 15 minutes because the colours will fade. On white cotton and linen, borax can be sprinkled directly on to the stain and flushed through with hot water.
Chlorine bleach (household bleach)	Always use diluted, and never on synthetic fibres including nylon. Always read the garment care label first and soak the whole garment, not just the stain. Rinse thoroughly and then wash to remove all bleach.
Household soap	Soap is effective at removing oil-based stains, but don't use it on tea, coffee and soft drink stains because it makes the tannins more difficult to remove.
Hydrogen peroxide	Better known as a bleach for hair, hydrogen peroxide, if used with care is suitable for soaking delicate fabrics – including wool and silk, but not synthetics. For hair use it is sold 10–20 percent volume, but for clothes and fabric use 3 percent volume only or dilute with water. Don't soak for longer than 30 minutes.

Lemon juice	Freshly squeezed or bottled lemon juice will remove rust marks (also called iron mould) from fabric.
Methylated spirits	This is a solvent, and so will remove grease and oil stains from non-washable fabrics (but not acetate or triacetates). It also removes traces of colour left behind by candle wax.
Prewash soakers	There are a number of branded products available. Always follow the manufacturer's instructions, and always soak the whole item, not just the stain.
Salt	Dissolve salt in cold water to soak fresh blood stains from fabric.
Stain removal products	These come in liquid, dab-on, paste and spray versions specifically designed to treat individual types of stains. Use as directed on the packaging, but don't forget to follow the other rules listed here for successful stain removal.
Talcum powder	A useful 'holding' agent for grease and oil stains. Sprinkle some on to absorb the excess oil.
Vinegar (clear vinegar)	The traditionally suggested remedy for removing perspiration stains from clothing. Soak in a solution of 1 part vinegar to 10 parts water.
Washing soda crystals	Good at shifting greasy stains. It also softens water to help detergent work more effectively.
White spirit	A solvent that will remove oil and oil-based paint from fabric.

Stain removal methods

There are often several traditional ways to remove a stain from fabric, so if you've heard of another way, it may work just as well as those suggested here. Always think about the type of stain you are tackling before you begin work.

Traditional stain removal methods

Stain	Removal agent	Method
Ballpoint ink	Methylated spirits	Dab with an absorbent white cloth and methylated spirits.
Beetroot juice	Borax and biological detergent	First rinse with cold water. Soak coloureds in a solution of borax for 15 minutes. For white linen, sprinkle borax on the fabric and flush with hot water. Wash with biological detergent.
Bird droppings	Borax, biological detergent and chlorine bleach or hydrogen peroxide	Scrape off excess droppings and sponge with a solution of borax or soak in biological detergent. If stains still remain, try soaking in dilute chlorine bleach (white cotton) or hydrogen peroxide (coloureds and synthetics, but not nylon).
Blood	Salt or biological detergent	Presoak fresh stains in heavily salted cold water or detergent.
Candle wax	Absorbent paper and a warm iron and methylated spirits	Scrape away the excess. Place kitchen towel over the residue and press with a warm iron until the paper absorbs the softened wax. Dab any colour residue with methylated spirits before washing.

Stain	Removal agent	Method
Chewing gum	Ice cubes	Freeze the gum with a bag of ice cubes. Once it becomes hard and brittle, break away the gum with a knife.
Coffee and tea	Detergent, vinegar and borax	Flush with cold water and spot clean with a solution of washing detergent but not soap. If staining remains, soak in a solution of 1 part vinegar to 2 parts water or a solution of borax.
Colour run in washing machine	Washing soda and colour dye remover	If you dye an entire wash load, soak in cold water with washing soda to avoid setting the colour. As soon as possible, machine wash again with a colour run dye reversal product.
Contact adhesives and glue	Acetate (nail polish remover)	Dab with acetate, following the rules for stain removal.
Cooking fat	Bicarbonate of soda and biological detergent	Add a few drops of water to bicarbonate to make a paste and spread over the stain. Leave for 30 minutes and then wash in biological detergent.
Crayon	Methylated spirits	Scrape away excess before dabbing with methylated spirits.
Curry	Biological detergent and hydrogen peroxide	Some curry stains contain strong natural dyes, which are almost impossible to shift. Dab with a strong solution of detergent before laundering. Soak stubborn stains in a solution of hydrogen peroxide bleach.
Dried fruit stain	Lemon juice	Place the stain side down on absorbent kitchen towel and dampen with lemon juice. Dab with hot water and wash.

Stain	Removal agent	Method
Fresh fruit stain	Borax or salt	Soak in a solution of borax for 15 minutes to neutralize the acid and then wash. Alternatively, cover the stain with salt and then wash.
Grass stain	Biological detergent or methylated spirits	Grass is a combination of protein and dye. Detergent should remove most stains. Dab any remaining dye with methylated spirits.
Ink on coloured fabric	Milk	Soak immediately in slightly warm milk and then wash.
Ink and felt-tip pen	Methylated spirits	Dab with an absorbent pad and methylated spirits.
Ink on whites	Salt and lemon	Sprinkle with salt and then rub with lemon. Rinse and wash.
Lipstick	Soap or methylated spirits	Rub fabric against fabric with soap or a little washing-up liquid and then wash. Dab with methylated spirits if the fabric isn't washable.
Mildew – dried	Salt or lemon juice	Rub with damp salt or lemon and leave in the sun for at least 12 hours.
Mildew on shower curtains	Chlorine bleach	Sponge or soak in dilute bleach and machine wash with detergent.
Mildew on white cotton and linen	Household chlorine bleach	Mildew is almost impossible to remove and is caused by damp. Soak in diluted bleach then thoroughly rinse and wash.
Mildew on white synthetics	Hydrogen peroxide	Soak in 1 part hydrogen peroxide to 9 parts water. Rinse and wash.

Stain	Removal agent	Method
Paint – emulsion and water based	Water	Sponge immediately with plenty of warm water. Dried paint can be scraped or picked off, but is difficult to wash off.
Paint – solvent based	White spirit	Dab with white spirit.
Perspiration	Clear vinegar or lemon juice	Soak or sponge with vinegar, but use lemon juice on wool. Rinse and wash.
Plasticine	White spirit	Scrape off as much as possible and dab dye stains with white spirit.
Pollen	Sticky tape	Lift away the pollen with sticky tape or the vacuum cleaner, but don't rub or you'll fix the dye.
Red wine	Carbonated or soda water	Dab or flush with carbonated or soda water and wash.
Rust (iron mould)	Lemon juice	Flush with lemon juice then leave for 15 minutes and launder.
Scorch marks		Scorch marks are permanent damage, but their appearance can be disguised by carefully shaving away the damaged fibres.
Shoe polish	White spirit	Dab with white spirit and wash.
Urine	Detergent, vinegar or shaving foam.	Soak in detergent and wash. For non-washable fabric, dab with a mild vinegar solution. On mattresses, sponge with a dab of shaving foam.

Time to relax

We all express different emotions to describe how we feel about cleaning, and the pleasure we experience afterwards. It's funny how some of us don't feel comfortable about relaxing, inviting round friends or going out until all the jobs are done, but the sense of satisfaction we feel when we finally do sit down and enjoy our surroundings is immeasurable.

Kim Oh it's dreadful when things need to be done; it really depresses me. When we moved into our new house, I didn't finish the unpacking before I had to go away filming, and I really couldn't bear to leave it. I was thinking about it the whole time I was away. There's not a day when I'm away that I don't think, 'Oh God, the dust is building up in my house!' It makes me happy to know that there's a place for everything and everything's in its place – it's like I've taken a vitamin pill.

Aggie Actually I find it quite difficult to relax – I very rarely sit down and watch telly. When the house needs to be cleaned, I feel anxious, irritable, annoyed and depressed. But when the work has been done, I'm transformed; I feel in control, liberated, unencumbered – as though my head's in the right place and anything's possible. That's when I feel content, dare I even say smug?

Kim I do think I'm over the top. Life is very short, and if there's a wee bit of dust, what does it matter? But you know, when I've finally done everything I sit down to watch TV, and my eyes start to wander off the screen and I'll just admire my lovely clean room, and I feel so satisfied.

Aggie Of course we all need to find a balance between a happy home and a healthy home. Most days my boys have the house full of their friends, but I must say they're all pretty good about leaving the place tidy – I think they'd be frightened not to!

Kim When I retire I look forward to having more time to keep my home 'spot on' rather than having to rush home from work and do it. My husband Pete says I'm fanatical.

Aggie When I finally do manage to stop, I love nothing more than to get on the phone and chat or do some cooking, baking, or enjoy a glass of wine with friends around the kitchen table. Once a fortnight I have a massage, which is my real treat.

Kim To relax, I'll break out the knitting or crochet if I'm in the mood. Otherwise I'll take out my catalogues; I'll plan all the things I might buy, but I rarely phone for anything. Mainly I like to look at clothes, handbags, shoes. I imagine all the gadgets we could own, but Pete says to me, 'Be sensible Kim, we'll never use that,' and he's right you know, we won't, so why have the clutter?

Stockists

One of the fun things about keeping home is you'll never be short of an excuse to shop. It's always a good idea to keep your eyes open for things you've long searched for in vain, or useful items that are too good a bargain to miss.

Shopping tips

Always visit specialist hardware stores on your travels. As you journey around the country, not to mention the globe, you'll discover all kinds of intriguing materials and specialist products to help you. Never miss out on a good traditional hardware store, they can be a real Aladdin's cave.

Check out '99p' and '£1' stores. They always have lots of gadgets, jumbo packs of cloths, branded cleaning products, batteries and light bulbs on sale much more cheaply than high street supermarkets. If in the past you've made the mistake of thinking these stores aren't for you, let us assure you they definitely are if you like a bargain – and who doesn't?

You'll always find some fascinating products overseas, especially in the large supermarkets and markets throughout Europe, the United States and the Far East. Lots of luxury hotels now sell the things they decorate their rooms with – including the bed linens (mattress sizes in Europe and the US are different; *see* The bedrooms, p. 236). Always check it's safe to transport any goods you do find abroad – you can't fly home with flammable or corrosive substances.

Online shopping and searching

The internet has revolutionized the way we shop. If you don't yet have access to it, you're sure to know someone who does. If not, larger public libraries provide public-use computer terminals with internet access.

Use a search engine such as www.google.co.uk and type in what you're looking for. For example, the search 'acid-free tissue paper' turns up lots of mail order suppliers who will easily beat prices you would pay in high street stationers. Modify your search to 'Pages from the UK' when looking for suppliers with lowest shipping costs.

UK stockists

There are too many stockists to mention all, but this is a range of suppliers covering the UK with retail or mail order services. They've been selected because among them they should be able to supply most of the specialist products referred to in this book.

Astonish A British manufacturer and supplier of their own brand of cleaning products, which they boast have no adverse effects on the environment. The range is sold individually and as value-added packs by mail order. Their website also carries downloadable material such as safety data sheets for their products, which list all the ingredients. www.astonishcleaners.com; 0113 236 0036.

Dri-Pak The UK's only manufacturer of soda crystals and soap flakes. Dri-Pak also produce the traditional cleaning products borax, bicarbonate of soda and laundry starch. The packs are stocked in many supermarkets and hardware stores and are readily available from wholesalers, so ask your local store to stock them. Also available mail order from www.dri-pak.co.uk; 0115 932 5165.

HG International Manufacturer of their own-label cleaning products, many of them specialist, for example for stone and ceramic surfaces, furniture and flooring. They are widely stocked in specialist shops (tiling and flooring). For local stockists and product information, visit www.hginternational.com/uk.

John Lewis department stores Nationwide. They stock almost everything imaginable for the home, from bedding to haberdashery, laundry and cleaning supplies. They offer a smaller range of goods by mail order at www.johnlewis.com.

Lakeland A specialist kitchenware and cleaning supplies chain, which also offers mail order. They stock the popular Astonish brand of cleaners. www.lakelandlimited.com.

Leyland SDM A London-based retailer of Leyland and Johnstone's paints, but also sells a wide range of hardware and specialist furniture and decorating waxes and finishes not easily found elsewhere. Some mail order; www.leylandsdm.co.uk.

Max and Buster brands This range from UK manufacturer Challs includes ammonia (10 percent strength), caustic soda and their own-brand cleaners. The products are available from hardware stores and by mail order at www.challs.com.

Poundland The name says it all: everything, including the leading brands, is £1. This rapidly expanding chain is found in prime locations on the high street of a growing number of towns. They provide excellent value on light bulbs, clothing care, cleaning and decorating supplies. Store locations only at www.poundland.com.

Robert Dyas A houseware and hardware retailer in the south of England, with eighty-five stores from Bristol to Colchester (but nationwide online shopping). Stocks a wide range of specialist cleaning materials, light bulbs, kitchen, garden and security products. Nationwide delivery to mainland UK; www.robertdyas.co.uk.

Stain Devils ACDOCO are the Bolton-based manufacturer of the Stain Devils range. You can find the eight differently numbered packs in the laundry aisle of most supermarkets and they are also sold direct at www.acdoco.co.uk, where there is an interactive stain clinic that advises which product to buy.

Index

Index

Kim & Aggie   The Cleaning Bible

Kim Woodburn is a professional cleaner who took up her first live-in cleaning job after moving to Liverpool, working from morning until night. She also founded a handmade knitwear company, and, in 1983, Kim made her television début modelling her range of knitwear on Pebble Mill at One. It was twenty years before television would rediscover her and she was asked if she would like to be considered for a new series. At the screen test she was introduced to Aggie and the rest is history.

Aggie MacKenzie has worked on a number of national magazines, and was associate editor in charge of the Good Housekeeping Institute, where they test all the latest consumer appliances, develop and test recipes and investigate new cleaning products and gadgets. Aggie now writes a regular column for *The Times*, and is in her fourth year of presenting the television series *How Clean is Your House?* with Kim Woodburn.